FAMILY SITUATIONS

FAMILY SITUATIONS

AN INTRODUCTION TO THE STUDY OF CHILD BEHAVIOR

By

JAMES H. S. BOSSARD

Professor of Sociology, William T. Carter
Professor of Child Helping, and
Director of the William T. Carter Foundation,
University of Pennsylvania

and

ELEANOR S. BOLL

Research Assistant,
William T. Carter Foundation
University of Pennsylvania

GREENWOOD PRESS, PUBLISHERS
NEW YORK   1968

The Library of Congress cataloged this book as follows:

Bossard, James Herbert Siward, 1888–1960.
 Family situations; an introduction to the study of child
behavior, by James H. S. Bossard and Eleanor S. Boll.
New York, Greenwood Press, 1968 [°1943]

 ix, 265 p.   24 cm.

 Bibliography : p. 243–260.

    1. Child study. 2. Family.   I. Boll, Eleanor Stoker, joint author.
 II. Title.

 HQ772.B63   1968   301.42'7   69–10071

 Library of Congress   [3]

REF
HQ
772
.B63
1974

Copyright 1943 University of Pennsylvania Press

Originally published in 1943 by the University of Pennsylvania Press,
Philadelphia

Reprinted with the permission of the University of Pennsylvania Press

Reprinted by Greenwood Press,
a division of Williamhouse-Regency Inc.

First Greenwood Reprinting 1968
Second Greenwood Reprinting 1974

Library of Congress Catalog Card Number 69-10071

ISBN 0-8371-0024-0

Printed in the United States of America

To
GERTRUDE BOSSARD
and
KATHRYN COLEMAN
Associates in our early family situations

PREFACE

THIS BOOK is the result of an unorganized coöperative venture. The two authors set themselves to two different but related tasks, and their conclusions are brought together here for their possible bearing upon each other. Dr. Bossard began with definite convictions concerning the situational approach to the study of behavior, the meaning of such an approach, what it should include, and its general importance. These convictions are presented in the form of theses, and are embodied in Chapters I, II, III, and IX. Mrs. Boll, beginning with the idea of classification in science, gathered the "specimens" of family situations in the existing literature and attempted to formulate them into a summary picture. The results of her work are found in Chapters IV to VIII, inclusive.

This volume is the second of a planned series of publications of the William T. Carter Foundation for Child Helping of the University of Pennsylvania. *Marriage and the Child,* the first volume, was issued in 1940. The facilities which it has placed at the disposal of the authors have made possible this volume, acknowledgement of which is hereby made with thanks. We are indebted to Professor Jeremiah Shalloo, of the University of Pennsylvania; to Professor Leonard S. Cottrell, of Cornell University; and to Professor T. E. M. Boll, of the University of Pennsylvania, who have read parts of this manuscript. It ought to be added that, although they made most helpful suggestions, they are in no way responsible for the views expressed. Mrs. Marion Davis, Mrs. Kathryn Heintzelman, and Mrs. Catherine Hall rendered helpful secretarial service.

The following publishing houses, scientific journals, and periodicals have given permission for quotation from publications to which they hold the copyright, acknowledgement of which is hereby made with thanks: *The American Journal of Sociology, the Annals of the Academy of Political and Social Sciences, The Family, The Ladies' Home Journal, The New Republic Publishing Company, Progressive Education, Social Forces, The Survey, The Writer,* D. Appleton-Century Company, The American Book Company,

The Commonwealth Fund, E. P. Dutton and Co., Harcourt, Brace and Co., Harper and Brothers, Henry Holt and Company, A. A. Knopf, Inc., J. B. Lippincott Co., Liveright Publishing Co., The Macmillan Company, the Manchester University Press, McGraw-Hill Book Co., Inc., the Oxford University Press, the Princeton University Press, the Russell Sage Foundation, and the University of Chicago Press.

JAMES H. S. BOSSARD
ELEANOR S. BOLL

Philadelphia, Pennsylvania
January 12, 1943.

CONTENTS

Part I

THE SITUATIONAL APPROACH

CHAPTER I

THE DEVELOPMENT OF THE SITUATIONAL APPROACH

THERE ARE two fundamentally different approaches to the problems of human behavior: one in terms of the traits and personality of the individual who behaves, the other by way of the situation to which he reacts. The first of these is the one that has been followed generally by professional and scientific groups interested in behavior problems, the second has only recently been recognized as an approach separate and distinct from the former. It is the purpose of this chapter to trace the development of this, the situational approach to behavior. By way of introduction, the rise of the term "behavior" will be referred to, as well as the sciences which are concerned primarily with its understanding. Following this, the situational approach will be defined briefly, in the sense of its first understanding. Since this approach is most characteristic of recent sociological studies, special attention will be paid to the meaning of the sociological approach to behavior problems and the sociological conception of personality. There is included also a brief survey of recent developments and emphases by sociologists in their approach to the study of behavior problems. The chapter ends with a restatement of the meaning of the situational approach.

THE RISE OF THE TERM "BEHAVIOR"

The word "behavior" has had a long history, in the course of which it has been given a variety of shades of meaning. One time-honored usage has been a general one, to comprehend a way of acting, both of persons and of things. Thus one spoke of the behavior of a ship at sea, or of an animal in search of food, or of the activities of a person. At other times, the word has been used more pointedly to refer to deportment, or etiquette, or the propriety of conduct, i.e., to a specific manner of acting in particular cases or circumstances.

3

Its first usage in the scientific field came several decades ago when some zoölogists, comparative psychologists, and others developed a specialized interest in studying "those visible movements of the animal organism which constitute the external physiological processes." These studies came to be grouped together under the phrase of "the science of animal behavior."[1]

Meanwhile, similar ideas of procedure were being entertained in the sciences dealing with human life and relationships. As early as 1897, Dr. Edgar A. Singer, now Professor of Philosophy at the University of Pennsylvania, had read a paper before the American Psychological Society on "Sensation and the Datum of Science" in which he anticipated the objective point of view of the later behaviorists.[2] This point of view was developed more fully by Singer in his papers on "Mind as an Observable Object," read before the 1910 and 1911 meetings of the American Philosophical Association.[3]

It was an insurgent school in psychology, however, which launched the term behavior on its scientific way in the human sciences. This school made its appearance about 1912. It arose, on the one hand, as a revolt against the older, introspective psychology, which contended that the starting point in mental analysis was the study of one's own mind, in terms of mental states such as "sensations," "images," and "affective tones." On the positive side, this new school insisted that the proper start was the study of what other persons did. The observation of human action, rather than the analysis of consciousness, was the essence of a scientific psychology. This school came to be known as the behavioristic school.[4]

Beginning as a sort of sideshow among the academic psychologists, the behavioristic school developed, in the decades following, to the proportions of an intellectual revolution, carrying implications far beyond its original scope. We are not concerned here, however, either with the premises of this school or their reception by students

---

[1] Maurice Parmelee, *The Science of Human Behavior*, Chapter 1.

[2] Cf. *The Philosophical Review*, Volume VII, No. 5, pp. 487-.

[3] Edgar A. Singer, *Mind as Behavior*, Chapters 1, 2, and 3.

[4] John B. Watson, *Psychology from the Standpoint of a Behaviorist*, and *Behaviorism*.

of human activities, but rather with the incidental by-product of the increasing use of the term behavior in these several sciences.

Within the last three decades, the word behavior has come to be recognized as a scientific term in a number of academic disciplines which are concerned with the study of what men do, and why. In its broadest sense, it has come to comprehend the entire response or adjustment pattern of the individual. Students prefer it to the earlier term "conduct," because the latter seems to have certain ethical connotations. A contemporary student of behavior problems speaks of the change in terminology and of its significance in these words:

The very word "behavior," which is used in contradistinction to the word "conduct" is significant of [a] great change in modern thinking. Conduct is a word which implies a judgment—approval or disapproval—for which praise or punishment may be meted out. Behavior is a scientific term which calls for a description of activities in terms of the constitutional stuff or personality—intellectual, biological, temperamental—out of which the child is made.[5]

THE SCIENCES OF HUMAN BEHAVIOR

Human behavior is a fascinating field for study. Its understanding has always intrigued human interest. Through the ages, man has observed the conduct of his fellows, and utilized his generalizations as a guide for his experience. Thus must one interpret the fables, legends, myths, proverbs, saga, sacred writings, literary tales, etc., which constitute the accumulated wisdom of the ages; they involved and reflected man's observations on what people did, and why. And this is the substance of human behavior.

With the passage of time, such observations grew in range and complexity; with the advent of writing and printing, they came to be recorded; with the growth of human learning, they became naturally more specialized. These developments coincided in point of time with the use of the modern sciences. The result was a natural one, no matter how slowly the logic of thought might move to its destined end: the study of human behavior came to be recognized as a legitimate field for scientific study. The point to be recognized, (and it seems an important one by way of proper

[5] Esther Loring Richards, *Social Work Year Book*, 1935, p. 43.

perspective) is that the modern sciences concentrating upon the problems of human behavior represent, then, so many current phases of an abiding and age-old aspiration by man to understand his fellows and, ultimately, himself.

The scientific study of behavior did not begin as such. That is to say, there was no conscious recognition among the early scientists of the scope of the study of human behavior as a whole. The period of beginnings was one of specialized sciences, attacking some one particular field or group of problems involving human reactions, often working independently of other sciences in related fields, and, at times, having no appreciation of such relationship or of the larger implications of their work. Each of these specialized sciences staked off its own claim, as it were; developed its own tools and techniques; and, in course of time, arrived at its own conclusions. It is only in recent decades that an appreciation of the underlying field of human behavior has come to be recognized as the common core in these sciences.

Obviously, the objective study of human behavior is not the monopoly of any one scientific group. The question may be raised with pertinence whether it is a science in a fundamental primary sense, or a sort of hybrid product of various sciences. The conclusion urged here is that it is a science in the sense that it is a systematic, objective study of a definite field, but that to its development many separate disciplines must of necessity contribute.

The foundation sciences naturally would be the physical and biological ones. As a basis for the study of human behavior, "There is," says Adrian, "a mass of information about the mechanism of the body. The behavior of any animal must depend in part on its general structure—its shape, size, number of limbs, arrangement of sense organs, etc., and with man there are the important structural modifications which allow the forelimbs to be used for wielding tools."[6]

Beyond anatomical structure are the physiological studies of processes involved. In addition to the older orthodox studies, there

---

[6] Edgar Douglas Adrian, in the Harvard Tercentenary Publications, *Factors Determining Human Behavior*, p. 4. Cf. E. Kretschmer, *Physique and Character*, and W. H. Sheldon, S. S. Stevens, and W. B. Tucker, *The Varieties of Human Physique*.

are the contributions of endocrinology, with its growing body of information about the hormones, "those chemical messengers produced by that specialized group of tissues known as the ductless glands," which play such an essential rôle in the maintenance of normal bodily functions.[7] In fact, there is much reason to think that there is a biochemical basis of life, both more specific and more important than has generally been supposed. The hope of a chemical psychology is not without foundation of fact.[8] Certainly the chemistry of the body is not the same in different persons, and it is not unreasonable to suppose that these differences will influence the reactions of persons to life's experiences.[9] Furthermore, there is the relation of the visceral organs to behavior, as stressed by Kempf.[10]

Every human being commences existence as a single living cell which contains all the possibilities and limitations of heredity. Just how specific and rigid these are is a matter of dispute, but enough is known to convince us of the existence of individual differences in constitutional capacities and of their transmission in accordance with the laws of heredity. Concerning the relative importance of the factor of heredity, there is today no substantial agreement. The winds of academic opinion shift from time to time, and if certain emphases in this country today tend to depreciate the importance of heredity, it is well to remember that this has not been the case recently among European scholars, nor has it always been the case here. At any rate, the biological sciences have much to contribute to the understanding of human behavior, not only for the light which they can throw upon the hereditary factor, but also, as Groves has pointed out, in their emphasis that behavior is the result of adjustment to environment.[11]

The psychological sciences have always occupied a central position in the studies of human behavior. The plural number has been used because there are different approaches to the behavior of man

[7] James B. Collip, in *Factors Determining Human Behavior*, p. 12. See also, R. G. Hoskins, *The Tides of Life*.

[8] J. Needham, "Lucretius Redivivus," *Psyche*, 7:10-13 (1927).

[9] W. I. Thomas and Dorothy S. Thomas, *The Child in America*, Chapter XI.

[10] E. J. Kempf, *The Autonomic Functions and the Personality*, Nervous and Mental Disease Monograph Series.

[11] Ernest R. Groves, *Personality and Social Adjustment*.

which come properly within the scope of psychology, just as there are many systems of psychology. The scientific study of the child, from the psychological side, has been made in large measure via the psychometric approach, concerning itself with studies of capacity, and thinking of behavior as a correlate or function.[12] Another group of psychologists have made what might be called the personality-testing approach. Their studies grew out of an interest in the correlation between intelligence and performance (i.e., behavior). The discovery that this correlation was not high led to an emphasis upon other traits and factors, such as temperament, character, etc. The number and variety of these studies may be gathered from the compilation made by Hartshorne and May.[13] Psychiatry may be included as one of the psychological approaches, even though it began as a branch of medicine. Concerned originally with the clinical treatment of the physiological causes of mental disorder, psychiatry represents today a framework of reference for behavior as a whole, with a variety of interpretations in socio-psychological terms and factors. The contemporary psychiatric viewpoint of mental disturbance as a failure of the organism as a whole to adapt to the conditions of life can have no other meaning but that psychiatry becomes an applied science (or an art?) of human behavior.[14] Similarly, one must include psychoanalysis in the psychological group. Like psychiatry, it began as a specialized therapeutic approach. As time has gone on, it too has become increasingly a study of the human personality, contributing concepts, emphases, techniques, as well as conclusions distinctly its own.[15]

Finally, there are the social sciences, which have turned increasingly in the last few decades to the study of human behavior. It is easy to understand the reasons for this development. In the first place, much of the work of the groups of sciences already mentioned reached into, or has implications for, the social sciences; in the second place, the more one delves into the study of behavior, the

[12] Thomas, *op. cit.*, Chapter VIII.

[13] M. A. May and H. Hartshorne, "Personality and Character Tests," *The Psychological Bulletin*, 23:395-411, 1926.

[14] Eduard A. Strecker and Kenneth Appel, *Discovering Ourselves*; Murphy Gardner and Friedrich Jensen, *Approaches to Personality*.

[15] Karen Horney, *New Ways in Psychoanalysis*; Ives Hendrick, *Facts and Theories of Psychoanalysis*.

more one sees that it is something which develops in relation to and with other people. Human personality is a product of social contact and communication, and its scientific study leads directly and inevitably into the field of social interaction. It is, then, to the analysis of this social or situational approach to human behavior that we next turn.

THE SITUATIONAL APPROACH TO BEHAVIOR PROBLEMS

The rôle of the environment as causative factor in the determination of human behavior has always been recognized.

From the earliest times [writes Conklin] it has been believed that species might be transmuted by environmental changes and that even life itself might arise from lifeless matter through the influence of favorable extrinsic conditions. . . . Many philosophers of the seventeenth and eighteenth centuries taught that man was the product of environment and education and that all men were born equal and later became unequal through unequal opportunities. . . . The equality of man has always been one of the foundation stones of democracy. Upon this belief in the natural equality of all men were founded systems of theology, education and government which hold the field to this day. Upon the belief that men are made by their environment and training rather than by heredity are founded most of our institutions with their commands and prohibitions, their rewards and punishments, their charities and corrections, their care for the education and environment of the individual and their disregard of the inheritance of the race.[16]

With the application of scientific method to the problems of behavior, it was natural that the prevailing emphasis upon environment should find expression in the resulting literature. Among the first students of crime to employ positive methods was Tarde, who championed the view that the criminal was entirely a social product.[17] Among the psychologists was Watson, already referred to, with an almost complete disregard for inborn or constitutional traits.[18] White, among the psychiatrists, is clear in his relative emphasis upon environmental factors in the causation of mental

[16] Edwin G. Conklin, *Heredity and Environment in the Development of Man*, pp. 214-215.

[17] Gabriel Tarde, *Penal Philosophy*, translated by Rapelje Howell.

[18] John B. Watson, *op. cit.*

disorders.[19] Adler, of the psychoanalytic group, reveals a similarly high estimate of the relative importance of environmental conditioning.[20]

The scientific study of behavior from the standpoint of environment came in time to be referred to as the "situational approach." Thus conceived, the term "situation" was used as a synonym for the stimuli which play upon the organism, these stimuli arising from conditions exterior to the organism.[21] More will be said in subsequent chapters concerning the meaning of this term, but for the moment this first, simple interpretation will suffice.

The procedure of studying behavior in relation to situations, thus defined, began with the physiologists, such as Loeb, Jennings, and others, in their work with "tropisms," i.e., reactions of organisms to light, electricity, heat, acids, etc. Next, it was applied by the psychologists,—Thorndike, Yerkes, Watson, Köhler—in their experiments with rats, dogs, monkeys, and babies. The procedure of both of these experimental groups was the same: they prepared situations, introduced the subjects into the situations, observed the behavior reactions, changed the situation, observed the changes in the reactions, and so on.

It was a logical next step to apply this procedure to the study of human behavior, and much of the emphasis in recent years has been in this direction. While the methodology was developed by the comparative physiologists and psychologists, the foundation for its extension to human behavior was laid by Pavlov, Krasnogorski, Bekhterev, Watson, and others, on the conditioned reflex. What this means is usually explained in terms of Pavlov's classical first demonstration with dogs. A dog is shown a piece of meat. His mouth waters in anticipation of eating it. The meat may be thought of as the original stimulus; the mouth watering, as the dog's reaction. Pavlov's experiments showed that repeated association of other stimuli with this original stimulus brought out in time the original response. The reaction to the associated

[19] William A. White, *The Mental Hygiene of Childhood.*

[20] Alfred Adler, *Understanding Human Nature.* Consult his book, *The Neurotic Constitution,* for his explanation of how the individual compensates for his organic deficiencies.

[21] Kimball Young, *Personality and Problems of Adjustment,* pp. 4, 5.

stimulus is called a conditioned reflex.[22] Applied to children, these experiments showed similar results, and made it clear how

fears and prejudices and prepossessions are produced, especially by the behavior of other persons. A single association may be sufficient to produce the reflex. There is on record, for example, the case of a youth who was the subject of an experiment with odors. The odor of roses produced a feeling of fear, and investigation disclosed that the subject had been injured in an automobile accident near a rose garden. A whiff of lavender may recall mother, and tuberoses remind us of death. We have here [concluded the Thomases] a most important approach to the formation of personality traits as dependent on situations.[23]

The idea of the relatively extreme modifiability of human nature, which is the essential implication of the work on conditioned reflexes, was supplemented by the conclusions of the psychiatrists concerning the early conditioning of the human personality. At the beginning of the century, most psychiatrists worked with institutional cases and thought largely in terms of organic and biological factors. By the third decade of the century, experience with non-institutional cases, and particularly with children, was leading to the conviction that situations prevailing in the first few years of life were of paramount importance.[24] One school of psychiatrists, (or should one say one group of schools?) the psychoanalysts, particularly emphasized infantile and preschool experience. Some of them have gone so far as to emphasize overwhelmingly the consequences of the prenatal environment.

THE SOCIOLOGICAL APPROACH TO BEHAVIOR PROBLEMS

Meanwhile the sociologists, recovering from their earlier inoculations of biological analogy, economic interpretation, and instinct psychology, saw in the situational approach very great opportunities for sociological emphasis. The situational approach to behavior by sociologists rests, of course, upon the striking concepts

[22] I. P. Pavlov, *Conditioned Reflexes*, translated and edited by G. V. Aurep.
[23] W. I. and Dorothy Thomas, *op. cit.*, p. 507.
[24] William A. White, "Childhood: The Golden Period for Mental Hygiene," in James H. S. Bossard, *Child Welfare, The Annals of the American Academy of Political and Social Science*, November, 1921, pp. 54-60; see also his *Mental Hygiene of Childhood*.

developed by the late Professor Cooley. His ideas of "the self as a social product," "the looking-glass self," and "the individual and society as two aspects of the same thing," had appeared as early as 1902,[25] but it was destined to be another decade and more until the implications of these concepts began to be realized for purposes of sociological study.

Following Cooley, the next major step in the development of the sociological approach to behavior problems came with the publication of Thomas and Znaniecki's monumental work on the Polish peasant.[26] In this work, the peasant is studied in process of moving from a European to an American situation, thus approximating the controlled change of situations with which, as has been pointed out, the physiologists and psychologists had been working experimentally. Throughout their entire work runs the fundamental theme of the relationship between personality and the environing culture. "Personality is always a constitutive element of some social group; the values with which it has to deal are, were and will be common to many personalities, some of them common to all mankind."[27] "Personal evolution can be understood only in connection with social life."[28] "Personal life records, as complete as possible, constitute the perfect type of sociological material."[29] "A social institution can be understood only if we . . . analyze the way in which it appears in the personal experience of various members of the group and follow the influence which it has upon their lives."[30]

Of particular significance in its effect upon subsequent sociological thinking was the emphasis upon the individual's definition of the situation. On the basis of his cultural and social conditioning, the individual meets the various social situations which confront him, and defines them with reference to his own behavior. Thomas further distinguished between those definitions of the situation which are laid down for the individual by his culture which he calls the moral or public definition, and those which represent the indi-

[25] Charles H. Cooley, *Human Nature and the Social Order.*
[26] W. I. Thomas and Florian Znaniecki, *The Polish Peasant.*
[27] *Ibid.*, Volume III, p. 6.
[28] *Ibid.*, p. 10.
[29] *Ibid.*, p. 6.
[30] *Ibid.*, p. 7.

vidual's own conception which he terms personal or hedonistic. The interplay between man and his culture is well stated in these words:

The human personality is both a constantly producing factor and a continually produced result of social evolution, and this double relation expresses itself in every elementary social fact; there can be for social science no change of social reality which is not the common effect of pre-existing social values and individual attitudes acting upon them. . . .[31]

Following the work on the Polish peasant, which Burgess identifies as "the starting point for the sociological explanation of personality and culture,"[32] Thomas carried forward his analysis of the cultural conditioning of personality in his paper presented to the American Sociological Society in 1926, with a particular emphasis upon the rôle of "critical experiences." "Behavior traits and their totality," he wrote then, "are the outcome of a series of definitions of situations with the resulting reactions and their fixation in a body of attitudes or psychological sets. Obviously, the institutions of a society, beginning with the family, form the character of its members almost as the daily nutrition forms their bodies, but this is for everybody, and the unique attitudes of the individual and his unique personality are closely associated with certain incidents or critical experiences particular to himself, defining the situation, giving a psychological set, and often determining the whole life direction."[33]

Two years later, in his presidential address to the American Sociological Society, he makes a clear distinction between different approaches to the study of behavior:

In approaching problems of behavior, it is possible to emphasize—to have in the focus of attention for working purposes—either the attitude, the value, or the situation. The attitude is the tendency to act, representing the drive, the affective states, the wishes. The value represents the object or goal desired, and the situation represents the configuration of the factors conditioning the behavior reaction. . . . The situations which the individual encounters, into which he is forced, or which he

[31] *Ibid.*, p. 5.
[32] Ernest W. Burgess, "The Cultural Approach to the Study of Personality," *Mental Hygiene*, April, 1930, p. 310.
[33] W. I. Thomas, "The Problem of Personality in the Urban Environment," *Publications of the American Sociological Society*, Volume XX, 1926, p. 31.

creates, disclose the character of his adaptive strivings, positive or negative, progressive or regressive, his claims, attainments, renunciations, and compromises. For the human personality also the most important content of situations is the attitudes and values of other persons with which his own come into conflict and coöperation.[34]

The next year, Thomas drew the line clearly between the constitutional and the situational studies of personality development, and defined the sociological approach. Studies which concern themselves with the stimuli to which the person reacts are situational studies. In these, the main objective is to discover how the behavior of the individual is determined by his relations to other individuals and a society, and this is sociological.[35]

Reinforcing the viewpoint of Thomas were the conclusions of Faris, Bernard, and others. In 1921, Faris indicted the explanation of behavior in terms of instincts,[36] and three years later Bernard's book on instinct appeared,[37] followed by his analysis of environments in 1925.[38] In his paper to the American Sociological Society in 1925, Faris foreshadowed the later sociological dictum of personality as the subjective side of culture in these words:

Individuality may then, from one standpoint, be thought of as character, which is the subjective aspect of the world the individual lives in. The influences are social influences, but they differ in strength and importance. When completely ordered and organized with the conflicting claims of family, friends, clubs, business, patriotism, religion, art and science all ordered, adjudicated, and unified, we have not passed out of the realm of social influence, but we have remained where the social group, taken separately, can be invoked to explain the behavior. Individuality is a synthesis and ordering of these multitudinous forces.[39]

[34] W. I. Thomas, "The Behavior Pattern and the Situation," *Publications of the American Sociological Society*, Volume XXII, 1928, pp. 1-2.

[35] W. I. and Dorothy S. Thomas, *op. cit.*, p. 310.

[36] Ellsworth Faris, "Are Instincts Data or Hypotheses?" *American Journal of Medical Science*, Volume 27, September, 1921, pp. 184-196.

[37] L. L. Bernard, *Instinct: A Study in Social Psychology*.

[38] L. L. Bernard, "A Classification of Environments," *The American Journal of Sociology*, November, 1925, pp. 318-332.

[39] Ellsworth Faris, "The Nature of Human Nature," *Publications of the American Sociological Society*, Volume XX, 1926, p. 29.

Utilizing the end of the third decade of the century as a convenient point to summarize, three developments may be identified as having taken place by 1930. First, the idea of the situational approach to behavior problems had been formulated, had been stated with clarity, and with some recognition of its wider implications. Second, the foundations for an understanding of the social conditioning of behavior had been laid. Physiologists and psychologists, working together, had proved the idea of the relative modifiability of human behavior; psychiatrists and social psychologists had explored the implications of this fundamental fact in their respective fields. Third, sociologists had formulated their own conception of personality, to which we turn next.

THE SOCIOLOGICAL CONCEPTION OF PERSONALITY

On the basis of this background there developed the sociological conception of personality. This conception is reflected, first, in the sociologists' definition of personality as "the more or less organized ideas, attitudes, traits and habits which an individual has built up into rôles for dealing with others and with himself. These rôles, with their supporting ideas, attitudes, traits and habits, grow out of the individual's participation in various groups."[40]

The sociological insistence is that personality, thus defined, is not inborn, but is acquired or achieved. On the basis of the individual's native or innate equipment, the human personality is a product of social conditioning. In the process of personality formation, two sets of conditioning factors operate. One of these is the interplay of person with person, which we term social interaction. Of outstanding importance in this connection, then, are the experiences of the person in his or her social contacts. But the influences of relationships with other persons are constantly modified or qualified by what these other persons have learned. Here is the second set of conditioning factors, viz., the cultural, embracing the more or less accepted ways of doing and thinking. "Hence personality is determined . . . by the conditioning power of the cultural heritages and social definitions of behavior which social groups preserve and which transmit from generation to generation."[41]

[40] K. Young, op. cit., p. 3.
[41] E. T. Krueger and W. C. Reckless, Social Psychology, p. 327.

RECENT DEVELOPMENTS AND EMPHASES

The decade of the nineteen-thirties was filled with studies which fall within, or which bear upon, the situational approach to behavior. These studies hail from many different sources and cover a variety of aspects. Several developments and emphases, however, stand out and may be identified

1. Definitely outstanding during the decade was the interest in methodology. How can behavior best be studied in its situational aspects? This, obviously, is a part of the larger problem of methodology in the social science field as a whole. Sociologists, particularly, have been interested in methodology. The decade under consideration was ushered in by the publication of the monumental work by Rice on *Methods in Social Science*,[42] and for several succeeding years the attendant problems of concepts as scientific tools seemed to preoccupy sociologists to the exclusion of other matters.[43]

Continued importance has been attached by sociologists to the life-history record in the study of the human personality. Identified as early as 1919 by Thomas as the "perfect type of sociological material," their use has been continued and their value reiterated during the decade of the thirties, with particular use in the study of delinquents.[44] Dollard has attempted to set up criteria which must be taken into account in the development of life-history material.[45] For a brief summary of this and other methods of studying personality, the reader is referred to Kimball Young's recent book,[46] and to a summary by Shalloo.[47]

2. A second outstanding interest of the sociologists in the study of personality during the fourth decade of the century was in the social processes involved. Obviously this is a broad field, and only selected aspects have been considered. One of these has been the processes of socializing the child. How is the child inducted into the family?

[42] Stuart A. Rice, *Methods in Social Science.*

[43] Herbert Blumer, "Science without Concepts," *The American Journal of Sociology*, January, 1931, pp. 515-534.

[44] Cf. Clifford Shaw and others, *The Natural History of a Delinquent Career;* Clifford Shaw, editor, *Brothers in Crime.*

[45] John F. Dollard, *Criteria for the Life History.*

[46] Kimball Young, *op. cit.,* Chapter XI.

[47] J. P. Shalloo, "Understanding Behavior Problems of Children," in the *Annals of the American Academy of Political and Social Science*, November, 1940, pp. 194-202.

What are the processes of family interaction? What is the rôle of other groups in child socialization? These questions have involved, among other things, much study of parent-child relationships; and of family functioning, both as an agency of orientation and as the selector and transmittor of the child's cultural heritage. Extended reference to this work will be made in subsequent chapters.

Another phase of emphasis has been upon the study of status systems, having to do with the person's polar position in reciprocal behavior patterns. Following the recent stimulating work of Linton,[48] particular attention has been paid to the significance of the status systems of our contemporary culture in the socialization of the child. These studies have emphasized the ascripted rather than the achieved statuses,[49] with analyses of the factors in the ascription processes, and the social typing of behavior which is involved.

3. Third have been the specific studies of the cultural conditioning of personality types. These have followed naturally the earlier descriptive studies of personality types in social situations, like Anderson's study of the hobo, Zorbaugh's analysis of rooming-house types, Wirth's picture of the Ghetto, or Hayner's picture of hotel life.[50] Wirth studied the rôle of cultural conflicts in delinquency.[51] Bossard and Dillon showed the segregation of divorced women in areas of social isolation.[52] Dollard pointed out that the psychotic person is one who has rejected the existing social organization and substituted a private version of culture which is organized and consistent, often even highly integrated and systematic.[53] Faris ad-

[48] Ralph Linton, *The Study of Man*, Chapter VIII.

[49] Kingsley Davis, "The Child and the Social Structure," *The Journal of Educational Sociology*, December, 1940, pp. 217-230; Allison Davis, "American Status Systems and the Socialization of the Child, *The Sociological Review*, June, 1941, pp. 345-354.

[50] Nels Anderson, *The Hobo*; H. Zorbaugh, *The Gold Coast and the Slum*; Louis Wirth, *The Ghetto*; and Norman Hayner, "Hotel Life and Personality," in *Personality and the Social Group*.

[51] L. Wirth, "Culture Conflicts and Delinquency," *Social Forces*, Volume IX, 1931, pp. 484-492.

[52] James H. S. Bossard and Thelma Dillon, "The Spatial Distribution of Divorced Women," *The American Journal of Sociology*, January, 1935, pp. 503-507.

[53] John Dollard, "The Psychotic Person Seen Culturally," *The American Journal of Sociology*, March, 1934, pp. 637-648.

vanced the thesis that the schizophrenic personality is the result of an extended period of "cultural isolation."[54] Stonequist identified the "marginal man" as a product of a cultural "no-man's land."[55] Sellin, exploring research possibilities in the sociological approach to crime causation, emphasized the rôle of cultural conflicts.[56]

4. Finally, there have been the very important studies of social behavior and the situational approach to it, made by students other than sociologists. Most of these have been made in the general field of child study. An earlier summary of them was made by the Thomases (1928).[57] In the years since, with the increasing development of nursery schools and institutes for child study, and the development of new techniques of observation and recording much progress has been made. Anderson summarizes excellently these studies in his article on "The Development of Social Behavior." Of particular interest is his identificaton of the factors conditioning social behavior: (a) the example set by elders and contemporaries; (b) social learning, which selects from a base of fluid relationships certain patterns for fixation and permanence and in which the direct observation of the various techniques is a very significant factor; (c) the quantity of social experience which the environment permits; (d) the availability of equipment that facilitates social relationships; and (e) the amount of participation in social activities outside the schoolroom.[58] Of unusual significance in this connection, and with particular reference to methodology, are the studies in social psychology by the Murphys,[59] Dashiell,[60] and others. An exploratory study of the roots of sympathy is presented by Lois

[54] Robert E. L. Faris, "Cultural Isolation and the Schizophrenic Personality," *The American Journal of Sociology*, September, 1934, pp. 155-165.

[55] Everett Stonequist, "The Problem of the Marginal Man," *The American Journal of Sociology*, July, 1935, pp. 1-13.

[56] Thorsten Sellin, "Culture Conflict and Crime," *Bulletin of the Social Science Research Council*, New York, No. 41, 1938.

[57] W. I. and Dorothy S. Thomas, *op. cit.*, Chapter XII.

[58] John E. Anderson, "The Development of Social Behavior," *The American Journal of Sociology*, May, 1939, pp. 839-858.

[59] Lois B. and Gardner Murphy, "The Influence of Social Situations upon the Behavior of Children," in Carl Murchison, *A Handbook in Social Psychology*, Chapter 22.

[60] J. F. Dashiell, "Experimental Studies of the Influence of Social Situations on the Behavior of Individual Human Adults," *ibid.*, Chapter 23.

Murphy.[61] The impact of culture patterns upon the personality, as seen through the eyes of the practising psychiatrist, was analyzed suggestively by Dr. Plant.[62]

SUMMARY AND CONCLUSIONS

It is hoped that the present chapter has succeeded in its purpose of establishing the following facts, which may be restated by way of summary.

1. Human behavior has been a subject which has challenged man's attention through the ages. The accumulated wisdom of the ages, however expressed, has concerned itself largely with how people behaved and why.

2. Within the past century, human behavior has become the focal point of a number of sciences. None of these has a monopoly of this particular subject, many are contributing now to the further understanding of the problems involved.

3. One definite approach to behavior problems is through the study of the situations to which behavior is a response. Building upon the earlier work of the physiologists and behavioristic psychologists the sociologists found in this approach an avenue peculiarly significant for this work.

4. The sociological conception of behavior is reflected chiefly in their studies of personality, which they see primarily as the result of social interaction and cultural conditioning. During the third decade of the century, the general principles of this conception were developed; in the fourth decade, they were fortified and illustrated by specific studies.

5. The situational approach, with its present assumptions and conclusions, is based not only on the work of sociologists, but also upon work done in such related fields as child study, psychiatry, education, social work, and the like.

[61] Lois B. Murphy, *Social Behavior and Child Personality.*
[62] James Plant, *Personality and the Cultural Pattern.*

CHAPTER II

THE MEANING AND IMPLICATIONS
OF THE SITUATIONAL APPROACH

Iт is one of the besetting problems of the social sciences that its students are using terms constantly with little or no attention to precision in their meaning. This is apt to be particularly true with words that have come to be associated with commonly used ideas or phenomena. For example, one can comb books on "progress" line by line without finding even a reference to its possible meaning. The word "education" is seldom defined in tomes devoted to its problems. "Communism" means many different things to persons speaking of it. The terms "situation" and "social situation" are no exception to this practice of the use of words without defining them. Examination of the literature reveals few references to the necessity of giving them any relative exactness in meaning, and even fewer efforts to do so.

Thus far in this volume, the word situation has been used to mean the stimuli which play upon the organism, these stimuli being external to it. This may have been satisfactory for the general purpose of surveying developments in the study of behavior centering around or related to this general approach, but for the further purposes of this volume greater precision in meaning is necessary. It is the purpose of the present chapter, therefore, to define more adequately the meaning of the term situation, to consider the different ways in which situations may be regarded, and to identify some of the problems which seem to inhere in the scientific study of social situations.

THE MEANING OF THE TERM "SITUATION"

Historical. One of the few organized efforts to define the term was made at the meetings of the Section on Sociology and Social Work of the American Sociological Society, in December 1930. In this symposium, Mrs. Ada E. Sheffield presented the idea of family case work as dealing, not with a client, but with "a dynamic field of experience, a field in which the individual or the family figures within an aggregate of interactive and interdependent factors of personality and circumstance . . . a segment of interactive experience involving clients in complex relationships with their physical and social setting."[1] This new unit she spoke of as a situation.

In defining the term for purposes of sociological analyses, Mr. Stuart A. Queen said:

A situation consists in relationships between persons viewed as a cross section of human experience, constantly changing in kaleidoscopic fashion, and affected both by material conditions and by relationships to other persons. Thus we make of the concept "situation" an intellectual tool similar to the anthropologists' concept "culture complex," in that both are quite flexible as to content, both are capable of subdivision, both are something more than the sum of discrete elements, both convey the idea of relationships, both present nuclei about which configurations gather, and both are constantly changing.[2]

General Ideas. When one turns from formal definitions of the term, such as those just cited, to actual usages in the recent scientific literature, certain definite changes in its connotations may be recognized. These have all been in the direction of greater precision in the meaning accorded to it. Beginning as a rather general term synonymous with environment, at least three general basic ideas seem to be included in the concept of the social situation.

1. The first is the idea that the stimuli included are all external to the organism. This implies at once that the term situation is not, properly speaking, synonymous with the word "environment." As Mead points out, environment means all of the factors to which the responding unit responds.[3] This obviously would include certain acquired internal aspects of the organism which would obviously operate as stimuli.[4] These internal stimuli are not included in the concept of the situation: we are concerned only with those which are external to the organism.

[1] Ada E. Sheffield, "The Situation as the Unit of Family Case Study," *Social Forces*, June, 1931, pp. 465-474.
[2] Stuart A. Queen, "Some Problems of the Situational Approach," *Social Forces*, June, 1931, p. 481.
[3] George H. Mead, *Mind, Self, and Society*, pp. 246-247.
[4] Kimball Young, *op. cit.*, pp. 4, 5.

Confining ourselves to the human organism, these external stimuli are said customarily to derive from two sources: (a) other persons, and (b) material objects. But such a classification would scarcely be satisfactory to Frank Buck or to Tom Sawyer and his dog. The rôle of domesticated animals obviously cannot be ignored in any consideration of external stimuli in human behavior. Even in so relatively simple a family situation as one may find in the home of a childless couple, the presence of a pet dog, for example, may carry as much or more significance than that of the husband's maiden aunt.

Something of the range and diversity of environmental factors is suggested by L. L. Bernard's excellent summary. While not all of the environments listed are external to the individual, the reader will have no difficulty in determining those which are or are not, so that the entire classification is here reproduced.

I. *The physical (inorganic) environments*
   1. Cosmic, 2. Physico-geographic, 3. Soil, 4. Climate, 5. Inorganic resources, 6. Natural physical agencies (falling water, winds, tides, etc.), 7. Natural mechanical processes (combustion, radiation, gravity, etc.).

II. *The biological or organic environments*
   1. Micro-organisms, 2. Insects and parasites, 3. Larger plants used for food, clothing, shelter, etc., 4. Larger animals used for food, clothing, etc., 5. Harmful relationships of larger plants and animals, 6. Ecological and symbiotic relationships of plants and animals acting indirectly upon man, 7. Prenatal environment of man, 8. Natural biological processes (reproduction, growth, decomposition, assimilation, excretion, circulation, etc.).

III. *The social environments*
   1. Physico-social environments: (a) Tools, (b) Weapons, (c) Ornaments, (d) Machines, (e) Transportation systems, (f) Communication systems, (g) Household equipment, (h) Office equipment, (i) Apparatus for scientific research, etc.
   2. Bio-social environments:
      A. Non-human: (1) Domesticated plants used for food, clothing, shelter, medicine, ornaments, (2) Domestic animals used as a source of food, (3) Domestic animals used as a source of power, (4) Medicines and perfumes of an organic character, (5) Animals used as pets and ornaments, etc.

   B. Human: (6) Human beings serving as laborers (slaves,
      etc.), (7) Human beings serving as ornaments, entertain-
      ers, etc., (8) Human beings rendering impersonal volun-
      tary or professional service, (9) Regimented human groups,
      such as armies, workingmen, etc., (10) Men coöperating
      voluntarily through the use of language mechanisms.

   3. Psycho-social environments: (a) The inner behavior (attitudes,
      ideas, desires, etc.) of individuals with whom we come in con-
      tact, (b) The uniformities of inner behavior occurring in col-
      lective units and perceived as customs, folkways, conventions,
      traditions, beliefs, mores, etc., (c) Externalized language sym-
      bols used to project the above types of behavior and to condition
      responses in ourselves and others, (d) Those inventions, pri-
      marily physical, which perform a similar service in conditioning
      psychic responses, but usually with less facility and completeness.

IV. *Composite or institutionalized derivative control environments* (derivative combinations of the various types of environments organized
   for purposes of social control).
   1. General in character: The economic, political, racial, esthetic,
      ethical, educational, etc., environments.
   2. Special in character: The American, Italian, Jewish, Scandina-
      vian, New England, Southern, Argentinean, Republican, Dem-
      ocratic, Catholic, Buddhist, revolutionary, conservative, femi-
      nine, masculine, etc., environments.[5]

   2. The second basic idea involved in the term situation is that
of the reciprocal relationship of these stimuli. In other words, they
do not just operate: they operate with, upon, and in relation to, each
other. A situation is, in other words, an organization of stimuli in
which each stimulus has a given relationship to every other one. It
is the particular relationship of these stimuli to each other which
gives them their meaning in any specific situation.

   This basic principle, that any fact derives its attributes and meaning from its relation to other facts, is pertinent to all scientific study.
And the failure to realize this in regard to social facts has handicapped greatly sociological analysis in the past. An example of this
principle from the mechanical field will serve as a simple illustra-

[5] L. L. Bernard, "A Classification of Environments," *American Journal of
Sociology*, November, 1925, pp. 318-332.

tion. A watch lies on the desk in the office wherein this is written. The time is at night. The building is almost empty of human occupants. There is no other watch or clock in the building. In relation to this particular office and its furnishings, this watch has certain meaning, and the possible questions concerning the watch tend to be limited by the other facts which inhere in the situation. At this point, I leave the office to visit in a friend's home. This friend has a large and varied collection of watches, clocks, sundials, hour glasses, and the like. Here and now, my watch appears in a new situation. New questions arise concerning it. Its significance is totally different from what it was an hour ago. It is, of course, the same watch intrinsically, but its meaning has been profoundly changed. It is so with the facts which serve as stimuli in a given situation. From the standpoint of the situation, the stimuli included exist in relation to each other, and from this obtain their meaning in the particular situation under consideration.

3. The third characteristic of the situation is that it is organized about, or in relation to, some focal point or person. It is this aspect of a special relatedness, with reference to some person or object, which has come to be the essence of the scientific usage of the situation concept. On the basis of this specific unity of organization, the situation becomes an emergent, by which we mean that this special relatedness becomes in itself an additional and effective factor.

The simplest illustration of the idea of an emergent is that of water—a combination of hydrogen and oxygen, in the very definite proportions of two parts of hydrogen and one part of oxygen. This special relatedness forms the liquid emergent known as water, which has quite different properties, i.e., behavior, than either of its gaseous components. Concerning its reality, Mead speaks in these general terms: "Anything that as a whole is more than the mere form of its parts has a nature that belongs to it that is not to be found in the elements out of which it is made."[6]

The existence and importance of this factor of special relatedness has been recognized by a number of thinkers of the nineteenth century. Such men as John Stuart Mill, Lester F. Ward, Spaulding, Wundt, and others were aware of it, and various terms, such as "creative synthesis," "evolutionary naturalism," "organicism,"

[6] Mead, *op. cit.*, p. 329.

"holism" and "heteropathic causation" were used to identify it. Mr. C. L. Morgan's term "emergent," however, has found most favor among contemporary philosophers, biologists, sociologists, and the like, who utilize the concept.

By the way of summary, then, a situation consists of a number of stimuli, external to the organism but acting upon it, organized as a unit and with a special relatedness to each other as stimuli of the specific organism involved. It becomes thus, as Lundberg[7] suggests, a "field of force," or a segment of life to which the organism reacts as a whole. Thus conceived, it becomes a tool of precision for the scientist in the study of the behavior of the organism, as definite and specific as the situation of the experimental physiologists and psychologists.[8]

THREE APPROACHES TO THE STUDY OF SOCIAL SITUATIONS

Having defined socal situations in terms of their basic aspects, it is pertinent next to distinguish between the possible approaches that may be made to their study. In speaking of these approaches for purposes of study, no reference is intended to the methodology to be employed, but rather to the nature and range of the phenomena considered. To introduce the distinctions in approach to be advanced, an illustration may possibly serve to advantage.

On the desk on which this chapter is being written there stands a Royal typewriter. Let us suppose that we are Martians engaged in an exploratory study of typewriters rather than Earthians similarly interested in social situations. In all probability we should begin our study by regarding the typewriter as a mechanical structure, made up of many separate parts. We would proceed to consider these parts—keyboard, letters, platen, ribbon, frame—inquiring and observing how they are related to each other, always coming

[7] George Lundberg, *Foundations of Sociology*, pp. 217 ff.

[8] The reader will find it worth while at this point to compare this attempt to characterize the situation with that of Leonard Cottrell, Jr., in his article, "The Case Study Method in Prediction," *Sociometry*, Volume 4, November, 1941, pp. 358-370. See also L. S. Cottrell, Jr., and Ruth Gallagher, "Important Developments in American Social Psychology during the Past Decade," *Sociometry*, Volume 4, Nos. 2 and 3 (May and August), 1941, for a statement of the main currents of change in contemporary social psychology. Another contribution by Cottrell is his "Analysis of Situational Fields—A Theoretical Orientation for Social Psychology," *The American Sociological Review*, June, 1942, pp. 370-383.

back to a recognition of the basic structural unity. Our questions, our problems, the facts we observe, the generalization we make, are those which bear upon the parts of this machine, their organization and special relatedness which is the essence of a Royal typewriter.

An operator of this machine, or structure, now approaches, and begins typing. Immediately, a whole new series of questions, observations, facts, and conclusions come to the fore. These have to do with the function of the parts of the structure. The field of study now centers basically around process, the process of operation. Each part of the machine is performing its rôle, this rôle at the same time related functionally to the rôle of every other part. This is a wholly new approach, distinct from the first-mentioned line of inquiry, yet a pertinent part of our study of the phenomena of typewriters and typing.

Sooner or later, in the course of our study, there will come the discovery that the typist is not simply operating a machine, but is using the machine to record and convey letters, words, sentences, and ideas. The typed page may be a report on research, a part of the presidential message, or a kidnapper's demand for ransom. It may be written in English, French, Latin, or American slang. The ideas expressed may be simple or complex, and the style may be direct or involved. Peculiarities of sentence construction and vagaries of punctuation and spelling attract our attention. In other words, an entirely new set of problems, facts, and interests engross us. We are now concerned, not with the structure of the machine, or the processes of operation, but with the material or content of the process.

The three ways of regarding the phenomena of typewriting may be identified under the captions of structure, process, and content, and the illustration just used serves to indicate the argument of the present chapter concerning the fundamental ways of approaching the study of social situations. The thesis here advanced is that social situations, just as social institutions and various other organized data in Sociology, can be regarded and studied from the three distinct points of view identified by the terms "structure," "process," and "content," and that much clarity and progress in their understanding would ensue if this distinction is recognized and maintained.

Structure. A social situation is, from one point of view, a structure. To analyze and describe it as such might be spoken of as a still-life picture. When we structurize a social situation, we see it in repose. Our interest is in the structural elements, their characteristics, and their position and relationships to each other. We are concerned chiefly with those relationships which are relatively continuous. What distinguishes a structure are the facts that it has form and that it is an organization, and the essence of both is continuity of relationship.

In the scientific study of a social situation, structurally conceived, we take it apart, examine each part as to its nature, and inquire into the way these parts are organized into a unit. This is one separate but important step in the understanding of the situation. If I understand him correctly, it is this that Lundberg had in mind when he wrote:

After the field, i.e., situation has been selected, the problem is to structure it so that the relationship of the elements in the field can be accurately shown. The method of doing this with which we are most familiar is, of course, to name with words certain elements or factors in the situation and then by use of the adjectives or adverbs of ordinary language we attempt to give an accurate statement of the relationships within the field.[9]

Similar would appear to be the thought of Mrs. Sheffield, in her paper of a decade ago: "The identifying of a pattern that is relatively constant helps us to bring order into our thinking about the variables which appear. It should clarify causative relations, should help us to follow social process, and to raise significant questions."[10]

Process. A second way in which a social situation may be viewed and studied is in terms of process. If the structural approach is a still-life picture, this second is that of the motion picture. We are concerned now with the interaction of the elements of the situation. The term "social interaction" is used constantly by contemporary sociologists, currently as the generic name for a whole set of processes taking place between individuals: thus, social interaction denotes the set of processes by virtue of which society exists. Here,

[9] Lundberg, *op. cit.*, p. 108.
[10] Sheffield, *op. cit., Social Forces*, June, 1931, pp. 471-472.

however, we are using the term intraction as a category of analysis, to identify the reciprocal or interdependent relationship between the elements in a situation. The basic idea involved is not one of the mere meeting or collision of these component elements, but something more pervasive and subtle, in the course of which each acts upon or somehow changes or modifies the other. Such interaction may take place between individual organisms, between persons, or between persons and their stimulating environment. Conceived thus in terms of process, the situation becomes an immediately related and functioning segment of human experience, as both Mrs. Sheffield and Professor Queen have indicated in their definitions cited in this chapter.

Content. Finally, from the third point of view, both structure and process are but vehicles or channels through which are transmitted a content of ideas, attitudes, words, and the like. This content we speak of as "culture."

The cultural content of the interactive process is confined to the human level. Before me on the floor, as I write, are puppies engaged in play. Here is an interactive process, most assuredly: there are gestures, grimaces, growls, with an evident rôle of attitudes, dispositions, emotions, and the like. This is process, but there is no cultural content. Culture is exclusively a human product, and a culture content of the interactive process is confined to human relationships. The interactive process may be thought of, then, as a series of functioning operations, conveying cultural items. Through this interactive process, these cultural items are being molded into a pattern which becomes the central core of the situation.

It is this cultural, or distinctive human, element in social situations which is apt to be overlooked by students who approach the subject from the background of certain disciplines whose approach is essentially organismic. An excellent illustration of this appears in a recent, and in many ways an excellent, volume.

Some phenomena of nature exist in the form of static structures, others in the form of reversible or irreversible processes. Examples of the first are geometrical forms, of the second, waterfall, wind, combustion, etc. The existential form of the organism is dynamic. This has been formulated by Jennings in his much quoted statement that "The organism is a process." In the last analysis, "organism" and "life" are identical concepts. The first term places the emphasis on the structural, the second on the dynamic aspect. The two aspects are inseparable from each other. The essential characteristics of the organism are, however, more clearly revealed in its function than in its morphological features.[11]

This cultural content, however, is a very specific thing in the case of any given social situation, in spite of what has been said about its pervasiveness. While culture is comprehensive, like the air we breathe, nevertheless the human personality is constantly selecting items and elements from the current culture, and is channelizing them through the interactive processes, so that any given social situation represents both a cross section and a cross selection of the contemporary culture, organized about a given focal point.

The distinction between process and content, as well as the specificity of the cultural content, is well set forth by Anderson in his analysis of family situations.

The examples set for the child by his parents, older persons, and associates operate from birth onward. Older persons transmit a variety of techniques and attitudes. . . . Two problems can be distinguished: first, the actual content of the pattern which is imitated. Thus the child observes his parents greeting neighbors and friends, hears the comments made by his parents on individuals, organizations, and activities, and is given examples of either good or poor sportsmanship when he plays with his parents. A boy sent to a clinic because of his unpopularity was socially isolated among his fellows because of his many caustic comments and criticisms. It was found that his father was known throughout his community for similar behavior. Here what seemed abnormal in the boy had been learned in the normal manner directly from a parent. Next, we may distinguish the effects of these patterns as transmitted upon the child's adjustment. If parents quarrel frequently in the presence of the child, he not only acquires quarreling as a mode of approach to others but may react with uneasiness and frustration. A child is sensitized to some social actions and hardened to others. Whether he becomes hardened or sensitized depends upon his total makeup and the character of his previous experience quite as much as upon the intensity or character of the stimulation given.[12]

[11] Andras Angyal, *Foundations for a Science of Personality*, p. 20.
[12] Anderson, "The Development of Social Behavior, *American Journal of Sociology*, May, 1939, op. cit., p. 849.

IMPLICATIONS OF THE SITUATIONAL APPROACH

Once the full meaning of the situational approach to behavior problems is recognized, it becomes important to consider the implications of such an approach, and it is to this discussion that we turn next.

1. It seems necessary to begin by emphasizing that the situational approach is a distinct and separate one, commensurate with the study of the personality which reacts to the situation. This fact would seem to require emphasis because such status has not been given to it in the past. Almost without exception, references to situations and situational factors in behavior have been made as though they were of secondary importance, a sort of by-product of the primary concern with the behavior of the organism. Studies of situations have been incidental studies, often casually made, and with secondary status ascribed to them. This has been true even when the avowed purpose was the study of the situation. Few studies of social situations have gone far without shifting consideration from the situation to the way in which the individual defines the situation and reacts to it.

Obviously, this has not made, nor can it make, for any considerable progress in the understanding of situations themselves. What has just been said is not to be interpreted, of course, as a criticism or depreciation of the emphasis in behavior studies upon the organism and its responses: the sole insistence here is that, once the rôle of the situation in behavior is recognized, the situational response must be recognized as a distinct and separate one, commensurate with studies of the organism and its behavior.

2. The second implication of the situational approach to behavior problems, and complementary to the first one, is a recognition of the situation as a *separate* field for scientific investigation. In other words, situations need to be studied, inductively and by themselves, without any reference to the way in which organisms react to them. This is said with particular reference to social situations, with which we are primarily concerned.

Emphasis upon this second implication again is necessary because of the past failure to recognize it. The reasons for this failure are easy to understand: they are natural products of the history of the situational approach. Recognition in scientific circles of the rôle of the situation in behavior began, as was pointed out in chapter I, with the physiologists in their work on tropisms. In these studies, simple situations were created, to which the reaction of simple forms of life were observed; in these cases, there' would have been little or no point to any major concern with the situation. The experimenters created them, and the elements involved were few and simple. For example, when a specific acid is dropped into water, in order that the reaction of the amoeba may be observed, the situation created is the combination of two liquids with specific chemical formulae. The situation was not only simple, but was also thoroughly understood. Naturally, the chief concern of the investigator was with the reaction of the amoeba. The case would be similar with the application of heat, or of light. The resulting situation was simple and could be expressed with the precision of a mathematical formula.

Following the physiologists, the situational approach was utilized by some of the psychologists. The situations employed by them were more complex, it is true, than those created by the physiologists. But the facts remain that they, too, were relatively simple, and that they were created by the experimenters. Moreover, the elements involved in their creation were physical elements, whose nature was known precisely, and whose relationship was a tangible and constant reality. Naturally again, the psychologist, once having created or established his situation, is concerned with it only incidentally, and as a vehicle to his investigation of the responses of his object to this situation. This remained true of scientists like Pavlov, Krasnogorski, Bekhterev, etc., in their work on the conditioned reflex. One who goes through the reports on their work finds but scant reference, other than brief, simple explanation, to the situations employed. All the emphasis is upon the reactions to these situations, and the possible meaning of their observations.

This is perhaps the place to recall that most of the studies of child behavior have been made by persons trained in the biological and psychological sciences. Even the sociological studies of young children have been made by psychologists, psychiatrists, and educators.[13] It involves no untoward criticism of their work to point out

[13] W. I. and Dorothy S. Thomas, *op. cit.*, p. 506; Ruth Pearson Koshuk, *Social Influences Affecting the Behavior of Young Children*, p. 6.

that, in their approaches to child behavior, they have shown the effects of their scientific backgrounds. Nor does it seem difficult to understand how such students would be prone to (a) minimize the rôle of the situation, or (b) to assume that social situations are understood adequately, and that the important fact is to see how the individual defines the situation and reacts to it. Most of them, naturally enough, have been disposed, therefore, to think primarily in terms of persons and their reactions, and when they have spoken of the situational approach, it has been with one eye turned to it and the other toward the behavior reaction to it.

The above assertions are based on an examination of the research publications on child development of the past two decades. Koshuk has summarized, in the reference just cited, the significant research material which has appeared in this field since 1925, and the reader is referred to this summary, not only for the specific bibliographical references but also for their terse and penetrating evaluations. The essential nature of these studies, in relation to the present discussion, is stated in the opening paragraphs of the summary as "dealing specifically with the influence of social factors, broadly defined, on the behavior of young children. . . . The emphasis turns out to be, quite naturally, on personality development within our own culture. . . ."[14] In other words, while the rôle of situational factors is recognized, the chief emphasis is upon the effect of the situational factor or factors upon the personality development of the child. Concern with the situational obviously is incidental: its understanding is tacitly assumed.

It is the whole emphatic insistence of this volume that a situational approach to human behavior is a wholly different matter. Social situations differ from mechanical or physical situations, and in a number of respects. In the first place, social situations are not created artificially as are those of physiologists and psychologists; they are accepted by the student as they are found. This changes the whole relationship of the student to the situation. In the one case, he creates a situation to see how the organism will react; in the case of social situations, he finds them ready-made, and must learn to deal with them as they are. Second, social situations are more complex than the physical, non-human situations which have

[14] Koshuk, *op. cit.*, p. 1.

been dealt with prevailingly in behavior studies. The physiologists and psychologists combine customarily a small number of elements to create their situations. In the case of social situations, the very nature of the human personalities involved excludes any such simplicity. The human personality is a very complex product, so that the simple combination of a man, a woman, and a child, in a family situation, would be far more complex than the combination of three chemical agents, for example. Again, the elements involved in a social situation cannot always be identified with clarity, nor can their rôle in the situation be expressed with the precision of a mathematical formula. For example, the degree and nature of tension between the father and mother may be an integral part of a family situation, with profound significance for the child, yet these aspects may be difficult to identify or express with any kind of satisfactory accuracy. The emotional quality of a social relationship is as real a social fact as the temperature of water, but no statistical thermometer has yet been devised to measure and express it. Finally, social situations differ from non-social situations in the inexorability with which they change. Most of the situations utilized by students of pre-human behavior were fixed, or changed slightly or slowly or both. This is not true of social situations, which are constantly changing, and at times with considerable rapidity. From one point of view, social situations are functioning processes, which places them into a category quite different from standardized psychological tests, for example.

The scientific study of social situations is possible only if they are regarded as objective and separate realities. This is the first step in their scientific investigation. We must begin by disregarding the ways in which individuals define situations or react to them. Further progress involves their analysis with reference to the nature and range of the stimuli involved; the ways in which these stimuli operate; the cultural content of the interactive processes in situations; and the manner of organization, or special relatedness of all the stimuli involved, with special reference to the object or person considered. Each of these must be defined with precision, and analyzed with appreciation of all the complexities present. Only after social situations have been thus studied, through the slow laborious technique of the scientist, are we in a position to consider adequately their rôle in the behavior of the individual. He who would study social situations would do well to analyze carefully the procedures of scientists who have dealt with situations at the pre-human level, and note the detailed precision with which they work. Ponder, from the standpoint of methodology, the following quotation from Pavlov:

While, as we have seen, very strong and even specialized stimuli can under certain conditions acquire the properties of conditioned stimuli, there is, on the other hand, a minimum strength below which stimuli cannot be given conditioned properties. Thus a thermal stimulus of 45 degrees C. applied to the skin can be made into an alimentary conditioned reflex, whereas at 38 or 39 degrees C. (approximately 2 degrees C. above the skin temperature in the dog) a thermal stimulus is ineffective. Similarly, while with the help of a very strong unconditioned stimulus it is possible to convert a very unsuitable stimulus—for example, one which naturally evokes a different unconditioned reflex—into a conditioned stimulus, it is exceedingly difficult or even impossible with the help of only a weak unconditioned stimulus to transform even a very favorable neutral stimulus into a conditioned stimulus. Even where such a conditioned reflex is successfully established, its occurrence results only in a very small reflex response. Some unconditioned stimuli may be permanently weak, others may display a weakness which is only temporary—varying with the condition of the animal.[15]

It will be noted, in the above description, that the difference of a few degrees in temperature of the stimulus determines whether it has conditioning properties or not. This is highly suggestive to students dealing with social stimuli, both in its implication of accuracy, and in the importance of the degree of strength or weakness of a specific stimulus.

3. This is perhaps the place to emphasize the interdependence of the sciences which the careful study of situations involves. This is a matter concerning which clear thinking has not always prevailed. The point of view presented here can best be explained through the use of examples. The physiologists, in their studies of the responses of organisms to varying situations, obviously drew upon the data of chemistry, bacteriology, physics, and the like, in order to create and describe accurately the situations to which the organisms were

[15] I. P. Pavlov, *Conditioned Reflexes*, p. 31.

submitted; and quite as obviously, no question concerning such a procedure would be raised. Similarly, psychologists, in creating situations or tests of a physical or mechanical sort to which their cases are submitted, draw without the slightest hesitation upon the the underlying physical sciences. That is to say, these earlier groups who utilized the situational approach to the study of behavior called upon all the scientific disciplines necessary in order to understand, as accurately as possible, the nature of the elements which they combined to create the situations which they utilized for their own specific purposes. When, now, one turns to the very much more comprehensive, complex, and difficult task of dealing with social situations to which human behavior is a response, it ought to be clear that the sciences which need to be called upon and whose findings need to be utilized must be far more numerous. Sociologists, then, in utilizing the situational approach, should have no hesitance or compunction in drawing upon the work of physiologists, physiological chemists, endocrinologists, psychologists, psychiatrists, psychoanalysts, historians, economists, political scientists, cultural anthropologists, horticulturalists, statisticians, and the like, as need may arise. The most extensive, and at times the most complete, utilization of the data of the complementary sciences by sociologists in their development of the situational approach is entirely in keeping with the scientific folkways, and in this case peculiarly proper because of the difficulties of the material involved.

SOME PROBLEMS IN THE SCIENTIFIC STUDY OF SOCIAL SITUATIONS

Reference has been made several times to the fact that the scientific study of social situations is not an easy discipline. It is important to recognize this. In fact, there are those who are so impressed with these difficulties as to conclude that it is impossible to apply the methods of science to many aspects of the situational approach. Without accepting such a conclusion, it does seem pertinent to consider at this point certain problems which arise in any attempts to study social situations scientifically.

One set of difficulties grows out of the fluidity of social situations. Conceiving of them in terms of social interaction, it is obvious that social situations are not only constantly changing, but that they are also being modified as they change. How then, one might ask, can one analyze with anything resembling scientific accuracy something that is in motion and changes as it moves?

One possible answer to this has been made by Rice.

No event, or unit of whatever kind [Rice pointed out], is ever repeated. Science must generalize from similar but different appearances, which it chooses to regard as if they were "repetitions" of the same event. The units with which science must work are conceptual units, artificially segregated by the human mind from the continuance of reality, and treated as if, in a given instance of scientific analysis, they were identical.[16]

Or again,

Science is dependent upon the conceptual repetition or recurrence of identities in a process of continuous change among the parts of a functional whole. But no part of this whole can in reality stand alone, in complete independence of the remainder; nor can it change without affecting, in however small degree, every other part.[17]

One other problem will be given consideration here, and this concerns the inclusion of non-human aspects or elements of social situations. Should they be included in the scientific study of these situations? The question is a debatable one, with certain logical arguments on each side. Against their inclusion is the fact that they are, in one interpretation of the term, not social at all, i.e., they involve no social relationships. Furthermore, there is the argument of expediency. In staking the claim for a scientific vein, the line must be drawn somewhere, and is this not the proper place? On the other hand, many physical stimuli have social implications. This is most evident if the physical circumstances are unusual. A university faculty could confer in a room with a temperature of 45 degrees, but the proceedings would be more brief than is customary. Dim lights are helpful when lovers dine together. A round table facilitates the art of conference. Cocktails enliven a party. Slums are depressing. Again, a great many of the physical appointments of modern living have been given social evaluation. That is to say, social standards have developed around these physical circum-

[16] Stuart A. Rice, "Units and Their Definition in Social Science," *Social Forces*, June, 1931, p. 476.

[17] *Ibid.*, p. 475.

stances, so that their presence or absence, the quantity and quality of their being, come to have great meaning to the persons involved, quite apart from any direct physical effects. Social interaction around a luncheon table in the Bohemian Club in San ·Francisco or the Union League in Philadelphia might change in other than nutritive respects if a chain restaurant with heavy china were substituted. Social situations are altered when a hovel is substituted for a palace. People suffer the pangs of hunger to keep up social standards, and it would seem ill advised for scientific analysis to ignore their ôle vhere they involve physical realities.

I₁ short, one comes to identify two types of stimuli arising from the physical bases of social situations, first, those which are physical, and second, those which are social. The latter arise from the evaluations which the interacting agents place upon them, thus affecting their attitudes, dispositions, judgments, and the like. And certainly these are important to one who seeks an understanding of social situations. One can agree wholly then with the Murphys when they write:

A large number of the most interesting problems in social psychology arise out of such irreducible patterns in which persons bear a special elation to he items in the material environment, instances in which the eparation of the behavior into "behavior toward people" and "behavior to vard things" would destroy the thing which is to be studied.[18]

SUMMARY

In this chapter, an effort has been made to bring out as clearly as possible the following main ideas:

1. It is a continuing need in the social sciences that terms be defined and used with precision. This applies to the term "situation."

2. The term "situation" is used in this volume to mean (a) a number of stimuli, external to the organism, but acting upon it; (b) organized and operating as a unit; and, (c) with a special relatedness to each other as stimuli of the specific organism involved. It is, thus, a "segment of life to which the organism reacts as a whole."

[18] Gardner and Lois B. Murphy, *Experimental Social Psychology*, pp. 19-20.

3. The thesis is advanced that social situations can be regarded and studied from three distinct points of view. These are identified by the terms "structure," "process," and "content."

4. The objective analysis of behavior along the lines just indicated constitute an approach to behavior problems commensurate in importance to the study of the individual and his traits. It is a separate, distinct, and highly important approach, and needs to be recognized as such.

5. Social situations need to be studied carefully and objectively, and without reference to the way in which organisms react to them. This has not been done in the past chiefly because, in the work of the physiologists and psychologists who first dealt with the rôle of situations, such situations were simple, ready-made and thoroughly understood. Social situations, however, are not created as a rule by experimenters. They are accepted as they are found. And they are found to be complex and fluid, comprising elements which are hard to identify and to appraise.

CHAPTER III

FAMILY SITUATIONS:
THEIR MEANING AND ANALYSIS

A SOCIAL situation was defined in the preceding chapter as an organization of stimuli, external to an organism and acting upon it, and with a special relatedness to each other as stimuli of the specific organism involved. Furthermore, the thesis was advanced that social situations, thus conceived, could be studied from three points of view, identified by the terms structure, process, and content.

The present chapter applies this framework of thought to the family. It includes, accordingly, a discussion of (a) the meaning of the term "family situation," (b) the importance of family situations in the situational approach to the study of human behavior, (c) the family as structure, (d) as a field of social interaction, and (e) as a vehicle for the transmission of culture.

THE MEANING OF THE TERM "FAMILY SITUATION"

The word situation, as used originally, tended to be synonymous with the term environment. Such usage seemed fairly satisfactory to scientific observers so long as the behavior of organisms below the human level was being considered and so long as the situations were created artificially with special reference to a particular organism whose behavior was being studied. With the application of the situational approach to human behavior, and with the necessity of accepting ready-made, rather than artificial, situations, students were compelled to identify situations with existing organizations of such stimuli, usually confined to some specific group of which the person was a member. Such a group is the family.

The term "family situation," as utilized in studies of behavior, involves, then, the application of our definition of the phrase "social situation" to the specific family group. A family situation may be defined, accordingly, as a unit of stimuli, operating within the confines of the family circle, and organized in relation to the person or object which serves as the focal point in the particular case being considered. Stated another way, the term family situation means a group of family stimuli, operating as a unit with reference to some polar point. This polar point may be some outside object, it may be a member of the family group, or some non-member observer or student of the family. It is important to keep in mind the rôle of this focal point, for what is implied is that the family situation changes as the polar point is changed. Speaking in very general terms, the family situation of a child is the unity of existing stimuli within the family circle as they operate upon the child; that of the husband or wife in the same family would be quite different. The change in the polar point changes the entire situation, with its involved stimuli and the relationship of these stimuli.

THE OBJECTIVE ANALYSIS OF FAMILY SITUATIONS

Once the situational approach to human behavior is made, the primary importance of the family becomes evident at once; once social situations come to be studied with complete objectivity, such analysis should begin with family situations. Basically, there are two reasons why the objective study of social situations should begin with those existing within the family. One of these is the unquestioned and very great importance of family situations in the determination of personality patterns and human behavior; the second is the fact that family situations seem to offer the best opportunities for the development of the technique which their objective analysis necessitates.

The importance of the family in the causation of human behavior is fully attested by all of the sciences which have participated in the development of the science of human behavior. Much of the recent advances in the fields of psychology, psychiatry, psychoanalysis, sociology, criminology, education, social work, and the like support the early, continuing, and pervasive significance of the family conditioning of the personality of its child members.

The priority of family situations in the development of the technique for the objective study of social situations derives from at least three characteristics. The first of these is the relative size and simplicity of family situations. In other words, one may begin with a social situation involving but two persons. If one is concerned with the situational approach to child behavior, one can begin with as few as two persons. Current census data reveal the general prevalence of the small family system. Speaking in quantitative terms, family situations involving but few persons are a normal feature in our contemporary life.

In the second place, family situations are of a continuing and recurrent nature. The interacting personnel remains normally the same, at least over considerable periods of time. Many of the characteristics of this personnel, as well as many of their relationships, are relatively permanent and stable. Particularly, again, is this true in the study of social situations from the polar point of the child. Ordinarily, changes in personnel are limited in number, particularly in relation to such changes in other situations; changes in the characteristics and relationships of this personnel tend to occur slowly; and often imperceptibly.

Finally, the relationships in family situations are peculiarly frank and intimate. Customarily, there is less dissembling in the family than in other human groups, certain occasional and conspicuous instances to the contrary notwithstanding. The connotation generally given by current usage to the word "intimacy" applies it to that relationship between people which is the essence of married life. Frankness and intimacy are characteristics, then, which are distinctly applicable to family life; they are characteristics also which are peculiarly helpful in the scientific study of family situations.

In short, one is tempted to make the rather dogmatic statement that family situations are the most important group of social situations, and relatively the easiest to study. Subsequent experience in the development of an objective situational approach to human behavior may lead to a modification of this conclusion; for the present, one is encouraged to proceed with confidence to their further analysis and description.

THE ANALYSIS OF FAMILY SITUATIONS—A PROPOSAL

In Chapter II, the thesis was advanced that social situations, as well as social institutions and various other organized phenomena in sociology, can be studied from three distinct points of view. These were identified by the terms structure, process, and content. This general thesis is now applied to family situations, and the more specific proposition is advanced here that a comprehensive, objective analysis of family situations must include these three distinct approaches. This in turn calls for a more adequate explanation of the kind of data and lines of inquiry involved in each approach.

THE STRUCTURE OF FAMILY SITUATIONS

To structurize a family situation for purposes of study is to view it in repose, i.e., to consider it as a form of organization. Thus considered, three lines of inquiry present themselves as of basic importance. These have to do: first, and by way of general background, with the structural form, or over-all organization, of the family unit; second, with the identification of the constituent elements of the structure, as well as the important characteristics of these elements; and, third, the nature of their continuing relationships. Each of these three merit further brief discussion.

The Structural Form of the Family

Obviously, a first step in the analysis of family situations is to consider the over-all organization of the family unit. People constantly use the word "family" as though no question concerning its meaning could possibly arise. Even experts in the field of family study tend to do so. There is, of course, some justification for this because, as Linton has pointed out, "all societies recognize the existence of certain close-knit, internally organized coöperative units intermediate between the individual and the total society of which he is a part,"[1] and to some one of these every person is assigned on the basis of a biological relationship clustering around a common ancestry. Applying the word family to such a unit, there is general agreement as to its meaning. When one proceeds beyond this point, however, the term family comes to mean something quite different from one culture to another. What begins as a rather standardized biological or reproductive unit comes to take diverse forms as a socially institutionalized phenomenon. Anthropologists have shown considerable interest in this problem of the structure of the family in the various cultures which they have studied.

[1] Ralph Linton, *The Study of Man*, p. 152.

Sociologists, concerned more with the contemporary culture, have given less emphasis to this, despite its very great importance in our own societal organization. It would be desirable, therefore, to consider briefly, by way of background, some structural forms of the family in our contemporary western culture, with special reference to the child.

Considering the family from this viewpoint, it is necessary, first, to draw a line between the immediate household unit and the larger body of related kinfolk. The distinction is a real one, and the term family has been applied in different cultures to each of these to the exclusion of the other. The student from a middle-class American home today, where the word family is synonymous with the reproductive unit of society, finds it difficult to realize that there have been many societies in which such units have not been so designated, and in whose everyday life such a domestic structure has played a rather minor rôle. In the translation of the documents used in the study of the Polish peasant, Dr. Znaniecki found it wholly impossible to use the term family in the sense in which American students use it. The family, to the Polish peasant, was a social group which included all the blood and law relatives up to a certain variable limit, usually the fourth degree. To designate the smaller grouping which we call the family, Znaniecki used the term "marriage group."[2]

It it well to remember that the transition in our own culture in the concept of the family in terms of the larger kinship group to that of the smaller household unit of today is a rather recent one.

My next discovery [writes Burgess] was a sudden perception of the tremendous difference between the modern family and the family of the past. How many of us realize how modern a phenomenon is the small family of father, mother, and children emancipated from the control of the wider kinship group of grandparents, uncles, aunts, and cousins. Do we perceive that it is to be found as a typical specimen perhaps only in cities, and particularly in the urbanized areas of our very largest American cities? The small family group in apartment houses or residential hotels is, no doubt, the most notorious illustration of effectual detachment from the claims of kinship. The absence in the city home of

[2] W. I. Thomas and Florian Znaniecki, *op. cit.*, Volume I, p. 87.

"the spare bedroom," that famous institution of the countryside, serves as a convenient defense against invading relatives.[3]

For the purposes of the present volume, the term "immediate family" is applied to family living within the household; for the larger, consanguine circle, the phrase "kinship group family" is used. These terms seem sufficiently clear and descriptive and shall be used henceforth.

While these two terms serve to indicate a fundamental difference in the structural form of family organization, precision in thinking compels a further subdivision of each of these two categories. The immediate family, as just defined, may include only the father, mother, and children, or it may include in addition other kinfolk, real and fictitious, who reside currently in the household. Both of these varieties exist with relative frequency, and to identify the distinction, and with particular reference to the child, the term "family of procreation" is applied to the first of the above; and the term "family of orientation," to the second subdivision of the immediate family.[4]

But each individual, it has been pointed out, is also a member of a larger kinship group family. William Brown, for example, is one of the Westchester County or one of the South Carolina Browns. This group contains all the relatives by blood or marriage up to a certain degree of relationship, a degree which varies from one family or culture to another. Here again, it is necessary to identify two subdivisions. Some of these kinship group families develop primarily through or around the male line; some, through the female line. The terms "patrilinear" and "matrilinear" are applied here to these, and the reference is not so much to a line of descent that is utilized as to the degree of social adhesion or isolation that follows upon the marriage. For example, when Mary Jones

[3] E. W. Burgess, "The Family as a Unity of Interacting Personalities," *The Family*, Volume III, p. 3.

[4] Some of the concepts here used are to be attributed to Professor W. Lloyd Warner, of the University of Chicago. The reader should consult also Drs. J. L. and J. P. Gillin's recent textbook, *An Introduction to Sociology*, The Macmillan Company, New York, 1942, Chapter 9, for a summary of family-type groups. Such comparison will reveal our preference for the term "kinship group family," rather than "extended family," as used therein. Also, our usage of the terms "family of procreation" and "family of orientation" are slightly different.

married William Smith, are she and her children now regarded as Jones or as Smith kinfolk, by each and by both? The answer to this question varies considerably from one family to another, and in different regions of this country. The distinction is an important one, particularly again with reference to the child and to family functioning in the development of its personality.

Perhaps something additional should be said here about the status of the kinship group family. There are societies in which the term "family" means only this particular type, but this is not true as a rule in our contemporary western culture, where its importance has been much reduced in recent years and its rôle tends to be of a secondary or supplementary sort. Perhaps most American children today are thought of as members of two types of families, the immediate and the kinship group, with the term "family" being applied somewhat indiscriminately to both types.

The hold of this kinship group family upon its individual members depends in this country generally upon the strength of the "we" feeling which it has developed. This depends in turn upon a number of factors. One of these is the spatial distribution of its members. In some areas still, and earlier quite generally, kinship groups lived quite closely together, with constant interrelationships among the members. When such a condition obtained from infancy, persons were conditioned from birth to accord much more importance to contacts with their kinfolk than when they are apt to be scattered over wide areas and when mobility may make uncertain their present whereabouts. A second factor is that of tradition. What has been the past history of the family in this respect? Some families have a history of close interdependence over long periods of time, and conscious effort tends to maintain this under changing contemporary conditions; other families have never "made much over their kin." This is affected in turn by a third factor: the reputation or prestige of the kinship group. There are family lines whose prestige has been such through the years as to confer distinction upon every person within the range of its membership. One is not apt to ignore his inclusion among the Cabots of Boston. Families like these tend to be "closed corporations" in many of the affairs of life. On the other hand, there are families which have been discredited, perhaps repeatedly, by the behavior of one or more members, with the result that the hold upon their kinfolk is weakened correspondingly. In still other cases, crises within or involving the kinship group call forth a sense of solidarity otherwise lacking.

The Structural Elements in Family Situations

The second line of scientific inquiry into the structure of family situations concerns itself with the constituent elements in these situations, and their characteristics. These constituent elements might be thought of as the polar points in the relatively continuous relationship in family situations. Concretely, these polar points would be ordinarily the persons included in the situation. That is to say, in the constituent elements in the structure of the family situation to which a child reacts might be a father, a mother, a brother, and a maiden aunt.

The characteristics of this constituent personnel next come to engross us. The simple fact of their number becomes an important fact. One of the most important things about a given family situation may be the number of persons in it. Similarly significant are the age, sex, age relationship, size, and physical appearance of the family members. Such facts have commonly been ignored, in the study of family backgrounds, yet the recent renaissance in the study of the rôle in the social structure of such simple factors as sex, age, and age disparity, suggests that similar facts may have very great meaning in the analysis of family situations, especially when considered in their relation to the behavior responses of children.[5]

Beyond the characteristics already mentioned would be the traits of personality which the social psychologists and other scientific groups have been identifying in recent years.[6] Particularly to be emphasized, in this connection, are those traits which are most important in parent-child relationships. Obviously, too, the particular characteristics identified or emphasized in any given family situa-

[5] Ralph Linton, op. cit., Chapter 8. See also Allison Davis, "American Status Systems and the Socialization of the Child," The Sociological Review, June, 1941, pp. 345-356; Kingsley Davis, "The Child and the Social Structure," The Journal of Educational Sociology, December, 1940, pp. 217-230.

[6] The reader is urged to consult here such classifications as those of F. H. Allport, Social Psychology, pp. 101-103; E. T. Krueger and W. C. Reckless, Social Psychology, pp. 352-353; Robert Park and E. W. Burgess, Introduction to the Science of Sociology, p. 70.

tion would vary with the nature of the individual case. For example, the mere ages of the parents, or their age disparity, might be of very great importance in the structure of one family situation, and very much less so in the case of another.

There arises at this point the question whether the human beings related in the situation are the only polar points to be considered. May an animate object, for example, serve as a polar point in a family structure? As this is being written, the author is studying a case of stammering. The case is that of an eight-year-old boy, who lives with his mother in a small apartment on the fourth floor of a large building. The flooring in the apartment is thin, and the mother has only a few small rugs to scatter about the floor. In discussing the case, the mother remarks that the largely uncovered floor is the most constant factor in her relationship with her son, their whole life being a series of repressions to prevent noise which will lead to the inevitable complaints of her neighbors. Concretely stated, is the thin floor in this apartment a constituent element in the structure of that family situation? It is the considered conviction of the scheme of study proposed in this volume that in this particular case the floor of the apartment is a constituent element of the structure of the family situation, on the ground that it is a polar point in a relatively continuing relationship.

It seems reasonable to insist, then, that the physical setting or background of family situations should be included among the structural elements, with particular reference to such characteristics that have significance for the relationships which exist and for the behavior which is called forth.

Structural Relationships

The third line of inquiry into the structure of family situations would center upon the relatively continuing relationships between the structural elements, as just described. Concerning these relationships, at least four aspects seem to be very important in this connection. First, there would be the character of these relationships, as they have become institutionalized and socially typed. Illustrations of this would be the father-mother relationship, that between mother and son, or between eldest and younger brothers. Second, there is the nature of the personality relationship, in terms of dominance and submission, for example. A third aspect would be the continuance and relative stability of such relationships. Are the particular relationships considered in any given case stable and permanent, fluctuating, intermittent, or temporary? Finally, what is the emotional tone of the relationship? Is it free and easy and happy, or is it tense, or is it uncertain and confused?

By way of summarizing the first approach to the study of family situations, as proposed in this volume, it is evident that a great deal of scientific work looking in this direction has already been made. Some anthropologists have concerned themselves with the structural forms of the family in different cultures, and a few sociologists have recognized the need for such studies of the family in our contemporary society. Again, studies of personality types and traits are available to serve as bases for the analyses of parental types and traits which we have identified as the structural elements in family situations. On the other hand, relatively little has been done in the analysis of structural relationships as such, but the definite nature of the data involved promises both ease of task and abundance of reward. The first approach to the study of family situations, in terms of structure, as proposed in this volume, involves then in part a series of new studies and in part a reorientation or development of studies already begun.

PROCESS IN FAMILY SITUATIONS

A second approach to the study of family situations may be made through the objective analysis of the interactive processes which take place between the elements (chiefly persons) in these situations. The constant interplay between the members of the family constitutes one of its fundamental features, and gives it such very great importance in the development of the personality of its members, particularly of its younger members. A family consists customarily of people of different ages and sexes, who are living together on the basis of a specialized and emotionalized relationship, in which there is going on a continuing interaction between its members. It is in this unit of interacting personalities that the child, for example, learns to live, and there are at least three reasons why this experience is of such overwhelming importance in the molding of the child's personality. In the first place, the family comprehends the earliest or first experience in living of the child; in the second place, those family experiences are repeated over and over again; and thirdly, they are tinged from the start by the emotional coloring which attends the relationships between parent and child.

Extended consideration has been given to this interactive aspect of family life, not only in the recent literature of the family and of parent-child interaction, but also in the more generalized studies of interpersonal relations. These studies tend to divide themselves into two main groups. In the first group are those which have concerned themselves with family interaction, primarily from the point of view of determining what it is that the child gets from this interactive experience, and particularly so far as its socio-psychological needs and development are concerned. The second group of scientific studies have centered about certain generic processes in interpersonal relations, with reference to family interaction. Turning here to the first group, a survey of the literature on child development reveals that at least seven contributions have been emphasized in recent years, and these will be summarized briefly.

1. One of the basic things which the family gives to its members is the satisfaction of what W. I. Thomas has called "the desire for intimate response." Every normal human being, and this includes every normal child, wants to be wanted, to be understood, to be appreciated, to be loved. This desire can best be satisfied in the family. Children get this satisfaction from their parents, and it is because of this that so much of their experience with their parents is so meaningful. It is this which is so instrumental in creating the bond which binds the child to his family emotionally, even where there are other unattractive and unfavorable aspects of the relationship. Persons who take children away from sordid surroundings and homes where they are badly and even cruelly treated, and place them in better homes or more attractive surroundings are frequently chagrined to find such children longing to return to the parental hand that abuses them. What the child is apt to miss in such cases is the emotional tie-up with persons who share this intimate reciprocal responsiveness. This affectional bond between members of the family, and particularly between parent and child, is of vital importance under any circumstances of family life; it is increasingly

and correspondingly important as other bonds—economic, protective, educational and religious—become less effective.

2. The family sets the stage to develop and utilize the child's abilities. Through its selection of toys, games, and playmates, the family establishes the first situations in which the child performs. At first these situations are apt to be centered around the child, to encourage and stimulate it alone; later, the element of competition is allowed to enter. Usually the earlier forms of competition are artificial or protected in character, devised for the purpose of showing what the child can do. Later that may be changed, and the children may be introduced gradually, or left to wander into, a natural or unprotected competition. It is of the art of parenthood to manage these changes deftly and aptly, and to the best development of the child. Obviously the difficulties of many children are due to the fact that they have grown up without being "emancipated" from a protected competition. Their problems are complementary often to those of the overly solicitous parent.

3. A desire for the approval of one's kind is a basic human need. Here again the family is important because it is our first audience. The giving or withholding of the approval of this audience operates as a powerful selective force in determining those goals upon which the child concentrates, and around which it develops skills.

Dr. Adler has emphasized very much the "talent"-finding result of proper parental encouragement.

Take for instance [he writes] a little three-year-old girl who tries to sew dresses for her dolls. She takes a few stitches which are certainly far removed from works of art, and her mother comes to her and says, "Do you know, that is a very good beginning. Now if you take a few more stitches like this" (showing the girl) "then you will have a beautifully dressed doll!" Such a mother, by encouraging this child in its efforts, giving it new fields to conquer, appealing to the child's ability to do more, is preparing the way for a "talent." Contrast another mother whose three-year-old daughter makes the same clumsy stitches in a doll's dress, and is met with, "For Heaven's sake, don't bother with that needle! You'll only prick yourself! Little girls can't sew doll's dresses!" In the first case the child is encouraged to find new combinations, new colors, new models, and develop its technic because its efforts are met by encouragement and applause. The second child loses all desire for activity in which its clumsiness is held up as a cause for shame and punishment. The first develops a talent. The second will complain all her life, "I have absolutely no talent for needlework!"[7]

Similar is the emphasis by Anderson. Our home environment, he points out, like our schools, seems to be so arranged that more practice is given the individual with much practice, and less proportionately to persons with less past practice. Here a child is furnished from early life with the opportunity to hammer nails. In the course of the next ten or fifteen years, the child has 100,000 opportunities to hammer nails, whereas a second child in the same period of time has only ten or fifteen opportunities to hammer nails. At the age of twenty, we may be tremendously impressed with the ease and accuracy with which the first child hammers nails, and ascribe it to an inherited ability perhaps, and be equally impressed with the awkwardness and incapacity of the second child, and its lack of innate ability. The differentiating effect of practice, the rôle of the family audience in its development, may be shown easily in regard to manual skills, and there seems no reason why the same is not true to other forms of behavior. The parable of the talents is apparently the statement of a fundamental principle.[8]

In addition to this selective effect upon skills developed, the family audience operates in other ways to influence the child's behavior. Too much praise from the family habituates the child to expect what no other group is likely to give for desirable behavior. The lack of praise may result in a search for attention-getting behavior of a less desirable sort. To ignore a child is to use a weapon which elicits many varieties of conduct.

4. The child receives from the family its first lessons in living with other persons and in making adjustments to them. The family is a miniature society in which the child comes slowly to discover that there are other persons whose presence, needs, and rights have to be considered. Gradually the child finds that he must limit his demands in the presence of others, and must adjust to them. The transition from the egocentric to the socialized stage takes place gradually and at varying times and rates in different children.

[7] Alfred Adler, "Character and Talent," *Harper's Magazine*, June, 1927.

[8] W. F. Dummer, *The Unconscious*. See Chapter III by John E. Anderson, pp. 82-83.

Sometimes, between eighteen months and three years, true social behavior develops, and chains of response of both the linear and circular type described by Allport put in their appearance.[9]

Certainly the child receives plenty of practice in this process of adjustment. He has to adjust, first of all, to the adults in his family group—parents, relatives, servants, etc.—and each of these adults is apt to be a good deal of a law unto himself. Then, if there are other children in the family, adjustment must be made to them on the basis of their personalities, age, and status in the family group. In other words, the young child has to learn early to shift gears, as it were, continually in his dealing with the other persons in the family group.

A part of this experience is the child's introduction to the study of human behavior. He learns how people act, how they react, how they differ. He learns that one adult talks much and does little, another is exactly the reverse; one threatens but does not punish, another does neither, a third does both. One is amazed to discover at how early an age children classify their elders on the basis of their behavior types. "My daddy don't pank, he just be cross," a two-and-a-half-year-old told her governess, when the latter threatened to report the child's conduct to her father, with the added threat that the father would punish her. Children sense, too, early how members of the family group differ in the ways in which they meet situations and deal with other persons, which techniques succeed and which do not. Mother has her own ways of dealing with daddy when he is angry, this is what grandma did to her neighbor, sister manages to win usually because of her technique, brother Charles seems to lose out so often because he acts thus and so. The family is, in other words, a psychological laboratory and school which is always operative, and in which human nature and relationships are most often seen in the raw, i.e., on the basis of that intimate and uninhibited responsiveness which is the essence of family life.

5. This is perhaps the place to discuss the rôle of the family in the determination of attitudes. The reality and the importance of attitudes has been much emphasized in recent years by the social sciences, as well as the prior and basic importance of the family in

[9] Ibid.

their determination. Among the attitudes formed through family experience are those which its members develop toward each other on the basis of their intimate and emotional relationships. Each member of the family group comes to develop an attitude toward every other member—child toward child, parent toward parent, parent toward child, and child toward parent. It is in this way that the child obtains his patterns for a varied number of later personal relationships.

The attitude of the child toward the parent has been emphasized particularly by students of behavior problems, chiefly because it has in it more than a person-to-person relationship: it involves also the relationship of one person to another who has powers greater than he. The parent, in other words, is not only a person, but also the symbol of authority, and the child's attitude toward the parent becomes also his attitude toward authority.

Dr. James Plant has written with appreciation of this, and in particular of the way in which this rôle of authority is established.

The validators, or criteria for enforcement, of personal authority are age, possession and idiomatic relationship. The validators of social authority are numbers, accomplishment, and acclaim. The validating factor of cosmic authority is its essential "unreasonableness" in the sense that its operation apparently transcends human control or rational planning.

The young child listens to the parent because she is older. "My mother is older, therefore she knows better." Age is of the greatest importance in all children's play. As the older child is orienting himself to new demands, social rather than personal, he says, "My mother is older, therefore she does not know better—she does not understand our age."

Without perhaps actually owning our children, we, as parents, yet attain all of the symbols of such ownership. Thus we feed, clothe, and bundle about the infant as we do other family chattels; and much of the authority relationship is that of "I am *your* mother; you are *my* child."

The third validator is termed idiomatic relationship, in the sense that some peculiar tie exists between parent and child that differs qualitatively from that between either and any other person. One harks back here to what was said as to the establishment of status. It is precisely those factors that enter into the question "Who are you?" that have that unreasonable or irrational element that is the basis of idiomatic personal relationship.

It is possible that certain identifications play a large rôle here, so that I care idiomatically for a person who seems to me to have certain traits in peculiar relation to certain traits that I consider my own. Whether this statement is anything beyond the rationalization of a situation, is beyond our present purview.

Thus the child's adjustments to personal authority come to mean his early conditioning to those factors of age, possession, and idiomatic relationship that enter into personal relationships throughout life. This patently rests a considerable burden upon parents that they act as though they were grown up, instead of merely proclaiming they are; that they show that possession of children is simply a formular expression for their own development and not an end in itself; that idiomatic relationship actually plays its sincere rôle of adding to the child's security.[10]

The importance of adjustment to authority as a pattern of behavior can best be appreciated when it is remembered that every individual lives his life constantly in the presence of forces greater than he. These forces may be cosmic, such as the forces of nature; or political, such as the state; or occupational, such as the employer; or domestic, such as one's mate; they may be all of these, and others, existing at the same time. All of us must adjust all through our lives to persons and forces greater than we.

Modern psychiatrists who contend that much adult behavior is the result of childhood patterns formed through family experience have emphasized greatly the rôle of the family in the creation, through parent-child relationships, of patterns of reaction to authority. Illustrative of this point of view is Mr. J. C. Flügel[11] who points out that the extent and the rapidity with which a child attains to independence are largely prophetic of the subsequent attainment of independence toward the world at large;[12] that much of the intolerance of, and resistance to, authority of certain individuals or even of whole sections of a community, are due to unconscious hatreds of parents; that much criminality is due to the same source; the displacement on to physicians, priests, etc., of feelings, originally directed to the parents, is frequent;[13] and that

[10] James Plant, "The Child as a Member of the Family," *The Annals of the American Academy of Political and Social Science*, March, 1932, p. 69.

[11] J. C. Flügel, *The Psycho-Analytic Study of the Family.*

[12] *Ibid.*, pp. 46-47.

[13] *Ibid.*, pp. 119-120.

resistance to political, civil, and educational authority is to be explained in many cases on the same basis.

6. We are on more objective ground when we proceed to point out that the child gets from the family many of the tools with which he acquires his later education. Particularly important in this connection is the acquisition of language. Words are the symbolization of experience, and the number, variety, and adequacy of the words the young child learns through his family experience, and the meanings which are fixed upon these words, become the tools of his subsequent instruction.

Sociologists have emphasized lately the importance of concepts, precisely defined, as tools essential to the development of their science. Many scholars appreciate how accurate thinking is handicapped by confusion in meaning of words used, even by savants. Every university teacher learns through experience how students misinterpret him because words mean one thing to him and another to the student. Most adults can recall how they carried through earlier years misconceptions derived from words not properly understood. How important, then, must be the word tools of a child in his ordinary instruction. We need to know much more about this than we now do.

7. Finally, the child gets through his family experience his first living habits, and because so many of these first habits remain through later life, this acquisition is of very great importance in the development of the person.

Living habits are specific things, both as to the area of life they comprehend, and as to the particular procedures involved. That is to say, eating habits revolve around the food needs, and they include foods relished and eaten, how and when eaten, with what regularity, in what combinations and amounts. We are dealing here not with vague general notions but for the most part with very definite concrete aspects of living. John develops the habit of gulping down his food; it is Mary's habit to eat no, or a scant, breakfast; Bill never eats liver.

It must not be assumed that these living habits are only those which have to do with eating, sleeping, bathing, bowel movements, and the like. They include many other things, such as method of walking, manner of speaking, gestures, grimaces, carriage, way of sitting, use of eyes and hands, care of personal appearance, and the like. Detailed studies of human interaction reveal surprising importance of many such matters, unfortunately often considered by parents as trivial.

Out of a vast amount of scientific data of recent years, two facts stand out in clear relief. One of these is that the foundations of human personality are laid down in early childhood; the second, that the chief molder of personality thus becomes the family. It is in family experience that we find the origin and fixation of the reactions of one individual to another.

Very early in life, almost at the cradle, our social schooling commences. It proceeds with rapidity and dispatch—for the amount of stimulation is tremendous and the motivation great. Fixations occur, habits run through their course to automaticity, more complex behavior is built upon them as foundations. . . . The behavior of the adult toward persons has its genesis in the behavior of the child toward persons. Social behavior is of a piece with all other forms of behavior and is governed by the same laws.[14]

It has been pointed out already that there is a second group of scientific studies which have concerned themselves with the generic processes in interpersonal relations. These studies have an objective far broader than our particular interest here, and the general area of investigation is one which must include perforce many scientific disciplines. It may be, as Cottrell and Gallagher suggest, that social psychology, conceived to comprehend such a field, "will be the biochemistry of the social sciences,"[15] but it is equally obvious that to study the generic processes of interpersonal relations, psychology, psychiatry, psychoanalysis, cultural anthropology, sociology, and other sciences all have their contributions to make. The analysis of family situations in terms of process is then a part of this larger area of investigation of interpersonal relations per se.

THE CULTURAL CONTENT OF FAMILY SITUATIONS

A third approach to the study of family situations concerns itself with their cultural content. Both structure and process are but

[14] Anderson, *op. cit.*, p. 90.
[15] Leonard S. Cottrell and Ruth Gallagher, "Developments in Social Psychology, 1930-1940," *Sociometry Monograph, No. 1,* p. 58. See also Kimball Young, *Personality and Problems of Adjustment.*

means to an end, and that end is the content which they serve to convey. This matter of cultural content is in many ways the basic aspect of a family situation, and yet it is perhaps the most neglected one in the study of family situations and of behavior problems. This is all the more astonishing when one stops to consider certain related developments in recent sociological thought. One of these is the sociologists' emphasis upon cultural data. In recent years, sociologists have been busy rewriting their theoretical framework in terms of the study of contemporary culture. An excellent illustration of this would be a textbook like that of Nimkoff and Ogburn's *Sociology*, which has had such a vogue in recent years. The second related development has been the undeclared but unmistakable search by sociologists for a distinctive approach to the study of behavior problems. In a measure, sociologists have busied themselves during the past two decades in rehashing and restating the psychiatric and psychological material on behavior problems, when all the while there has been at their very front door this rich vein of sociological material, so aptly a part of their field of investigation and so pregnant with meaning for the interpretation of behavior.

As a basis for this phase of the study of family situations, it seems pertinent to examine briefly the culture-transmitting function of the family, so far as the child is concerned. This is one of the fundamental services which the family renders to the child. It is through the family that the child gets its first introduction to the culture of its era and area. And, for a number of years, the family remains the chief agency through which the child has its contacts with the larger cultural scene.

The family, however, is more than a mere vehicle for the transmission of culture to the child. Speaking more precisely, the family performs customarily three additional or supplementary functions: (a) it selects from the existing surroundings that which it transmits; (b) it interprets to the child that which it transmits; and (c) it evaluates that which it transmits. The child, in other words, sees its cultural heritage through the eyes of its family; it learns of it through the symbols which the family uses; it shares the family's feelings toward it. Knowledge of, and attitude toward, the culture are intertwined in the child's mind from the very beginning, and when, as the child grows older, other agencies compete with the family in these transmitting and rating processes, they but build upon an emotionally tinged foundation already established by the family.

In the objective analysis of the cultural content of family situations, consideration should be given to such aspects of this cultural content as are significant to an understanding of human behavior as affected by family situations. At least six such aspects can be identified readily.

The Ethos, or the National Cultural Pattern

The child is born to a particular cultural pattern in the contemporary world, usually national in scope, and as of a definite historical epoch. From the beginning it is swept along on the tide of this culture, accepting it for the most part without question.

The distinguishing pattern of culture of a particular society was called *ethos* by the ancient Greeks, and William Graham Sumner, pioneer American sociologist, utilized the term to apply it to the totality of characteristic traits by which a society is individualized and differentiated from other societies.[16] It is in the ethos, or its societal character, then, that the United States differs fundamentally from Fascist Italy, modern Persia, ancient Judea, or the interior of China in 2000 B.C.

To this ethos, or national cultural pattern, the child is introduced by his family. This introduction is in part formal, but much more it is incidental and imperceptible. The ethos surrounds the child at every turn, he learns it because he knows no other. It is like the air he breathes or the landscape he sees. It is to him but a natural part of the scheme of things. And all the time, as he learns the culture he absorbs too the family attitude toward it. He shares this attitude with his parents, and because of his emotional relationship to his parents his attitude toward the culture becomes emotionally tinged. Thus originate those feelings toward one's country, and about other countries whose cultural pattern is different, with which we are so much concerned in recent years.

The identification of the family version of this national culture pattern is highly important in any country; it is peculiarly so in the United States because of the heterogeneity of our population.

[16] William G. Sumner, *Folkways*, pp. 37-38.

In 1930, the last census tabulation available at the present writing, one-third of the population of the continental United States consisted of persons who were foreign born and native born of foreign parents. Included in these two elements were twenty-nine nationality groups consisting of more than 100,000 persons, sixteen of more than 500,000, and eleven of more than a million.

In many cases, considerable numbers of persons in one nationality group have lived together in a relatively compact manner so as to maintain various features of their alien culture despite many years of American residence. In the study of family situations from the point of view of cultural content, it becomes important to ask questions such as those which follow. Is the family version of the ethos of this American-reared child an American version, an American-Sicilian one, or an American-Bulgarian one? Do the father and mother represent the same national culture? Is that of the immediate family and that of the larger kinship-group family the same? Here, concretely speaking, is a young man, born and reared on the lower East Side of New York, son of an Italian father and an Irish mother. What is his national culture pattern, as transmitted by his family?

The Regional Pattern

Recently, social scientists have broken down the nation into regions. The region is a unit part of the larger society, identified first in geographic terms, subsequently on the basis of trade and other economic considerations, and now increasingly on cultural bases. Much of the research work on the region today is on the basis of identifying selected traits which lend themselves to statistical treatment. Dr. Howard Odum has made a noteworthy contribution by dividing the states of the nation into six groups on the basis of outstanding similarities of culture.[17] The Division of Social Research of the Works Progress Administration makes an interesting report on *Cultural Regions within the Rural-Farm Population*. It identifies twenty-nine cultural areas and 210 sub-regions within these areas.

[17] Howard Odum, *Southern Regions of the United States;* H. W. Odum and H. E. Moore, *American Regionalism;* National Resources Committee, *Regional Factors in National Planning and Development.*

These cultural areas are not mere academic distinctions. Under one name or another, they have long been recognized in popular parlance as well as in more intellectual discussions. The Southerner differs from the Maine Yankee, and the Iowan in Hollywood is unlike both; the Prussian and the Bavarian have never "spoken the same language"; the North Italian is different in many respects in his ways, his speech, and his ideas from the Sicilian.

The region has its distinct cultural features. It carries

certain dominant motifs which serve as selective norms and as centers with reference to which conduct is directed. . . . It is this complex regional culture which produces the personality patterns of its inhabitants through the stimuli which it radiates, the preferences and choices which it offers, and the distinctive placement of persons or groups of persons, which constitutes its structure.[18]

The region, in other words, is a distinctive social system, supplying a plan for personality patterning. It is this regional or sectional variant of the national cultural pattern which is imposed through the family upon the child.

Concretely again, here is a child living in Massachusetts, in a city in which the community cultural pattern is American Irish. The child lives in a family of South Carolinian rearing and descent. What version of the regional culture is transmitted by the family to the child? What is the relation of this family pattern to that of the community?

The Class Culture

The population of any national and regional society is divided in turn into classes and groups. The bases for such divisions are numerous, and vary in the importance accorded to them.[19] Some of the resultant groupings are of less importance, but others, and these are the ones with which we are concerned, rest upon differences which have marked meaning in the general society, and come to be distinct and rather fixed in character. Particularly important are those divisions which rest upon race, national cultural origin,

[18] J. O. Hertzler, "Some Notes on the Social Psychology of Regionalism," *Social Forces*, March, 1940, pp. 331-332.
[19] Cf. C. C. North, *Social Differentiation*.

economic resources, hereditary privileges, and intellectual attainment.

As social classes become distinct and fixed, they develop common interests, a spirit of coöperation and mutual aid, a feeling of consciousness of kind.

There are built up a set of common attitudes, habits, sentiments and values upon which the members agree, which give them a basis for understanding each other, and upon which they may act in harmony. To belong to a caste or class is to know how to act in prescribed ways. It gives a fixity and a predictability to behavior which may be important in the smooth running of the social order.[20]

Other features which develop are marked feelings towards other classes, both higher and lower in the societal hierarchy. In other words, social classes develop their own culture patterns.

The family transmits the cultural pattern of its own class to the child, together with the class attitudes toward other classes. The family influence upon the child is particularly significant in its rating of social classes, placing its own class in the scale and determining attitudes toward other classes. Here one finds marked emotions, for these matters of class distinctions go far below the surface. Prejudice and appreciation, antagonism and coöperation, pride and a rankling sense of injustice—these develop as by-products of the transmission of the class culture. Class bias has its roots in the family setting of the child, and has taken form before the family turns the child over to other culture-transmitting agencies.

Highly instructive in interpreting the differences in class culture and their meaning for the child are the recent publications of the Yankee City Series. Warner and Lunt have shown how the child's physical contacts, its school associations, its curriculum selection, its clique memberships, and the rôle of the ceremonial in its home— all of these and other aspects of the child's life are dictated by the family's place in the class structure of the society.[21]

By way of illustration of the deeply rooted and abiding nature of family attitudes toward other groups and classes, one might recall Donald Young's study of race attitudes of 450 university

[20] Kimball Young, *An Introductory Sociology*, p. 475.
[21] W. Lloyd Warner and Paul S. Lunt, *The Social Life of a Modern Community*.

students, and the effectiveness of objective university instruction in changing such attitudes. This study indicates but slight changes as the result of such instruction. "Apparently the 15 weeks of logic, facts, and figures in 30 classroom hours of a semester course is not an adequate counter-irritant to 15 years or more of attitude-building in life situations."[22]

In summary, the child gets from the family pattern a way of living, based on the fact that he is born in a certain class in a given religion in a particular nation. It learns the life of Boston rather than of Burma; of the flat or the farm; of the slum or the suburb; of the Sicilian concrete mixer or of the Fifth Avenue surgeon. In other words, the child gets from the family his class cultural orientation. As a functioning element in the cultural content of any given family situation, there must be considered, then, the family version of the class culture which has been transmitted to the child.

Status

As the child is being introduced to his cultural heritage, there arise other questions of a more personal nature. Who am I? What am I? What is my own particular relation to this cultural situation in which I find myself? What is my peculiar place in it? What is my status?

These questions arise early, and are insistent. Parents may sense them before children develop to the point of formulating them. Social workers recognize the craving in adopted and foster children to learn about their own parents—who they were, what sort of people they were, regardless of how they may have been treated by them. The press is replete with stories of grown persons seeking knowledge of parents never known to them. The study of genealogy is a very human and understandable quest.

Sociologists and psychiatrists have made much of the concept of status. They define it to mean position in society, the standing accorded to the individual by his fellows. Status, in other words, is place on a prestige scale. Linton defines it in terms of polar positions

---

[22] Donald Young, *American Minority Peoples*, pp. 15-16. See also Donald Young, "Some Effects of a Course in American Race Relations on the Race Prejudices of 450 Undergraduates at the University of Pennsylvania," *Journal of Abnormal and Social Psychology*, October-December, 1927, pp. 235-242.

in the patterns of reciprocal behavior between individuals and groups.[23] Perhaps one might summarize by saying that status involves one's personal orientation in his cultural setting.

One of the most important things which the family does for the child is to give it status. Or rather, one should speak of the statuses which the child gets from the family. There is, first of all, its status within the family of procreation. With the coming of another child, this status is modified, often quite materially so. Again, the child has its status within the family of orientation, if that differs from the family of procreation. In these statuses within the immediate family, sex, age, and age relationship are the chief determining factors.

It is with reference to the child's status in the larger society that the family serves a most important function. In this connection both the immediate and the kinship group types may be of very great importance in giving the child its status in the world of its fellows. The family does this by means of two things: it gives the child a name and a social position. Without a name, the child is but an undifferentiated human organic unit. When he is named, he becomes "somebody." Then, by virtue of his family, he obtains a place in the social group. He is now what sociologists call a "person," i.e., an individual with status.[24]

What has just been said suggests the tremendous rôle of a family name and tradition in the development of a child. Professor Nimkoff contrasts in this connection the histories of several well-known American families. As an example on the positive side is the well-known Adams family, which for two centuries has been distinguished for its record of public service. John Adams (1735-1826) was the second President of the United States. His cousin, Samuel Adams, was an outstanding leader in the American Revolution. His son, John Quincy Adams, was our sixth President. His son, in turn, Charles Francis Adams, was U. S. Minister to England. The latter's son, Henry Adams, became a distinguished historian, and his son, in turn, Charles Francis Adams, was Secretary of the Navy in the administration of President Hoover. As illustrations on the

[23] Ralph B. Linton, op. cit., Chapter VIII.
[24] Robert Park and E. W. Burgess, An Introduction to the Science of Society, p. 55.

negative side may be cited the Juke and Kallikak families, so well known to students of American social problems. It requires but little imagination to appreciate the tremendous handicap imposed by these family names upon their successive generations.[25]

This factor of status is related closely to two other concepts much emphasized in the recent literature of social psychology and psychiatry. One of these is the matter of security. We all seek security throughout life. Very early in life the child senses security or insecurity as a member of the family group. He feels that he was wanted or not wanted; that he was a boy when his mother wanted a boy, or the reverse; that he came too soon, or when he was wanted. Later on, he seeks security through membership in secondary groups, through achievement of one sort or another. Many a personality pattern of extreme aggressiveness or incessant restlessness or an insatiable drive for power results from deep-seated insecurity formed during this period. Still later, people seek security in marriage. The pattern of many marriages is not one of romance, but of a drive for that security which the chosen mate may give. A part of the quest for security is for physical and economic safeguards against the threats of an external, foreboding world; but much of it is psycho-social—a wanting to belong.

Status has a great deal to do with conduct through its effect upon one's conception of one's self. The rôle of the conception of one's self has been grasped by many students of human nature. William James used to remark that a man had as many selves as there were persons who recognized him and carried an image of him in their minds. The poet Masefield writes:

> And there were three men went down the road,
>   As down the road went he.
> The man they saw, the man he was,
>   And the man he wanted to be.

Status is a factor in the determination of one's conception of the self, and this conception in turn is a determinant in the behavior of the person. This, then, is another element in the cultural content of a family situation which should be considered.

[25] M. F. Nimkoff, *The Family*, pp. 68 ff.

Cultural Values

The culture to which the child is born is too vast, too comprehensive, too diverse, to be transmitted in its entirety, either by the family or by other agencies subsequently assisting it. This is particularly true of ideas, beliefs, and values in the culture. As has been pointed out already, from the very beginning of the adjustment of the child to his culture, there is going on through the family a selective and evaluating process which determines which elements of the culture are transmitted, and what attitudes accompany the transmission.

There are a number of factors which determine in turn this selective and evaluating process. It is in part a matter of the parts of the culture which the family knows; in part, it depends on what in the culture the family has access to; in part, it is a product of the family's experience with different aspects of the culture; finally, there is the powerful influence of the hopes of the family. Each family is prone to see its children as its future, so that domestic hopes and ideals are imposed upon the children, often with more emotional accompaniment than are the realities of the culture. In other words, every family transmits the cultural heritage in its own way. More than that, it transmits its own version, compounded out of what it can see of the culture, how it does see it, and how it wants to see it.

The result of this selective and evaluating process by the family is the formation of the child's sense of values, both in regard to personal pursuits and social behavior. The culture to which the child is born has its folkways, its mores, and its scale of rewards for differing schematizations of living. But it is within the bosom of the family that judgments are formed, conflicts in culture are resolved, choices are made or at least influenced. Life is varied and complex, infinitely full of possibilities. Personality development is a constant series of choices. These choices represent the person's values, and modern scholarship concludes that these values are the result in large part of family conditioning.

Striking statistical confirmation of the relative importance of the family in this respect can be found in a study made by Hartshorne and May of the sources from which children derive their ethical concepts. The methodology pursued in this study was to note the degree of correspondence between the moral judgments of the child and those of other persons with whom he was closely associated. The correlation between the children's ideas of right and wrong and the scores of their associates revealed the following results:

Child and parents .... .545
Child and friends .... .353
Child and club leaders .... .137
Child and day-school teachers .... .028
Child and Sunday school teachers .... .002

A perfect correlation would be represented by 1,000, so in interpreting the above figures, whatever other questions may be raised, it is clear that the most significant correspondence exists between the judgments of the children and those of the parents. The study also found that the judgments of the children were more closely allied to those of the mother than of the father.[26]

So fundamental is the rôle of the cultural values transmitted by the family and operating in any given family situation, that the fullest consideration must be given to their identification and operation. Unfortunately, sociologists have shown a reluctance to deal with values, apparently on the ground that their intangible and subjective nature made their objective study impossible. Being relative newcomers in the study of behavior problems, sociologists seem to have leaned over backward in their desire to confine themselves to data and methods similar to those of the older and more established natural sciences. It is an implication of the outline of study proposed in this chapter that culture values can be studied objectively. An illustration taken from the records of a juvenile court case may clarify this contention. A fourteen-year-old boy has been guilty of stealing. After a court hearing he is committed to a probation officer. In the course of his contact with the boy, the probation officer leans that the boy's family habitually steal the coal consumed in their home from the coal cars in a railroad siding nearby. During the past six years, the family has bought no fuel, stealing to the amount of its needs. These systematic thefts, furthermore, are spoken of by the family, and are rationalized on various grounds

[26] H. Hartshorne and M. A. May, "Testing the Knowledge of Right and Wrong," *Religious Education*, October, 1926, pp. 539-554.

by the adults in the family. Also, a number of neighboring families behave similarly in regard to their fuel needs. Here, it certainly would seem, is a family value, which can be identified through overt behavior extending over a period of years.

The foregoing reference to the cultural content of family situations is obviously but a brief description of some of the more important aspects which must be considered. The adequate analysis of family culture, its relation to the culture of the community on the one hand and to the child on the other, must be far more comprehensive and specific than the foregoing description has served to show. Such analysis is yet in its infancy. Some further implications of it will be discussed in the concluding chapter of this volume.

SUMMARY

In this third chapter, an effort has been made to bring out in particular these six ideas, which are stated again in summary form.

1. The term "family situation," as utilized in this volume, involves the application of our definition of the phrase "social situation" to the specific family group.

2. The situational approach to human behavior should begin with the study of family situations, not only because of their very great importance in the development of patterns of behavior, but also because they seem to offer the best opportunities for the development of an adequate technique for study.

3. The objective analysis of family situations should consist of three distinct approaches: in terms of structure, process, and content.

4. The study of the structure of family situations should include the structural organization of the family, the characteristics of the constituent elements in family situations, and the nature of their continuing relationship.

5. Studies of process in family situations may be divided into two groups. First are those dealing with the interactive aspect of family life, and second are those which center about the generic processes in interpersonal relations.

6. The cultural content of family situations constitutes perhaps their basic aspect. Both structure and process are but means to an end, and that end is the content which they convey. The study of the cultural content of family situations is, on the other hand, rela-

tively neglected: this in spite of the sociologists' emphasis upon cultural data and of the family's obvious rôle in the transmission, selection, interpretation, and evaluation of culture for the child.

7. The adequate analysis of the cultural content of family situations must recognize at least five aspects—the national culture pattern, the regional pattern, the class culture, the status of the family, and its cultural values. Each of these must be analyzed objectively, for the family situation as a whole.

CHAPTER IV

CLASSIFICATION IN THE GROWTH
OF KNOWLEDGE

THE FIRST chapter of this volume made clear, it is hoped, how the situational approach to human behavior came to be developed, and what are the basic implications underlying that approach. Chapter II sought to explain what the term "social situation" has come to mean, and in what ways it can be studied by scientific students. In the third chapter, the general outline of the study proposed was applied to family situations, to show the lines along which the objective analysis of family situations could proceed with advantage.

The next of the theses to be presented in this volume brings us to the subject of classification. Once family situations come to be analyzed on the basis of anything resembling a comprehensive outline, once such analyses can be "mounted" on the cards of the "scientific collector," once the number of such descriptive analyses begin to accumulate, the question of their classification inevitably presents itself. It is the contention of the present study that, following the objective analyses of family situations along the lines indicated in the preceding chapter, the next logical step is their classification. It is the purpose of the present chapter to show: first, that such a sequence corresponds to what has taken place in other fields of knowledge; and second, that the actual beginnings in the development of a classification of family situations have already been made.

THE BEGINNINGS OF CLASSIFICATION

To classify means to arrange according to a system. That man should classify his ideas and facts very early in human history seems quite obvious; that the desire to do so grew with the accumulation of his knowledge is equally clear; and that such systems or classifications have been an essential instrument in the expansion of his knowledge may also be taken as self-evident.

In the simplest of cultures, man has always found a need for grouping the many materials and objects that have formed his world. When primitive man separated his hunting tools from his household utensils, so that each might be in the place most accessible to his needs, he was grouping them according to his description of the uses of those tools. When he began to think of animals as dangerous, as harmless, or as useful, and of plants as being medicinal, edible, or poisonous, he was separating them according to differences and grouping them because of likenesses which he had learned from experiences that directly affected him. These groupings enabled him to think of many separate entities in terms of some broad generalization, freeing him from the burden of carrying the knowledge of each one as an individual experience.

The centuries that brought the growth of civilization and complexity of cultures gave a tremendous stimulus to the desire and need to put things in order. Erik Nordenskiold says:

As long as man's knowledge of nature is limited to what he can observe in his immediate vicinity, he has little difficulty in controlling the objects of his knowledge, but when his range of vision widens, there arises the irresistible need for combining the individual objects that have been observed under general expressions, which seem to fix the knowledge of them and to impart it to others.[1]

"Native Australians," says W. A. White, "have one word for a sheep's tail, another for a cow's tail, another for a dog's, but no word which would include them all."[2] Think of the almost hopeless complication it would be to modern zoölogists, with their knowledge of thousands of animals, if the properties of each had not been classified, in our language, as common appendages—legs, heads, and tails. In other words, there are so many people in a world so full of a number of things, that it is impossible to grasp them all, to share and to study them with others, if they have to be thought of singly.

From the beginning of life the processes of differentiation and conjunction have been reacting upon each other. As soon as man combines objects into systems to simplify life for himself, he releases just that much more physical and mental energy with which

---

[1] Erik Nordenskiold, *The History of Biology*, p. 190.
[2] William A. White, *Mechanisms of Character Formation*, p. 83.

to satisfy his eternal curiosity and explore the differentiations occurring within the separate systems. In the immaterial, as well as in the material world, he concerns himself with the observation of new phenomena until he is again faced with the need for recombination. This is the story, in short, of the development of man's life from the age of primitive man, whose days were spent in learning the tools for the sustenance of life and the propitiation of the gods, to that of modern man who deals in politics, religion, business, education, the arts and the sciences, and still looks around for some activities with which to fill his leisure time.

THE ACCUMULATION OF DATA IN THE SCIENCES

To speak of *the sciences* themselves is to speak of one of the results of the process of differentiation. Physical and social sciences have become separate categories. Within them, physics, chemistry, botany, biology, sociology set up their autonomy. And as they do so, the concentration upon each brings to man's hand an ever-increasing amount of material pertinent to each discipline. Then, again, within the autonomies, the process of combination starts to appear. It becomes impossible for any one discipline to handle all of the material within it, for the purpose of any kind of study, without reducing it to some lower denominator. In the development of every kind of science, conscious, studied attempts at classification have commenced just whenever the bulk of data in the field has begun to grow impossibly unwieldy.

Thus far, then, classification has come about through certain definite steps. (a) There are phenomena which men observe; (b) these phenomena are described as they appear to men; (c) the number of phenomena and the descriptions increase; until (d) the attempt is made to reduce them into groups for the purpose of easier comprehension.

PROGRESS OF CLASSIFICATION

Just as these classifications have grown from simple groupings, almost unconsciously made, into complicated and studied systems, so have the theory and methodology of classification itself changed. The subjective point of view, which grouped objects as like or different in terms of some particular use to or effect upon man, the center, has gradually given way before the more objective viewpoint, that of classifying objects on the basis of their own structure, and of their interrelationships of sequence or of cause and effect—quite independent of their relation to man, his advantage or his morals. This second change in the system of classifications has been infinitely more slow and difficult in the achieving than that growth which merely accompanied the accumulation of more classifiable data.

In explanation, William Locy remarks,

The animated world impressed itself naïvely on the senses of primitive man. . . . Scientific insight aims at the representation of things of nature as they are. But things are not first seen as they are; they appear as our minds make them. The mind of primitive man opened slowly to vague wonderings of the relations of cause and effect—gropings toward the meaning of natural phenomena—a higher step than mere sense-impressions.[3]

When man did take the higher step that looked for cause, he found it in something outside of himself and the manifestations of nature. Some power, unbound by any law save its own unpredictable will, became the ultimate answer to every searching question.

So long as this was the case, there was little incentive for the search after natural laws. Though there might be a plan for the universe, it was subject to change without notice. The sun might stand still, or the earth be consumed by fire. But there was an even more potent barrier to research. The fear of the sacred prevented minds and eyes from prying into natural phenomena, and those who were the high priests of the sacred jealously guarded the right to their knowledge against more common folk. The ability to bear bravely and unquestioningly the vagaries of this life, for ultimate rewards in the hereafter, was the prescribed purpose of the ordinary man.

Inanimate objects first were divorced from the power of the sacred. Gradually living things which, men declared, had no souls, were freed for objective scrutiny. But whatever touched closely upon the heart and soul of man himself was strictly taboo. This enslavement of man to his own beliefs is sufficient reason why, for

[3] William Locy, *The Growth of Biology*, p. 8.

century after century, while life itself separated into many different disciplines, and observable material accumulated, the basis for many classifications remained at the level of sense-impressions, and why those in the social sciences emerged last of all from that realm.

CLASSIFICATION IN BOTANY

The history of systematic botany shows how, step by step, this change finally took place. Until the sixteenth century there had been practically no study of plant groupings which were in any sense of the word scientific. Interest in plants had been almost exclusively derived from their medicinal qualities. Existing descriptions of specimens were inaccurate and hazy, and made only with the purpose of fixing them in their relation to man's health. The emphasis, then, was on the use of the plant to man, and not at all upon the plant itself. There was, therefore, no particular incentive to examining carefully the structure of plants, but just to naming, describing them and their medicinal properties generally, and philosophizing upon their natures. By the sixteenth century, the confusion caused by this lack of accurate observation was great. Botanists disagreed widely as to which plant was the one actually described; found that plants of the same name were not the same plants at all in different parts of Europe; were uncertain if a plant found in one part existed at all in another. There came about then the attempt to settle the confusion by more accurate descriptions of the plants. Writes Julius von Sachs:

Thus was made the first beginning of a really scientific examination of plants, though the aims pursued were not yet truly scientific, for no questions were proposed as to the nature of the plants, their organization or mutual relations; the only point of interest was the knowledge of individual forms and of their medicinal virtues.[4]

However, accurate description by direct observation, with a minimum of philosophic brooding, brought about in a very few years an accomplishment in the science greater than had been gained since the beginning. For now, though medicinal use to man was the object, it was no longer the basis for classification. The very desire to identify more clearly those plants which were edible, poisonous,

---

[4] Julius von Sachs, *History of Botany*, p. 2.

or medicinal had swung the emphasis on to the *structure* of the plants themselves. These structural elements became the likenesses noted in plant groupings, and the uses of the plants, though they inspired the classification, actually became incidental to it.

So, the accumulation of more detailed descriptions brought the awareness of likenesses and differences and relationships between plants, quite separate from their relations to anything outside themselves. Interest was excited, and botanists found that they gained greater recognition by recording their own observations than by compiling the works of their theorizing predecessors. Inevitably, as the number of investigations increased and new specimens were found, a universal method began to develop, bringing similarity of vocabulary, description, estimate, and separation of forms; in a word, "methodical diagnosis."[5]

As a result, there came about huge catalogues of descriptive material. For purposes of reference they were classed according to natural affinity, those plants with the most marked differences being set into different groups, within which sub-groups designated slighter variations.

Just at this point there appeared the lag which seems to occur at a similar point in the history of every science, the lag between the accumulation of data and the discovery, or acceptance, of some scientific truth that puts lifeblood into the system. According to Deane Swingle, "The ideal classification must embody two qualities. It must show actual genetic relationships and it must be reasonably convenient for practical use. If it fails to show true relationship it is spoken of as 'artificial,' and does not satisfy the discriminating thinker."[6] But the use of "true relationship" presupposes the knowledge of that relationship in scientific terms. The origin of plants was still thought of in metaphysical terms, the constancy of species being the basic assumption. As long as this was the case, the classification had to remain merely a reference or a short cut to handling material. And it did so remain, though constantly growing, until 1859, when Darwin disproved that theory. When the principles of natural selection and variation revealed the effects of known causes, which were in natural law, were open to study, and not dependent upon

[5] *Ibid.*, p. 19.
[6] Deane B. Swingle, *A Textbook of Systematic Botany*, p. 7.

the caprices of their creator, there "arose a real blood-relationship, and the natural system became a table of the pedigree of the vegetable kingdom."[7]

Today, plant classification is a highly organized science. It is not a completed one. New types of plants are continually coming into view, and old orders have to be rearranged on the basis of new knowledge. But after long centuries of groping, the two essentials have been established: the natural relationship of plants according to the laws of plant evolution; and the placing of them within that relationship by the analysis of their own specific structure.

CLASSIFICATION IN BIOLOGY AND MEDICAL SCIENCE

The systems of biology and medical science have run a course very similar to that of botany. For that reason they will be discussed here only in the light of the increasing difficulty with which an experimental science becomes more objective as it becomes more closely associated with man, his body and his soul.

The outstanding difficulties for medical science have been fourfold. First, superstition clings longer and harder to man, who is assumed to have a soul, than to plant or animal, which is not. The idea that whatever happened to man was ordained by God was relinquished with terrible slowness. Second, actual experimentation upon the body and mind of living man is suspect and dangerous, especially so at a time when knowledge is scant. Again, there is the lag which comes to each science when it awaits a new truth or discovery to give it a factual base. In this case it was the wait for the discovery of instruments for seeing and measuring both the germs that cause diseases and the minutest organs affected by them. It was impossible that these causes or effects could be understood when human eyes and hands, unaided, could neither see nor feel them. And last, social standards and values are imposed upon scientific truths already known whenever they touch living man, making their application difficult or impossible. One has only to consider the resistance with which known treatments and cures of venereal diseases were met to understand the height of this last hurdle.

For a long time, then, medical science was hampered in gaining anything like a scientific classificatory system because diseases could

[7] *Ibid.*, p. 12.

not be separated from their manifestations in a patient, and could be described only in those terms. The study of disease, conforming to this method, had brought to light much unrelated and ill-defined data, and more philosophic speculation, with the same kind of confusion resulting that had formerly worn thin the patience of clear-thinking botanists. "Because of this," writes Dr. Shryock, "physicians had the same reason for desiring a grand synthesis as had Newton. There was real need to bring order out of this chaos in medicine, if [it] was to serve any other interest than mere curiosity."[8] And systems were accordingly devised. Classification in medical science reached the stage at which we found systematic botany when careful analysis and accurate description brought about a universal method. But,

The chief basis upon which Sydenham and his successors could distinguish diseases was that of clinical symptoms. This was well enough in the case of a few relatively clear-cut conditions; but as the study of symptoms proceeded with enthusiasm there seemed to be no end to these phenomena. Physicians tried to classify all symptom-diseases, in much the same way that they were classifying plants and animals. When their nosographies listed as many as eighteen hundred presumably different illnesses, it became apparent that good intentions had made confusion worse confounded.[9]

Obviously there was enough medical knowledge to deserve a better system, but there was not yet enough to point the way toward making one. And thus the science stood, indeed even slipped backward, until the microscope and its related instruments led the way to objective measurements and to separated studies of the causes and relationships behind the symptoms of diseases. "With such means of observation and with the quantitative recording of data, the medical science at last emerged on the plane of modern methodology."[10]

SUMMARY

In short, then, a science itself goes through a certain evolution in developing its system.

[8] Richard H. Shryock, *The Development of Modern Medicine*, p. 24.
[9] *Ibid.*, p. 25.
[10] *Ibid.*, p. 166.

Apparently every science, whether we begin with dynamics in the sixteenth century or end with sociology in the twentieth, goes through certain phases. The first stage reveals a minimum of observation and a maximum of theoretical synthesis; the second an early attempt at objectivity and measurement, characterized by pioneer enthusiasms; the third reveals a partial reversion to speculative synthesis and a partial lapse of quantitative procedures—due to difficulties encountered in carrying out the quantitative program; the fourth level witnesses a revival of the quantitative procedure, this time upon a firmer factual basis and with a technique so improved as to make possible a final victory for modern methodology.[11]

When a science has completed these steps in its evolution it has then the foundations for a firm system of the classification of its data; a framework of relationships within which are set the data as their own observed structure places them.

CLASSIFICATION IN THE FIELD OF HUMAN RELATIONS

There is a field for study, an art and not a science, which holds out the need for classification without presenting all of the difficulties found in the sciences. Therefore, though the most natural step would be to proceed directly to an examination of the history of the later social sciences, which will form the content of the following chapter, it seems wise at this point to take a look at the methodological system of this art. This exploration goes into the field of literature and the drama. All of the material of literature is made up of actual life data, combined and recombined. Because of this, it forms an interesting bridge between the physical and the social sciences and the different kinds of data with which they deal. For, to objectify plants, germs, and bones, and separate them from their relationships to man is one thing; to objectify and measure life situations made up of and by man is quite another. In literature these situations are, to a large extent, already objectified. The author deliberately tampers with situations. He holds all the elements in his hand and juggles them to create certain effects upon his book people. The life situations in books may be held up as examples of the morality or evil nature of the author or his characters. But there is no strong taboo against their analysis for classification, for the

[11] *Ibid.*, p. 147.

people concerned in them are only figments of fancy, and the sacred
privacy of personalities will not be violated by the reader's prying
into their situations.

The material needed for a classification has already been at hand,
and on the printed page, for generations—and even centuries. In
the novels, short stories, poetry, and drama of the world there
lies, just for the reading, the whole gamut of man's activities, emotions, and relationships. The completeness of a literary life situation
brings a bit of solace to the heart of a student of actual human
relations as he turns to it after scanning case record after case record.
There is a great deal to be gained for both the art and the science
in the supplementing of these two fields of investigation into human
life. From the clinical record, the writer can learn of the critical
realities of life. He, in turn, with the keen perception and sympathetic imagination that always mark a real artist, can round out
those critical realities into a situation of subjective living that seems
more humanly real, more believable and understandable. Nor is
the student of human nature apt to be misled by fantasy, if, in
using literary situations, he avoids the frankly escapist literature.
For realistic literature which survives does so because its situations,
in their elements, are real and pertinent to all literate people in all
ages. Almost, in reading what has survived, one can read what is
elemental.

The need which has made itself felt and has resulted in the
classification of life situations in the literary field is a very material
one. A plot does not usually spring full-born from the brow of any
pretender to literary fame. Variety is a goal, but situation elements are, after all, limited in number. Therefore it is a stimulus
for the struggler in Grub Street in finding beside him a simple
grouping of all the elements that have gone into the making of
classic situations. Here he can find what situations have been most
popular, and he can make his choice of an unworn one, or he may
so mix the elements as to make a worn one seem novel. Though
there may be nothing new under the sun, there can surely be an
easier avoidance of the trite if all of the old is scanned and in-
geniously recombined.

Classifications of life situations have been attempted in the literary field, then, both because the necessary material is readily available, and because the results of sorting it are directly usable.

A CLASSIFICATION OF DRAMATIC SITUATIONS

A pioneer in the classification of life situations was Georges Polti. His particular interest was in discovering how many different situations had been used in the drama and the relative frequency of each. Gozzi, he knew, had stated that there were but thirty-six. Schiller had not been able to find so many. But neither one had left much evidence for their conclusions. Polti decided to attack the evidence first, and work toward a conclusion. Thus in its general procedure, Polti's work in *The Thirty-Six Dramatic Situations* is true to the best scientific tradition.[12]

More than a thousand classic works of literature formed the material for this study. Polti examined them for each separate situation which they held, and attempted to group together those situations most nearly alike in their structure. He describes, thus, his own method of examining these structures:

To obtain the nuances of the Thirty-Six Situations, I have had recourse almost constantly to the same method of procedure; for example, I would enumerate the ties of friendship or kinship possible between the characters; I would determine also their degree of consciousness, of free-will and knowledge of the real end toward which they were moving. And we have seen that when it is desired to alter the normal degree of discernment in one of the two adversaries, the introduction of a second character is necessary, the first becoming the blind instrument of the second, who is at the same time invested with a Machiavellian subtlety, to such an extent does his part in the action become purely intellectual. Thus, clear perception being in the one case excessively diminished, it is, in the other, proportionately increased. Another element for modifying all the situations is the energy of the acts which may result from them. Murder, for instance, may be reduced to a wound, a blow, an attempt, an outrage, an intimidation, a threat, a too-hasty word, an intention not carried out, a temptation, a thought, a wish, an injustice, a destruction of a cherished object, a refusal, a want of pity, an abandonment, a falsehood. A third method of varying the situations: for this or that one of the adversaries whose struggle constitutes our drama, there may be substituted a group of characters animated by a single desire, each member of the group reflecting that desire under a different light. There is, moreover, no Situation which may not be combined with any one of its neighbors, nay, with two, three, four, five,

[12] Georges Polti, *The Thirty-Six Dramatic Situations.*

six of them and more! Now, t se combinations may be of many sorts; in the first case the situations develop successively and logically one from another; in the second case they dispose themselves in a dilemma, in the midst of which hesitates the distracted hero; in the third case, each one of them will appertain to a particular group or a particular rôle; in the fourth, fifth, sixth cases, etc., they are represented according to two, or according to all three of the cases already brought together in one situation.[13]

There is here a surprising grasp of situation analysis. Polti has considered as *structure* numbers of relationships, kinship, affectional relationships and degree of intensity, dominance-submission —and in the classification itself he gives heed also to sex and status relationships. The *specificity* of situations is suggested. Further, he has noted the content of situations as it affects different members differently, and as it is derived from both internal and external factors. And finally, he has suggested the *process* which builds up one situation, changes it and produces yet another situation.

But analysis is only the first step to classification. As we have already seen, there must be a logical framework of relatedness within which the structures, separated by analysis, are to fit. This framework must be objective, dependent for its meaning only upon the phenomena under scrutiny. When Polti arranged his situations into a system he reduced his classification to the semi-scientific type that was in use when plants were considered only in the light of their effects upon man. For Polti's real interest was not in the situation but in the drama. And drama is born of man's emotions. Thus the framework of Polti's classification became the kinds of passions roused in man by certain situations, and they all had to be squeezed in to fit under the heading of the appropriate response they raised in man.[14] Perhaps Polti had some justification, because of his specific

[13] *Ibid.*, pp. 129-130.
[14] Polti's classification runs as follows:
  1. Supplication.
  2. Deliverance.
  3. Crime pursued by Vengeance.
  4. Vengeance taken for Kindred upon Kindred.
  5. Pursuit.
  6. Disaster.
  7. Falling Prey to Cruelty or Misfortune.
  8. Revolt.

purpose, in that emotion is the beginning and the end of drama. But as the drama unfolds, an emotional relationship is only one of the structural elements of a life situation. To subordinate all others to it as if they were merely variations of it is to oversimplify. For a sex relationship, an age or status relationship is not just such a variation. Each one has its own meaning and effects, quite apart from any emotion concerned in them.

Selections from a sample category, summarized, will show how all classes of structure were subordinated to the one fact of the kind of emotional relationship they happened to create:

Rivalry of Superior and Inferior
(Emotional relationship arising from status)
Necessary elements: The Superior Rival, the Inferior Rival; the Object.
A. Masculine Rivalries. (sex relationship)
    1. Of a Powerful Person and an Upstart. (status)

---

   9. Daring Enterprise.
  10. Abduction.
  11. The Enigma.
  12. Obtaining.
  13. Enmity of Kinsmen.
  14. Rivalry of Kinsmen.
  15. Murderous Adultery.
  16. Madness.
  17. Fatal Imprudence.
  18. Involuntary Crimes of Love.
  19. Slaying of a Kinsman Unrecognized.
  20. Self-Sacrifice for an Ideal.
  21. Self-Sacrifice for Kindred.
  22. All Sacrificed for a Passion.
  23. Necessity of Sacrificing Loved Ones.
  24. Rivalry of Superior and Inferior.
  25. Adultery.
  26. Crimes of Love.
  27. Discovery of the Dishonor of a Loved One.
  28. Obstacles to Love.
  29. An Enemy Loved.
  30. Ambition.
  31. Conflict with a God.
  32. Mistaken.
  33. Erroneous Judgment.
  34. Remorse.
  35. Recovery of a Lost One.
  36. Loss of a Loved One.

2. Of Rich and Poor. (economic status)
3. Of a Man Who Is Loved and One Who Has not the Right to Love. (emotional and status)
B. Feminine Rivalries. (sex)
   1. Of Lady and Servant. (status)
   2. Double Rivalry. (number)
   3. Oriental Rivalries. (culture)*

Polti's contribution to the classification of situations can be compared to that of Linnaeus to systematic botany. Raymond Pool has said,

On the whole the system of classification and nomenclature that Linnaeus gave us is a truly remarkable one when we consider the relatively few plant characteristics that were employed in making it. If he had only hit upon the greater value of a larger number of characters he doubtless would have introduced a system that would be in use to this day. But that is probably expecting too much from even one of the world's greatest men at a time when civilization had only lately emerged from a long period of superstition and almost impenetrable darkness.[15]

Polti, because of his keen ability as an analyst, might have constructed a scientific classification of as great use to students of life as to students of the drama, had he considered more characters as of equal importance.

A Study of Marriage Situations in the Drama

There is a study of life situations in literature, by Donald Koster,[16] which is of interest for two reasons. First, it is a concentration upon one particular kind of life situation, the marriage situation. And second, it is strong, for our purpose, where Polti's was weak, in the framework within which the results are suspended.

Dr. Koster's study is of all the plays written in America since 1785, in which the theme of marriage is treated. Though its intentional emphasis is on analysis and not on classification, the latter was inevitably resorted to for orderly presentation. But this simple

---

* Parentheses contain author's analysis of units which should be considered as independent elements of a situation and not as different causes of one emotion.

[15] Raymond J. Pool, *Flowers and Flowering Plants*, p. 134.

[16] Donald N. Koster, "The Theme of Marriage in the American Drama," dissertation, in manuscript.

and incidental tool of the author's, in the very labeling of its classes, discloses that objective consideration of the material studied which is essential to any present-day classificatory system.

Some of the designations run as follows: *The Marriage of Convenience, The Marriage for Love, The Triangle, Barriers to Marital Happiness, Relations Between Parent and Children* (in so far as these relations influence the marriage of either parent or child or both), and *Love Triumphant over Obstacles.* The structure and content elements are then classed under those headings. Within *The Marriage of Convenience,* for instance, we find: parental arrangement, desire for money and luxury, social position, control over others, companionship, desire for respect as an individual, and so on.

The situation here is given its autonomy. It depends upon no relation to anything outside of itself, not the drama from which it was picked, or the individuals it will affect, but only upon how one marriage situation seems to be different from, or like another. The elements analyzed out of a situation can then fall into place where they naturally belong in the relation of a part to the whole.

This is the situational approach in the classification of life data. The situation itself must receive its autonomy before it can be classified according to both of those scientific essentials: accurate analysis and natural interrelationship.

SUMMARY

The purpose of this chapter, in discussing the history and development of certain classifications, has been to highlight certain facts.

1. Classifications have always existed in the form of spontaneous expressions of man's need to group the data known to him. These are simple groupings expressing either superficial similarities as they appear to man, or similar properties as they affect man.

2. As new data are gathered, they are analyzed in terms of their structural elements to be properly identified. If the descriptive analysis is only incidental to some particular subjective use of the data, then the classification is not yet constructed in accordance with the ideals of modern methodology.

3. At some point in each system, the discovery of some principle or tool makes possible the study of the data of each system in their own relationships, and not in their relation to something outside of themselves. Then an attitude of complete objectivity is reached and the classification may become truly scientific.

4. Systematic botany and medical science have progressed through these stages slowly, but with relatively greater ease than the later social sciences because the objective study of man and his life is obviously more difficult than that of plants and diseases.

5. Classifications attempted in literature and the drama are an intermediate step between those in the physical sciences and those in the later social sciences. They deal, not with tangibles which can be physically separated from man, but with the inextricable elements that compose situations in the life of man. Thus they encounter all of the difficulties of the analysis of intangibles. At the same time they have the advantage of being separated from man and his resistance to self-analysis because they are not reality but are constructions from reality.

6. Two specific studies of literary situations have shown: (a) that life situations can be analyzed in terms of structure and content; (b) that these situations can be classed as objective entities, independent, and having meaning both in themselves and in their interrelationship.

CHAPTER V

THE CLASSIFICATION OF FAMILY
SITUATIONS: A HISTORICAL REVIEW

A STRIKING parallel has occurred between the developments of classification in science and in family situations, though the latter has been quicker in its pace. The four stages of evolution in classification, as seen by Dr. Shryock in the field of science (see Chapter IV), are clearly discernible in the literature of family life. These stages are not so easily separated by dates as in other systems, for the whole field of the study of family relationships is so new, relatively, and has progressed so rapidly, that while enterprising ground-breakers were ushering in a new development, the majority of students in the field were still doggedly producing volumes of material from a far less enlightened point of view. Certain beacons, however, shine out as the guides which have brought the classification of family situations to the stage in which we find it today, and it is to a review of these that this chapter is devoted.

THE PERIOD OF PHILOSOPHIZING IN TERMS OF SOME
SUBJECTIVE VALUE

Just as botanical classifications were based on the medicinal qualities of the plants, and as diseases were identified with the symptoms they produced in man, so, for a long time, all families were labeled according to the "good" of the child. Almost until the beginning of the twentieth century, this "good" was synonymous with "morality."

Immorality, it was assumed, was caused in two ways; either by the faulty discipline of moral parents—since all children were amoral little creatures and had to be trained to decency—or through the example of an immoral home. The cure for immoral adults lay, of course, in religion, and the guide to proper training in the tenets of the church. Thus, for the most part, discussions and descriptions of family life resolved into preachments upon discipline and religion in the home.

Now and again, some moralizer would reach a little farther into the future than did his contemporaries. Excerpts from Christopher Anderson's *Parent's Book: The Genius and the Design of the Domestic Constitution with its Untransferable Obligations and Peculiar Advantages*, shows how nearly he touched the twentieth century, and yet how far from it he remained. In the introduction he says: "One of the most favorable indications of the present period is the fact, that so much attention is directed to the consideration of domestic relations and duties,"[1] and he continues, "Though in every instance of its [the family's] existence, itself brief and transitory, and to cease with the last generation of men on earth, its influences go down from generation to generation and from age to age, into and all along the ages of eternity. They, more than any other, commonly, form the future man and woman, and direct their influences, in their various relations, and on succeeding generations."[2] He realized that sometimes, even in Christian homes, all was not completely satisfactory, for "Even after the dominion of sin has been broken; after the Parents themselves have been turned to the Lord their God, there is, alas, still in many, if not in all, some remaining tendency at least to failure."[3] And he felt that practically all of these failures expressed themselves either in undue severity, overindulgence, inequality of treatment, or partiality.

These ideas expressed in more modern verbiage can be found in many current articles on family affairs, along with his four chosen family situations. But there the analogy would end. For the point of Anderson's book was to show that this "tendency to failure" had one cure, just a little bit *more* Christianity. For "Whatever men may say, genuine Christianity alone can rectify the disorder which sin has introduced, whether into the soul, into our families, or the world at large."[4] And so the family, classed as a sacred institution, was opened to but limited secular scrutiny, and any imaginative speculation concerning it was restricted, for as long as the family conformed outwardly to the ideals of the church, the souls of its

[1] Christopher Anderson, *Parent's Book*, pp. iii-iv.
[2] *Ibid.*, p. 229.
[3] *Ibid.*, p. 242.
[4] *Ibid.*, p. 243.

members were guaranteed their rich reward, if not on this earth, then in heaven, where it was to last through eternity.

Toward the close of the century, with the firmer establishment of humanitarian ideals and new scientific disclosures, the "good" of the child came to be thought of in terms of education and health as well as of morality. This was indeed a step in advance as far as general child welfare was concerned. Further, it extended the number of factors under observation in classifying family situations. But unfortunately it also served to crystallize the preoccupation with obvious external and detrimental factors. Now any family hampered by poverty, ill-health, death, or absence of a parent, immorality, or unconventional standards was automatically a "bad" situation, because it interfered with the health, morality, educational or economic advantages of the children. Assumed was the resulting corollary that any children unhampered by such difficulties would, in the normal course of growth, become satisfactory citizens in an adult world, and ultimately members in good standing of the Kindgom of Heaven.

Gertrude Tuckwell of London, Editor of *The Women's Trade Union Review*, wrote a little book in 1894 on *The State and its Children*. In it she drew some dramatic pictures of certain unusual kinds of family life.

The long barges which are drawn up and down the network of canals which intersect the country, bearing a freight of clay, bricks, or sometimes "mud, manure and the refuse of our large towns," contain also the tiny dwellings of the barge drivers. . . . Here lived, not only the bargee himself, but his wife, children, and often his mate as well, and a typical instance of the overcrowding is the account of the sleeping arrangements of a cabin containing 150 cubic feet of space. . . . All day long the boats slowly moved from place to place so that there was no possibility of schooling for the children, instead, they drove or led the horse or donkeys which drew the barge, while father sat and smoked upon the deck. Ignorant, often, of their own ages, the children learnt nothing but the oaths and foul language for which the bargee is especially famed, while their occupation, as drivers, was occasionally enlivened by witnessing the drunken fights which followed on their parents' orgies at the various public houses.[5]

[5] Gertrude M. Tuckwell, *The State and Its Children*, pp. 90-91.

As a preview to present-day wholesale migratory life, she wrote another vivid bit.

Whenever a race or village fair is going on throughout the country, the Gypsies' vans are to be found. They move continuously from place to place through the warmer months, generally settling in one place through the winter. . . . The van people earn a livelihood in various ways: some sell baskets; some set up their "merry-go-round" booths or shooting galleries at the fairs; and some make a living by cocoanut shies, or fortune telling. . . . The living room inside a van is very small, as are the tents or small hovels which the gypsies set up when they are stationary for a time, yet in the small area there sleep the father and mother, and often eight or nine children. Gypsy families are very large . . . but many of the little souls die off before they are old enough to become seasoned to a life of continual hardship and exposure.[6]

And finally, as a hint of the influence of certain occupations on family life, there is this picture.

The children employed in theatres and circuses are to a great extent the children of the people who follow these professions themselves. In the circus the parents who have earned their own livelihood on the trapeze or as riders or clowns bring up their children to their trade, and on the stage, many of the little people employed are children of the dressers or theatre employés. . . . The children seem very reasonably proud of their family traditions. . . . Messrs. Sanger arrange that the children employed in their circus shall work in shifts; the group of children accompanying the circus, while it is under tents in the summer, and giving performances then, is relieved in the winter when the circus is stationary by another group, and the children who are not performing attend school, so that half the little employés are at school in the winter, and half in the summer of the year.[7]

The significant facts deduced by the author from these glimpses of ways of life, were what the children did *not* get—educational opportunities equal to those of stationary families, and proper health facilities. The rich possibility of discovering what these colorful lives *did* mean to children and to their families, in terms of family life, was completely disregarded in the desire to show the state what it should do for the good of the child.

[6] *Ibid.*, pp. 95-96.
[7] *Ibid.*, pp. 119-121.

Just as long as all family life was thought of in terms of its subjective value to the child, a situation had to be rated as "good" or "bad" according to current ideologies and known facts, though good and bad are not facts in themselves. The current ideology, in the ninetenth century, was still that of right and wrong being dictated by words on tablets of stone, though those words were being interpreted with more humanism than formerly. The known facts of the results of adherence to, or the breaking of, these laws upon personality and behavior were very few. Thus, the study of family situations was at the level of a fumbling and undirected search for some information which would cast the light of direction upon it. It was to be stalemated at this level until some new knowledge should start it on its progress toward the goal of objective science.

THE PERIOD OF OBSERVATION, TESTS, AND MEASUREMENTS

Fortunately for the course of progress, it is infinitely easier to count broken homes, poor homes, and obviously immoral homes, than it is to count homes with different degrees of religious conviction or adequacy of discipline. It is equally more simple to measure health, nutrition, and education than the degree to which a child honors his father, his mother, and his God. As the century turned, these tangibles were seized upon with the fervor born of the new scientific method. Books, pamphlets, and articles were published in ever-increasing abundance. The growing bulk and coherence of social service files made more statistics more easily available, and increased enrollment in public schools rendered up great numbers of children as the readily obtainable guinea pigs in test after test. Dr. Goddard added tremendous momentum to this snowball of testing when he introduced to America the form which he declared would measure genius, imbecility, and all the intermediate stages of mental development.

Characteristic of this kind of study is one of the "Parental Conditions of Wisconsin Girl Delinquents."[8] Here a selected group of girls, whose adjustment was beyond question unsatisfactory to society, was studied for factors significant in producing that condition. These were found to be: low socio-economic status, larger family

[8] Katharine DuPré, Lumpkin, *American Journal of Sociology*, September, 1932, pp. 232-240.

than the general population, broken homes, stepparents, foster parents, social defective tendencies (such as delinquency, alcoholism, sex irregularity), and low intelligence. Result: a bad situation and a bad girl.

For a while, just as Dr. Goddard's study of the Kallikaks was used to show that feeble-minded people breed feeble-minded children, and the few normal children of feeble-minded parents who happened to have been raised in normal families went unnoticed, so the tests which showed dire results to children in bad homes were used to strengthen the old philosophy. However, before long the very number of tests began to make the hitherto unnoticed so noticeable that it could no longer be explained away. The actual fact was that some so-called immoral homes raised some very moral children, while the neighbors were shaking their heads at the ministers' sons. Some youngsters seemed to be much happier and better adjusted to life with their mother as their only parent and support than other youngsters who lived with both parents in economic ease. Often sparks of genius came from unexpected places, while children of intellectuals failed to make a hundred plus in their intelligence tests. Conflicting explanations had again made confusion worse confounded. It was time to sit back and think for a while.

THE PERIOD OF SPECULATION, AND RECASTING OF PHILOSOPHY

All the while, during the frenzy of hit-or-miss testing and measuring, something of vital importance to the study of the family had been filtering into the consciousnesses of its students. The family was not just an institution ordained by God for the rearing of children. A family was people!

Unspectacular as this discovery may sound, its effects have been far from modest. One of them was that for the first time parents became a part of the family as human beings rather than as robot-monitors. Then psychology and the growth of interest in personality development, along with the increase of controversy between schools of heredity and environment, had made mere people something to conjure with. People were no longer the simple results of their goodness or badness. People were no longer doomed to one fate because their own parents had borne them, nor were they the simple outcome of the critical experiences of their lives. Individuals, it was seen, come into the world with certain drives; they struggle with and against their environments; they develop, as a result, certain "sets" or tendencies which recondition their struggles and the effects of life upon them. In short, people are infinitely more complicated than had been generally assumed. Social theory had long claimed that social relationships make their mark on the personality of every participant. If, then, a person was largely a product of all that had happened to him in life—his environments plus his own tendencies—and if other people were a part of his environment, the family became a group of personalities reacting upon one another, within which group all of the common relationships and activities, as well as the outside influences which intruded, affected one and all members of the family, and with them the whole family situation.

Murmurings of this sort showed themselves in literature at rapidly decreasing intervals. In 1921 Nora Milnes wrote:

The underlying impulse on the part of the worker to make life a little more endurable for those who are hard pressed may be there, and good may result to her from her desire to see things better. But if that desire is to be of practical value she is bound to recognize that such ministration alone is insufficient. . . . She will quickly appreciate the fact that between her and those among whom she is working, there exists a gulf that she fails to bridge and that she fails to understand the minds of others because she knows so little of the forces that have gone to make those minds; that, largely because she is ignorant of the environmental conditions that have played so great a part in determining the type, she is but applying a palliative, not a remedy. Then she will discover that she is faced, not only with the problem of a child but with all the problems of the parents of that child. Gradually she will recognize the truth that no child lives in isolation, that in fact such isolation is impossible. Then she will appreciate how true it is that the problems of the child are never the beginning, they are but the end of other social problems.[9]

Again, in 1927, Phyllis Blanchard stated that heredity places limits within which the personality is pliable.

If some one response is continually evoked, it is likely to crystallize into an habitual reaction, and to color the attitude toward other individuals

[9] Nora Milnes, *Child Welfare from the Social Point of View*, pp. 16-17.

in the wider social group outside the home. . . . The child who is subjected to many experiences that call out the fear response develops a timid, fearful attitude toward the world.[10]

It is in the family, she explains, that the first responses are set, and whether they are responses of fear, suspicion, defiance, or love makes all the difference.

In a discussion of broken homes as a causative factor in juvenile delinquency, Joanna Colcord reported that the two cannot at all be considered in a direct causal relationship, for broken homes must be classified according to the more subtle aspects of family relationships. Homes may be voluntarily or involuntarily broken. The results of the severance may be either beneficial or damaging to the family. The member who leaves may be the one who has given the family stability, or he may be the one who has caused the disharmony.[11]

And finally, in 1930, after a great wealth of such material had been produced, Foster and Anderson declared that interest in the young child had changed from emphasis on the child as an entity to the child as a part of his home situation, his relationships to his parents and to their attitudes.[12]

All these subtle influences and relationships, divorced from values of good or bad, had to be acknowledged before a family situation could even begin to be seen for what it is, how it differs from other family situations, and before any question of relative values could be placed. This new philosophy was the result of careful brooding over the application of scientific data to the results brought to light during the period of testing and measuring.

THE RETURN TO THE QUANTITATIVE METHOD BASED ON AN OBJECTIVE FOUNDATION

A new and objective philosophy of the study of family situations is not the attainment of a goal. It is only the beginning of cutting a new and better path to that goal. The path is still in its first mile,

[10] Phyllis Blanchard, "The Family Situation and Personality Development," *Mental Hygiene*, January, 1927, pp. 16-17.

[11] Joanna C. Colcord, "Discussion of 'Are Broken Homes a Causative Factor in Juvenile Delinquency?'" *Social Forces*, May, 1932, Volume X, pp. 525-527.

[12] J. C. Foster and J. E. Anderson, *The Young Child and His Parents*.

but some of the toughest trees are down, and light is beginning to shine through.

Two different methods are coming to be most widely used to uncover the intricacies of the whole family situation. One is a continuance of the former quantitative testing method, vastly improved. Its procedure is the testing of three groups: one a control group representing a certain kind of adjustment; the second a control group showing the opposite kind of adjustment; and the third a group selected at random. The individuals in all three groups are then tested, similarly, for a number of home situation factors, such as personal relationships, activities, attitudes, as well as health, education, religious training, presence or absence of parents, and so on. If the tests are wisely prepared and well administered, and if the frequency of certain factors varies noticeably from one group to another, then it is assumed that a hint of causal relationships between certain home factors and certain types of adjustment has been found. Moreover, less and less often are claims being made on the basis of one causal factor. Rather, series of factors showing high frequency are claimed, in their interrelationship, to be conducive to a certain kind of adjustment.

An example of this kind of study is the one made by June Carpenter and Philip Eisenberg on "Some Relations between Family Background and Personality."[13] Introducing the results, the authors explain:

Few doubt that the family is important in the development of personality; the problem is rather to relate the *organization* of *specific elements* in the family background to the development of personality. . . . Our specific problem is to uncover any relations which may appear between some aspects of family background and the personality trait, dominance-feeling.[14]

The results were as follows:

1. Socio-economic status higher and with greater prestige.
2. Treatment by parents.
   a. more independence and freedom.

[13] June Carpenter and Philip Eisenberg, *The Journal of Psychology*, 1938, Volume 6, pp. 115-136.
[14] *Ibid.*, p. 115.

      b. individuality emphasized.

      c. children visit away from home.

      d. given allowance.

      e. not dependent on family for social life.

      f. solve own problems.

3. Relationship with father.

      a. dominant women more like father and closer to him.

      b. less difference between age of dominant women and father than between other women and father.

4. Relationship with mother.

      a. opposite of above relationships.

      b. mother apt to be very weak character.

      c. mother apt to be very demonstrative.

5. Relationship with siblings.

      a. not significant.

      b. more dominant women idealized by sibling, especially brothers.

6. Only child.

      a. no significant relations.

7. Outside social relations.

      a. independent of family.

      b. fewer contacts with adults than with children.

      c. most contacts with children older than self.

      d. most contacts with mixed groups.

This sort of study is the beginning of an attempt to show a picture of the whole background out of which a kind of personality is apt to emerge.

The second method of studying family situations is the descriptive method. Through family case studies, historical, biographical, and autobiographical material, pictures of actual family situations are revealed in their intimacy. Naturally the accuracy of them depends on the artist or interpreter, just as the accuracy of the testing method depends upon the inventor and tester. But as more and more material is being brought to light, it becomes impossible to get any idea of its accuracy or its value, indeed even of its scope, unless there is some way by which to reduce the material so that it may be more easily handled. Classification of material has always been the means to manageability and clarification in other sciences. Classification becomes now a need in the science of family situations.

The Emphasis on Person-to-Person Relationships

In the enthusiasm over the discovery of the people in the family, the complications of their relationships to each other were often given undue emphasis in the whole picture of family life. Two other aspects of the family situation were largely disregarded. These were the external influences, health, poverty, occupation, and the like, which do enter and affect a situation; and, second, the complexes built up within a family, the values, ideals, activities, and attitudes around which the family is organized. The natural tendency in starting something new is to discount everything that belonged to the old, forgetting that some elements of it must be kept to carry over if the new trend is to become more than just a fad. This tendency, however, does have a value—that the newer aspect is put under glaring and concentrated light, and may thus be more quickly understood and shown up, at length, for its relative position in the scale of things. The new classifications of family situations escaped neither this tendency nor its advantage.

One classification illustrative of this trend is found in an article by Bertha Hattwick on "Interrelations Between the Pre-School Child's Behavior and Certain Factors in the Home."[15] Kinds of situations found here are:

1. Over-attentiveness in the home.
   a. parent favors child.
   b. is over-solicitous.
   c. treats child as a baby.
   d. household revolves around child.
      (Result: withdrawing behavior, infantilism)
2. The irresponsible or negligent mother.
   a. means well, but cannot be depended upon.
   b. fails in proper care; not enough attention.
      (Result: aggressive behavior)
3. The calm, happy home.
   a. parents usually happy.
   b. home usually calm and secure.

[15] Bertha W. Hattwick, *Child Development*, Volume 7, 1936, pp. 200-226.

(Result: coöperative behavior and good emotional adjustment)
4. Homes which display signs of nervous tension.
   a. mother nervous.
   b. mother fatigued.
   c. mother impatient.
   d. mother quarrelsome.
      (Result: uncoöperative behavior and poor emotional ad-
      justment)
5. Home where responsibilities and play interest are shared by parents
   and children.

Obviously, this classification is concerned only with person-to-
person relationships, for their effects upon behavior—the child's
behavior. All other things being equal in these homes, a certain
kind of adjustment might consistently occur in each separate
classification. But all other things are not equal, even within the
category of the calm, happy home.

Another, more inclusive study on *Intra-Family Relationships and
Pupil Adjustment*,[16] has its results classified under the headings:

1. Home membership.
   including absence of mother or father, presence of persons other
   than normal family, education of parents, employment of
   mother.
2. Supervision.
   of outside activities, entertaining, manners, etiquette, spending
   money.
3. Discipline.
   physical punishment, administration of punishment, continuance
   of punishment, fairness, consistency, and reasonableness of discipline, attitude of parents in discipline.
4. Parent-child relationships.
   nagging, favoring, worrying parents, parents who treat child
   as adult, who consider child's point of view, who keep promises,
   who provide happy home life.
5. Relations between children.
   coöperative and considerate, quarrelsome and jealous.
6. Relations between parents.
   friendly, coöperative, affectionate, kind, thoughtful, considerate,

[16] Theodore R. Myers, *Intra-Family Relationships and Pupil Adjustment*.

courteous, sharing direction and management.

conflicting, quarrelsome, inconsiderate, dominating one over the other.

There is here a considerable extension of elements. There is a hint of the intrusion of external factors which even thoughtful parents cannot prevent from interfering with family adjustment. There is also the realization that a happy relationship between husband and wife does not certify so happy a one with their children or between the siblings in the family. But still there is the lack of any relation between the elements which would produce the semblance of a picture of any real family life.

In two separate studies there were attempts to capture the thing that is lacking in the above classifications. In the one, that of the Gruenbergs, the classification is called "Family Patterns"; it notes the following categories:

1. The patriarchal family.

    which still persists, more often subduing or driving children out than being successful.

2. Families in which members go their own respective ways, yet manage a semblance of unified life.

3. Married couples intending to have no children, with a minimum of household equipment and machinery.

4. The one-child family.

    a. mother preoccupied in a variety of activities and giving care of child to others.

    b. mother working outside home and still assuming full control.

5. The "father in the city" family.

    appearing weekends as a friendly visitor.

6. Solicitous families.[17]

In the second study, Helen Witmer's "classification of homes in terms of family relationships" speaks of:

1. The close-knit home.

    affectionate and harmonious, with interests and recreation centered in the home but not to the exclusion of outsiders.

[17] Sidonie M. and Benjamin C. Gruenberg, "Education of Children for Family Life," *Annals of the American Academy of Political and Social Science*, March, 1932, pp. 205-215.

2. The socially conforming type of home.
   appearance of happiness, but considerable rivalry between the siblings, and parents only moderately fond of each other.
3. The loose-knit home.
   harmonious, little quarreling, each member going his own way with no comment or supervision.
4. The very seclusive, introverted home.
   all interests centered in the home to the exclusion of outsiders.
5. The very unhappy home.
   constant quarreling and friction, drunkenness, immorality, neglect, etc. Children sometimes left outside parents' quarrels, sometimes drawn in to take sides.[18]

We begin to see in these classifications some glimmer of the configuration of family life. But at the same time external pressures have again been lost, and as yet there is no mention of the internal complexes built up within the family. They are, then, purely and simply expressed in terms of the personal relationships between parents and children and whoever else may happen to make up the family circle.

Dr. Burgess summarizes this kind of classification in his comments upon his own discussion of types of parent-child relationships. He says:

The various elements in parent-child relations, such as unbroken homes, the child's confiding in parents, demonstration of affection, regularity of health habits, parental initiative in sex education, have been found to be definitely associated with the well adjusted personality of the child, as determined by teachers' ratings, personality tests and by the autobiographies of college students.

This analysis of the influence of the home upon the personality development of the child may, perhaps, be carried a step farther. If it has been shown to be possible to determine the relation of a given factor, such as lack of criticism of the father and mother, to the personality development of the child, why should it not be feasible to combine these different indices of the influence of the home environment and

---

[18] Helen L. Witmer, "The Childhood Personality and Parent-Child Relationships of Dementia-Praecox and Manic Depressive Patients," *Smith College Studies in Social Work*, June, 1934, Volume IV, no. 4, pp. 289-377.

so to secure a total score of family relations making for desirable character traits and well adjusted personality?[19]

But, he adds, it must be remembered that the home conditions that make for good adjustment in one group do not necessarily mean the same in another. They vary from age to age, culture to culture, city to country, with girls and boys, with different racial mixtures, with all sorts of conditions. In other words, these classifications go just so far. They are valuable as a start, if their intentional emphasis, and therefore their limited scope, is realized and accepted.

A Classification Combining Personal Relationships and External Factors

To one investigator who had wide experience in actual contact with children in their family situations, personal relations did assume a relative position. It was all too clear, in case after case, that economic status does affect a family, that physical and mental diseases obtrude themselves and change a family, that cultural differences create their own coloring of a situation. Personal relations, as important and basic as they may be, are altered by these conditions. Blanche Weill gave due weight to them in this classification:

1. *Poor personal relations.*
   domination by one member.
   interfering relatives.
   favoritism.
   unwanted child.
   clash of authority.
   dissension between parents, overt or otherwise.
   over-solicitude.
   over-severity.
   neglect.
   jealousy.
   step-parent.
   ineffectuality of parent.
2. *Disabilities.*
   a. physical.

[19] E. W. Burgess, *The Adolescent in the Family,* White House Conference on Child Health and Protection, p. 271.

deafness of member of family.
blindness of member of family.
crippled member of family.
invalidism.
acute illness.

b. mental.
mental defect in either parent.
mental defect in member of family.
neurotic member of family.
psychotic member of family.

3. *Maladjustments.*
a. social.
racial differences.
nationality differences.
religious differences.
differences in conventions or standards.
foster home.
institution home.
broken home.
divorced member.
widowed member.
imprisoned member.
member in sanatorium.

b. moral.
broken home.
deserted home.
disgraced home.
immoral home.
acute.
chronic.

4. *Economic pressures.*
insufficient income unaided.
insufficient income aided.
mother working out.
father out of work.
undigested wealth.[20]

Though there are here personal relations, external factors, and cultural backgrounds, there is still something missing in a classifica-

[20] Blanche C. Weill, *The Behavior of Young Children of the Same Family.*

tion of this sort, especially from the point of view of a sociologist. In social relationships not only are the participants altered, but something new is created that is more than the sum of the effects upon the individuals. In the family, part of this something new is the crystallization of these relationships and attitudes about these relationships into complexes: family activities, family interests, family goals, standards, values, the physical and mental tempo of the home, the emotional tone of the whole family set-up.

Difficult as it may be to analyze or to describe in words, it is just this part of the family situation which makes one feel the differences between the families of one's close friends. We classify in our minds likenesses and differences in the homes we know well, not on the basis of the number of children in them, or whether the mother wanted her babies, the income the family enjoys, or the state of its health, but on the basis of the tone of the whole family complex which meets us when we enter it, and leaves its lasting impression upon us.

Each family has its own culture. Part of it is the general culture of the community in which it lives. Part of it is the culture of each of the parents, and that which the children have taken for their own from their own special social relationships. But the whole of it is a unique culture—a reassembling and modifying of cultural elements according to the specific needs and attitudes and values of the combined family group.

Until an attempt is made to capture in words this intangible, there can be no question of a true situational approach in the classification of family situations.

Classifications Expressing the Whole "Feel" or Tone of the Family Situation

The first clear expression, in literature, of the sorts of situations which are necessary to a complete classification, is found in an article written in 1920 on "Salvaging the Family."[21] Though it is not a classification in form, the text bears quoting for the clarity with which it catches the spirit of some of the differences in American families.

[21] Edward W. Yeomans, *Progressive Education*, Volume III, October-November-December, 1926, pp. 283-288.

There is the problem of the rich family, or the family attached to caste and social position, dragging with it its class loyalties and fastening them around the neck of each child as a kind of sacrament: prep school, college, university club, business success.

And then there is the poor family beset by the bitterness of a fight for self-respect which Arthur Clough's "say not the struggle naught availeth" would not alleviate one little bit.

And in between there are, besides the intelligentsia, all the grades that find expression in the antics of the Shriners, the Kiwanis and the Rotary clubs—and so on, to fantastic fringes very hard to define.

Besides these there are the distinctive problems of the city dwellers and the country dwellers and the small town dwellers. . . .[22]

This is a description, in few words, of the different cultures of different families. Dr. James Plant has said, "The man coming to his daily task brings his family with him."[23] He does not bring just his pleasures and worries over his children, and his anxiety about the monthly bills, but all the special slants and prejudices and attitudes about life, his fellows, and world affairs which are peculiar to him because he is a member of a small-town family, or a family in the Social Register. "The family," Plant continues, "must be considered in terms of what it means or provides to the individuals within it,"[24] and what it does mean and provide is not a series of disintegrated factors, but the whole family milieu.

From the histories of college students whose family maladjustments had caused them some grief at school, Louella Pressey listed the situations she discovered. They are:

1. The "foreign-social-background" home.
2. The "inadequately-financed" home.
3. The "lower-social-level-than-college" home.
4. The "high-pressure" home.
5. The "antagonistic-to-college" home.
6. The "interfering-and-clinging" home.
7. The "chronic-dissension" home.
8. The "prejudiced-in-favor-of-one-child" home.

[22] *Ibid.*, p. 285.
[23] James S. Plant, *Personality and the Cultural Pattern*, p. 17.
[24] *Ibid.*, p. 160.

9. The "overly-religious-and-narrowly-moral" home.
10. The "recently-disrupted" home.[25]

This is a considerable narrowing down of Yeoman's broad definitions, for even within a relatively selective group—families sending their children to a certain college—all of these contrasting tones, and doubtless many others, are to be found.

One of the most recent classifications of this kind is based on the organization of the family around its central interest. Charlotte Bühler conducted a study of families with the help of experienced child psychologists who actually visited with the families at close intervals over a period of from three to six months. The visitor's first task was to prevent the normal course of home life from being interrupted by her presence, and then to observe individual activities and contacts with others. These contacts included approach or response, kind of response, the situation out of which the communication arose, and the intended purpose of it. From the analysis of the results, five distinct kinds of family organization around a central interest emerged. In summary they were:

1. The family in which the child formed the center of interest as a child.
   a. Affection for child was the decisive motive.
   b. Contacts were primarily intended to give something to child.
   c. Objective obligations and adult cares were kept from child.
   d. In presence of child, adults adjusted to him and his private world.
   e. General tone was of affectionate and joyous participation in family unit.
2. The family in which the child formed the center of interest as an educational object.
   a. Responsibility for child was the decisive motive.
   b. Child was not an object of elation and affection, but of duty for development.
   c. Child was kept apart from adult worries and objective obligations but was always impressed with his own moral and other obligations.

[25] Louella Pressey, "Some Serious Family Maladjustments among College Students," *Social Forces*, December, 1931, Volume X, no. 2, pp. 236-242.

3. The family in which the social unity of the family was of primary importance.
   a. Harmonious development of family life, and not the child, was the center of interest.
   b. Child was the adults' social partner in conversation and social life.
   c. Instruction and guidance were chiefly pointed in this direction.
   d. Child had to accept duties for the family good, and responsibilities for proper organization of family life.
4. The family in which the household was the center of interest.
   a. Order of the house was the primary motive.
   b. Social unity of the family was a protective organization for smooth running of household.
   c. Children were members on an equal par with adults for this purpose.
   d. Child, as such, was neglected.
   e. Human side of social life lost importance.
5. The family in which the struggle for existence was the center of interest.
   a. Guiding motive was economic welfare.
   b. Adult world replaced completely that of child.
   c. Child was accepted into it as a partner with equal rights and duties.[26]

All of these families studied were deliberately chosen from an upper middle-class level, with from one to three children, preferably of school age, in order that no extreme divergences in pattern might be obvious at the outset. Yet such a wide range of patterns did emerge.

SUMMARY

In this chapter, the systematic study of family situations has been viewed historically and has been found to have progressed through stages matching those in the evolution of the other sciences.

1. In the first stage, the family was examined only subjectively, in its relation to the "good" of the child. For a time this "good" meant morality alone, but ultimately such factors as physical and

[26] Charlotte Bühler, *The Child and His Family*, translated by Henry Beaumont, pp. 108-110.

mental health, education, and economic status came to be included in the subjective value.

2. The easily detectable factors of health, education, and economic status helped to introduce the second stage, or the period of observation for testing and measuring. The procedure for the study of the family developed into those of examining the situations of individuals with specific behavior irregularities in order to find which of these measurable factors were most constant in the homes of the maladjusted.

3. Analyses of the results of many of these tests brought a realization of the fallacy of the philosophy that certain unhealthy factors must inevitably produce unhealthy home situations. The third stage became, then, one of speculation, resulting in the casting aside of preconceived judgments and the adopting of a new philosophy of objective and deductive study of family situations themselves.

4. Advanced knowledge of the facts of personality formation and of social interaction gave rise to new procedures with which to put the new philosophy into operation. These new quantitative procedures have brought the family situation into focus as a group of interacting individuals, influenced by special sets of circumstances, to which the family reacts in specific ways. Given a known set of interrelated factors within a family situation, then that family may be susceptible to certain known effects of those factors.

5. The very number of random studies developed according to the new philosophy has brought about a need for systematization. This need has resulted in such attempts to classify family situations as have been reviewed in this chapter.

Part II

STUDIES OF FAMILY SITUATIONS: A SUMMARY

INTRODUCTION

THE FIRST part of this volume dealt with a series of developments
and theses in the situational approach to the problems of human
behavior, with particular reference to situations in the family. Part
II is an effort to summarize and synthesize the many specific studies
of family situations already made.

In preparation for this task a survey was made of the available
literature on family life, parent-child relationships, and family situations. This survey covered the literature for the years 1926 to 1940
inclusive. Some seven hundred case records and analyses were gathered, as well as sixty summaries of selected types of case histories.
It is believed that this task, to which about a year was devoted, is
reasonably complete.

In presenting the results of this survey, two general procedures
were available. One was to classify the "specimens" by name, content, or outstanding feature, and to offer the findings in a somewhat
tabular form. The other possibility was to attempt a summary of
them in the form of a representative or synthetic picture. For a
variety of reasons, the second of these alternatives appeared the
more feasible one.

When the various cases were all brought together and analyzed,
they seemed to divide themselves into three groups. The first dealt
solely with the personal relationships within the family. The second
added to these structural relationships the external pressures which
modify them. The third studied the whole configuration of the
home: the people, the external factors which intrude themselves,
and the content, or culture, of the inner family situation. These
groups, in developing from the first to the third, have been cumulative in the number of factors under analysis. Each one has included the elements of the former group and has added some new
element.

In order to set these situations into a meaningful classification it
has been necessary to employ two devices. First, artificial barriers
have had to be constructed among the three groups into which the

cases fall. In being classified, these groups have had to be regarded not as cumulative but as separated in terms of the factors which they contain. No one family situation is a pure type, a result of the influence of one special factor. Each one has the elements of many as the causes of its condition. But they have to be classified as pure types. A family situation, then, is regarded here as it stands out at a certain moment in time, as a sort of stereoscopic picture, taken by a magic camera. Regarding the family as portrayed in such a kind of static projection, we have looked for the factor which looms largest in the foreground of the image. We have then separated and labeled that situation according to its conspicuous factor.

The second device has been that of interpolation. Of the classifications referred to in the preceding chapter none is complete in its listing of subsumed varieties. Possibly no classification will ever keep abreast of the discoveries of kinds of family situations. But every day of research brings the unknown into the realm of the knowable and classifiable, and it has seemed only reasonable to add the new. The attempt has been made, not to catch every set-up of family life, for there are as many set-ups as there are families, but to draw a line from one extreme, through the normal to the opposite extreme, marking, wherever possible, the points at which enough change has occurred to make a visible difference in the situations. Therefore, wherever in this synthesis of actual cases analyzed there has seemed to be an obvious gap which would lose the thread of continuity in tne structure of the classification, selected situations have been found, or constructed, and interpolated to preserve the line from one extreme to the other.

This synthesizing of case records and analyses of family life, aided by the devices of separation and interpolation, has resulted in a system of classification based on three broad categories. In the first, which we call *Intra-Family Relationships*, there are the people who live together. In the second, which we name *Family Patterns*, there is the content of the family group. And in the third, which we designate *External Factors*, there are those irresistible forces which enter the family from the outside—health, poverty, community culture, and so on. Descriptions of these three groups will constitute the three succeeding chapters.

TABLE I

A CLASSIFICATION OF FAMILY SITUATIONS

Intra-Family Relationships

I. Affectional relationships

A. Excess of Affection
- 1. The Possessive Home
- 2. The Over-Solicitous Home
- 3. The Over-Indulgent Home

B. Normal Affection
- 1. The Companionable Home

C. Discrimination in Affection
- 1. The Divided Home
- 2. The Favored-Child Home
- 3. The "Impartial" Home

D. Inconsistency of Affection
- 1. The Bickering Home
- 2. The Unreliable Home

E. Displacement of Affection
- 1. The Home with a New Member

F. Lack of Affection
- 1. The Nagging Home
- 2. The Frigid Home
- 3. The Neglectful Home

G. Frank Rejection
- 1. The Home of the Unwanted Child

II. Subjectual Relationships

A. Repression
- 1. The Mother-Controlled Home
- 2. The Father-Dominated Home
- 3. The Overly-Demanding Home

B. Anarchy
- 1. The Child-Dictated Home

C. Confusion
- 1. The Home with Too Many Bosses

D. Approaching Balance
- 1. The Democratic Home

Family Patterns

A. Size
- 1. The Large Family
- 2. The One-Child Family

B. Organization
- 1. The Coöperative Family
- 2. The Independent Family
- 3. The Incomplete Family

C. Activity

1. The Nomadic Family
2. The "Joiner" Family
3. The Family of the Intelligentsia
4. The "Cliff-Dweller" Family
5. The Community-Benefactor Family

D. Values and Goals

1. The Social-Climber Family
2. The Materialistic Family
3. The Overly-Religious Family
4. The Scientific Family
5. The Superstitious Family
6. The Conventional Family

External Factors

A. Socio-Economic Status

1. The Inadequately-Financed Home
2. The Suddenly Wealthy Home
3. The Large-Inheritance Home
4. The Mother-Supported Family
5. The Family Marked by Peculiar Occupational Characteristics
6. The Home of Culture-Conflict
7. The Disgraced Home
8. The Family in the Public Eye

B. Neighborhood

1. The Farm Family
2. The Small Town Family
3. The City Family
4. The Summer Resort Family
5. The Misfit-in-the-Neighborhood Family
6. The Family in a Sub-Standard Neighborhood

C. Health

1. The Home of the Invalid
2. The Home of the Defective

CHAPTER VI

INTRA-FAMILY RELATIONSHIPS

WITHIN the intimate circle of every family group there are two kinds of relationships existing between its members which, in terms of personal interaction, set it apart as a certain kind of family. These are the relationships of affection and subjection. The significance of these relationships to the modern family is plain. Dr. James Plant has pointed out that everyone, in order to have any security and happiness in life, must have a feeling of "belongingness" to a group. In a country which has nurtured individualism as vitally as has America, and particularly where a tremendous proportion of its families live in the anonymity of large cities, what other group beside the family holds out, immediately, a chance for the satisfaction of "belongingness?"[1] As for the subjectual relations, there can be no doubt that the general set-up of the home, the choices open to its members, their activities and their chances for growth are, to a large extent influenced by whichever person in the family it happens to be who holds the whip hand.

It is, then, to the synthesis of the intra-family relationships that this chapter is devoted, with the quality of the affectional relationships and the nature of the subjectional relationships as the focal points from which the synthesis is drawn.

I. AFFECTIONAL RELATIONSHIPS

It is obvious to the most casual observer that every member of a family in which the personal relationships include warm and sincere affection finds himself in a vastly different situation from those members of a family where animosity and discord prevent even a minimum of security in the affectionate loyalty of the family group. But these situations are the extremes. Between them lie endless possibilities of variations, and infinitesimal shadings of these bonds of affection, each lending its own special hue to the whole blend of the family situation.

[1] James S. Plant, *op. cit.*, pp. 150-154.

113

Percival Symonds states these differences graphically. In every family, he says, there is a straight line of acceptance-rejection, and of dominance-submission, and each member of every family is plotted at some point along these lines. With the lines intersecting at right angles, the point of intersection is the theoretical ideal—a perfect balance between excessive affection and rejection, and between dominance and submission. But every point on the graph is a possible plotting point.[2]

The attempt here is to give a name and a description to those points on the graph which can be clearly differentiated one from another. For names are the tools with which to study data. For the artist, it has been necessary to give a name to the primary colors, and then, gradually, to name more and more different combinations of them as they become distinct to his eye. Just so must the student of the family situation label those shadings of personal relationships which, through repetition, have become familiar to him as distinctive shadings. However impossible it may be to catch the differences between each and every family, only by such a process can any approach be made to a complete color-card of family relationships. The following classification is one of the steps in that process.

EXCESS OF AFFECTION

The Possessive Home

In case studies analyzing the personal relationships existing in family situations, the kind of relationship which enjoys by far the greatest incidence is possessiveness. Furthermore it is the mothers who most frequently adopt the possessive attitude in affection even though it is the father who most usually puts on the appearance of actual physical proprietorship. From the psychological point of view, this transgression of the female parent is a natural corollary to male dominance.

In his drama of mother love, Sidney Howard portrays a family situation grown out of the fierce possessiveness of a woman who had made a supposedly "great match" with a man fifteen years her senior. He had managed to shatter his wife's illusions within a week after their marriage day. But Mrs. Phelps, in her own words,

[2] Percival M. Symonds, *The Psychology of Parent-Child Relationships*, Chap. I.

explained that she did not lose romance. Instead, she found it—in motherhood. "I found it in doing for them [my sons] myself all those things which, nowadays, nurses and governesses are hired to do. To spare mothers! I never asked to be spared. . . ."[3]

Typical is the scene in which Mrs. Phelps is eagerly displaying baby photographs to the bride and the fiancée of her two grown sons:

I used to study their photographs, month by month, just as I did their weight. I wasn't satisfied to watch only their bodies grow. I wanted a record of their little minds and souls as well. I could compare the expression of David's eyes, for instance, at nine, with their expression at eight and a half, and see the increased depth. And I was never disappointed.[4]

These services for her two sons had won from them a slavish dependence and a sense of duty toward her that made everything else in life of secondary importance. But such ties were, for her, only a tool to satisfy her greed for their demonstrations of love, and actual physical contact with them. She begs David's bride to leave her a "little, little part" of her boy's heart. And by that she means separate bedrooms for her son and daughter-in-law, with never a moment for them to be alone, a change in her son's career which would permit him to remain at home with Mother always; in fact, a complete pushing aside of the possibility of her son's loving anyone but herself, living any life separate from hers. So possessed are the boys that their healthy young appetites for the love of normal young girls becomes soiled in their own eyes, when held up for comparison, by their mother, to the supposedly sexless, selfless devotion existing in the Phelps family.

It is only to the outsider that the family devotion has a look of something more than spirituality. Nevertheless its effect on the family is that it dooms the one son to a life of unnatural sterility in the service of his mother's love, and the other to a complete break with family ties when the call of youth becomes even stronger than his mother's will.

[3] Sidney Howard, "The Silver Cord," in *Representative American Plays*, edited by Arthur Hobson Quinn, p. 1056.
[4] *Ibid.*, p. 1030.

In the case of the Phelpses, the mother's possessiveness was a means to gain compensation for the marital love which was denied her. Many other women resort to possessiveness of children as a compensation for other satisfactions which they miss in present-day life. In times when the mother had to produce by her own handiwork most of the material needs of her family, she obtained great satisfaction in the importance of her rôle in the home. Now almost all family needs can be supplied as services outside of the home, with the exception of the need of the members for intimate family affection. Case records show that many modern mothers seize upon this need for affection and try to intensify and prolong it in their children in order to sustain the satisfaction in their own importance.

Even the size of the modern home reduces satisfactions and fosters possessiveness, for there are not so many affectional relationships as there used to be. There are fewer grandparents and old maid aunties and other dependents to need care and affection in the home, for these have their pensions and prefer to live separately—or are invited to. Father is away from home, at work, most of the time. There are fewer children, and they are prepared for and spaced so that they come when Mother is young and her health can best stand childbirth, and so that the children will be more congenial. The result is that Mother does stay young and healthy longer than she used to. And long before she begins to grow old and tired enough to enjoy the feeling of slack reins in her hand, her babies are growing up and away from her into a world where outsiders supply their needs better than she can. How great, then, is the incentive for the modern woman of the so-called "maternal type" to keep her children as babies, make them dependent upon her, and have them regard mother love as the supreme bond. Babies are by far the easiest and most satisfactory, though not the only, victims of the demand for this kind of satisfaction in an individual-centered world.

A composite picture of all the situations in which possessiveness dominates is very close to that picture of David and Robert Phelps and their mother, though not always so dramatic in the unfolding. Possessive love begets not love but a sense of duty struggling with a desire for freedom. Resentment against parents goes hand in hand with a feeling of guilt over that resentment. There is always conflict deep beneath the surface in this family, between the natural process of growing up and away from parents, and the parents' opposition to that process. If the conflict comes to a climax and the parents win, the child is denied the ability to cope with an adult world, and the well-worn term "the perfect s-mother" is justly applied. If the child wins, the one bond upon which this family relies for its alliance is broken.

The Over-Solicitous Home

A survey of the literature of family life leads to the belief that nervous American parenthood is practically vibrating with the awareness of all the pitfalls which its children may encounter. There are so many homes in which the outstanding characteristic is over-solicitiousness.

Martin's mother rushed him to the hospital on his eighth birthday because he was thin and "going down so." He had had three mild childhood diseases, during all of which he had "nearly died" and driven her frantic. She had been taking him from one doctor to another and changing his diet ever since, forcing him with milk, cream, and rich dishes, to fatten him. He was not allowed to play with other children, because they were too rough for him—not even with his own sister, who was lucky enough to have been raised by another member of the family during her mother's long illness after her daughter's birth. But Martin's mother had never, in all her visits to doctors, been able to get a satisfactory diagnosis for her son, and she was going to persist until she did. Martin, incidentally, though he was a real thorn in the family, was above average in intelligence and in perfect health. But it is quite conceivable that he might not have remained healthy had his mother's efforts continued unchecked.[5]

Severe illness in childhood often causes parents such concern for the little patients that long after the need for special care is gone the over-solicitous attitude continues and unbalances the whole family. But, though over-solicitousness intimates some kind of anxiety along with excess affection, health is only one source of that

[5] Leo Kanner, *Child Psychiatry*, p. 94.

anxiety. There are parents who, through their very real interest in the answers to child development and mental hygiene, emphasize the possible dangers in the lives of their children, and guard against them so carefully that they hazard their family's natural life as definitely as did Martin's mother. Children have a sixth sense with which they feel the emotions and attitudes that lie beneath the words and actions of their parents. And while the actual physical protection from supposed dangers, that goes along with the Over-Solicitous Family, prevents a good deal of needed experience for the children, the sensing of the parents' anxiety over something that the children do not quite understand can instill a deep, unreasoning fear, and a feeling of inadequacy in their own powers that persist throughout their whole life.

While the possessive family which conforms outwardly to its ideals of behavior can maintain an appearance of harmony until some crisis of wills occurs, the Over-Solicitous Family seems to show a more ruffled surface. The children are quick to use their parents' solicitousness to gain their own ends, and the resulting little tricks are hard to handle for such parents. Lacking the courage for firmness that is found in the Possessive Home, these parents often blame each other for the children's unfortunate behavior.

Norma Lessing had discovered very early in life that her mother was much upset when her daughter vomited. Norma was a very intelligent little girl, and used her discovery to distract her parents whenever her will was crossed, or when she was confronted with a new and unpleasant situation. She used it to gain attention when her baby brother seemed to usurp her place; she clung to it when she was sent to a kindergarten that she did not like. And her little weapon was always successful because of the anxiety it caused her over-solicitous parents. Norma became a little tyrant and very wearing to the nerves of her family members. Her father said her mother was too easy with her. Her mother was sure it was the father's fault.[6]

Norma's childlike cleverness, combined with her parents' over-concern, might have destroyed the child's natural charm and reduced her family to a state of continuous irritability and conflict

[6] Blanche C. Weill, *Through Children's Eyes*, pp. 150-163.

had not a consultant psychologist put some wisdom into both Norma and her parents.

One fact which stands out in the cases of over-solicitousness is that many of the parents are products of that change in economic status which, from generation to generation, has been so marked in this country. These parents often rationalize their desire to love protectively with the conviction that it is their duty to keep their children from certain of the hardships they themselves had to undergo as children. The Over-Solicitous Family that is able to do this carries the program to such an extreme of sheltering the children that the whole family lives on a false basis—the parents denying the very facts and experiences that they themselves lived, and the children being shielded from the knowledge of the existence of what they must almost inevitably discover in the future.

The Over-Indulgent Home

Cases of Over-Indulgent Homes fall easily and definitely into a class separate from the Over-Solicitous Homes. A more positive kind of relationship exists where excess of affection among the family members takes the form of over-indulgence. While over-solicitousness stresses the negative duty of preventing ills and dangers, over-indulgence takes action in the determined giving of objects and opportunities. A change in the status of the parents of this family means that the children are presented gratis with as much of what their parents lacked as they can obtain for their children.

It might seem that in this family there is lacking the frustration that accompanies the vampire tactics of the possessive family, as well as the feeling of inadequacy invited by the Over-Solicitous Family. But case histories belie that assumption. There was a great deal of frustration and disillusion in the heart of the little boy who lay on the floor of the Franklin Institute and screamed himself purple because his father would not open the glass case and buy the model steam train for him to take home. It was beyond his understanding that the parents who had always provided for him every single desire had at last met their limit. The parents' expressions of mingled embarrassment, exasperation, and unhappiness deepened with the realization that their soft coaxing explanations and bribes could work no cure, for their son had just had his first meeting with the harsh aspect of reality.

The converse phase of this sort of situation which the literature discloses is that of children creating an atmosphere of over-indulgence by their treatment of a parent. In many families where there is a great deal of affection, the children are encouraged to make a sort of pet out of one of their parents, so that a mother or a father is pampered into as great a state of demandingness as that of the child in the museum.

Mr. Day,[7] the likeable ogre in an extremely popular play, enjoyed seeing his wife's relatives. They were charming girls. But *he did not want them staying overnight in his house*, for then the bathroom was always full of women when he wanted to shave. He had got used to his wife and sons' tiptoeing to his whims. But even this devoted family could not prevent reality—and relatives—from encroaching upon the family circle. And when the latter did, at the Days', everyone in the family, including the guests, paid with their nerves and Mr. Day's adult tantrums for their inability to give Father his own way.

The charm of an arrogance that always expects its own way may assume glamorous proportions upon the stage, but in the real situation of the family it is all too lacking in glamour. For every hero who demands and gets, there are the other members who must do the giving or suffer the consequences, the ones who have to face reality in order to prevent the over-indulged one from facing it. Where there is no fairness there is bound to be resentment. Where one expects too much, there is almost inevitable disappointment. And where there is no preparation for disappointment, there is no sane and reasonable technique for dealing with it. A family built on these foundations will not be apt to generate that feeling of secure and coöperative friendliness which tends to make healthy nerves and homes.

NORMAL AFFECTION

The Companionable Home

At some point in the line of family affection—and it comes close

[7] Howard Lindsay and Russel Crouse, *Clarence Day's Life with Father.*

to that theoretically ideal point[8]—there is a disappearance of that emphasis on affection that betrays over-compensation, or substitution for emotional starvation in some other sphere of life. In a home where every member of the family is loved and accepted by all the other members, and is himself assured of that acceptance, there is no need for the reassurance of undue protestations.

Burgess describes this sort of home as one in which there are friendly relations between the parents, a minimum of dissension and quarreling, a sharing of recreation and play, a feeling on the part of the children that they are understood, and a liberal system of discipline in which the children concur.[9]

Affection shows itself here in spontaneous good-fellowship, but there is no particular desire to show it off to others. Neither is there the blindness to the true character of the family members which an overpowering sense of duty toward them tends to create— nor is there subsequent rage because of their imperfections when they are found out.

One has to turn almost exclusively to fiction or biography to find pictures of this ideal state in family affectional relations. Time after time in order to approach a norm, we must look to fiction for the material. This fact reveals one of the weaknesses of depending entirely upon case record analysis in sociological investigation. For, almost up to the present day, case records have by their very definition precluded normalcy. So all-important to a home is the framework of affectional relations that the family situation in which they are satisfactory is one of those least likely to be studied as a "case."

William Lyon Phelps's autobiography is a living picture of this kind of family situation. He could analyze his family members critically, describe their virtues and faults without over-glorying in the one or resenting the other. Taking his family just as it was to him, and remembering it that way, he loved it. "My mother" he says, "was highly-strung, and sometimes suffered from acute nervous despondency. But most of the time she was in high spirits and full of gaiety. She was insatiably fond of playing games and was so amiable, so kind, so sympathetic, so warmhearted that she was intensely beloved by innumerable individuals."[10]

[8] Percival M. Symonds, *op. cit.*
[9] E. W. Burgess, *op. cit.*
[10] William Lyon Phelps, *Autobiography with Letters*, p. 4.

An introduction straight into the heart of this companionable family is this scene.

I wanted to be a preacher and public orator. When I was eight years old, I began to preach sermons to the family on Sunday afternoons and I kept this up for two or three years. I wrote these sermons out on "sermon paper" and every Sunday afternoon I conducted a regular service, the audience consisting of my father, mother and two brothers. I remember how desperately hard it was for me to think up enough material to fill four pages of manuscript. The family assembled with a perfectly straight face, for I was tremendously in earnest; I read the hymns before they were sung, and preached a sermon, which whatever it lacked in literary merit, was uncompromisingly orthodox. The family managed to listen seriously, until, one afternoon, while reading a hymn I came to the line, "Deep horrors then my vitals froze," and I had the misfortune to pronounce the word as "vittles." The family burst into roars of uncontrollable laughter. . . . I could see nothing funny in it, and their attempts to explain the connotation of cold storage were lost on me, as I had never seen the word "victuals."[11]

Here, in biography, is caught the spirit of the Companionable Home.

There is, fortunately, one scientific analysis of this sort of family situation. The study, a very recent one, leads to the hope that there may be more like it. For it has proved the value of investigating family situations which are not so marked by some imperfection as to resort to clinics as self-considered cases.

In a carefully planned, scientific study of the living situation in different homes,[12] actual contacts and conversations were recorded as illustrative of the spirit of the family relationships. In the home which in our classification would come under the category of the Companionable Home the following are typical of the contacts made between Gertrud, six, and her sister Steffii, three.

Steffi and Gertrud are picking flowers.
Gertrud: "There are some more over there. See, there's another one."
Steffi walks over and picks it up.
Gertrud picks buds off the shrubbery and gives some to Steffi. . . .
In a card game, Gertrud gives Steffi several extra cards to help her win, though this is against the rules of the game. . . .

[11] *Ibid.*, pp. 19-20.
[12] Charlotte Bühler, *op. cit.*

Gertrud is cutting out stars. She says, "Now I'll make a green one
to give to Steffi.". . .
Mother is feeding Steffi and says: "I'd like to eat my own dessert.
Hurry up, Steffi, so I can eat too."
Gertrud: "I'll feed her, Mama." . . .
Steffi is setting the table. Gertrud offers to do it for her.
Steffi: "Now wait, I'll do that."[13]

When the father of this family comes home from work, the first
thing he is interested in is knowing what Gertrud and Steffi have
been doing and learning, and their mother encourages them to tell
him themselves. All of the members of the family are actively interested in sharing their ideas and activities, and in doing services
for each other, not with any thought of reward, or for the duty or
looks of the thing, but spontaneously.

In homes like those of Gertrud and Steffi, and of William Lyon
Phelps, the driving desire for security in "belongingness" is satisfied as it can be nowhere else. There are substitutes for it; but the
earliest, deepest, and most lasting security, which few later events
can completely shatter, is found in the natural, normal relationships of the companionable home.

DISCRIMINATION IN AFFECTION

The Divided Home

Unfortunately a home does not necessarily breed the same kind
and degree of affection in all of its members, if indeed it ever can
do so. The case study of affectional relations in a family is not the
story of how one person responds to another. It is a complex of
affection and responses among the individuals, unlike, uneven, and
discriminating. In marriage, the affection between the two partners
is not similar and equal, for the two are the results of totally different conditions which make them regard each other with different
evaluations. When the babies begin to arrive, no matter how much
more unity they may bring to the home, each one introduces a new
personality that is going to evaluate his family as his own peculiar
conditions dictate; and he will be evaluated by them in the same
way.

[13] *Ibid.*, pp. 143-145.

Some of the conditions which foster deep discrimination in affection within the family are shown to be as accidental and trivial in themselves—though not to the family—as those chances which cause us to make firm friends of certain people and to avoid others who are equally accessible for friendship. Some of the more outstanding of these conditions as they are unfolded in case histories are sex, physical resemblance, and age.

The division of labor between the sexes is still marked by a firm line in the average home. If the line is crossed, the family situation is considered extraordinary. The man who does the dishes for his wife when she is pregnant is chivalrous, but if he makes a general habit of it he is very apt to be called Mr. Milquetoast. Sometimes the wife who really enjoys spading up the garden and shoveling snow feels compelled to restrain herself to prevent the sympathy she evokes from her neighbors. Children sense these lines of distinction early. One little girl whose mother very decidedly held the reins of household management was surprised, when she learned to read, to find her father's name on the front door of the house. "The house is your's though, isn't it, Mummy, and not Daddy's?" she asked.[14]

This value of the relative places of the sexes is accentuated for children even in their own earliest life. The girls dress like their mother, and the boys like their father. Mother understands and enjoys most of the toys made for her small daughter, dresses their dolls and shows them how to make candy on their own little stoves. But Father knows the intricacies of electric trains and toy machine guns, and later, of football. Further, the attitude of adults themselves seems to instill in children the horror of being "sissies" or "tomboys."

In a home where affectional ties are balanced, this distinction between the sexes may be only a complementing of functions working to the benefit of the whole régime, and fitting the sons and daughters for their ultimately different rôles in later life. But where a combination of factors prevents balance, sex lines up against sex in keen rivalry and hostility. Particularly where the relationship between mother and father is not sound, the man's side of the family

[14] *Ibid.*, p. 66.

and the woman's side may be deliberately drawn into two camps where the younger members are propagandized, through similar interests, into scorn for the other side.

Usually, such are the chances of heredity, a child is apt to resemble either his own mother and her family, or his own father and his paternal ancestors. And almost as usually, unfortunately for the child, there is a history of strained relationships between the parents and the in-laws on either side. What is more natural than that a mother will be drawn to the child most like her, and will glorify it in an attempt to lower her husband's lofty ideas about his parents. "Jane," she will say, "has been given the leading rôle in the Sunday School pageant. The teacher says she has great dramatic ability. You see, she is just naturally following my father's career. She has always been just like us. And Edith," she will declare, "has failed again to be promoted, though she *is* good in her Home Economics course." By which she means that Edith takes after her paternal grandmother, and that she will probably be a good cook and absolutely nothing more. Now, while Father may instinctively feel that a stage career will only lead Jane down the primrose path that her maternal grandfather traveled, and that Edith will be performing an honorable duty, he nevertheless understands what his wife means; and so do Jane and Edith. Jane will decry Edith's earthiness, and Edith will not waste any opportunity to deride Jane's uselessness around the house, for Edith's father will assuredly take her part.

The merest accident of age has separated many a home into cliques. It is a commonplace that children born close together bear a unique relationship to each other; in a friendly home, theirs is a companionship association. More widely separated siblings often club together in a protective association. But where groups of children of different ages are in the same home, the prerogatives which each group holds—one because of advanced age, the other because of baby status—can raise hostile barriers which never break down. Cases have been found in which this particular age structure resulted in the attempts of both groups to try to break up each other's special games from which they had been excluded. Though the years iron out the natural differences of interests in age groups, they do not so easily erase the hostile structure. For the attitudes which grow up about divisions within the family crystallize firmly, and become independent of any first causes.

Division because of age affects the parents as well as the children of a family. Frequent allusions are made to middle-aged parents whose ways of life have become set, and who resent the intrusion of a baby's pattern of living into their home, even when they have longed for the child. The home can well become a battleground on which childish eagerness and adult obstinacy clash. And just as common is the incidence of those very young parents who, because of babies, could not fulfill their youth, and want to keep it. In these homes there is the continuous drive of the children to grow up, of the parents to disguise their ages. The thirty-three-year-old mother of an attractive sub-deb was heard to remark with thinly concealed resentment in her voice, "Babs and I have just one thing in common. She is trying to look as if she were twenty—and so am I."[15]

In families such as these, we see the truth of Edward Yeoman's comment when he writes, "How shall we exchange competition for coöperation in family life, for competition is what exists, a nervousness to see who can control the situation, a race involving agony on both sides and too often despair sharper than a serpent's tooth."[16] For here competition divides a family into camps; sets sibling against sibling; and even alienates parents and their children.

The Favored-Child Home

Through the stories of family life there runs a theme of dissatisfaction with certain children in comparison with others in the same family. Time and time again it expresses itself in the words of parents. "If only all my children were like Margaret," or, "I don't know why my son is so naughty. His brother is such a good boy." Blanche Weill, in studying a case which will be described in a later category, found that the mother was always, and unconsciously, balancing the behavior of her problem daughter with that of an older and quieter son. Blanche Weill saw here two distinct personality problems. The mother recognized only one. What caused these two different viewpoints?

[15] Case record from author's files.

[16] Edward W. Yeomans, "Salvaging the Family," *Progressive Education*, Volume III, no. 4, 1926, p. 285.

From the moment that any interested man and wife discover that they are about to become parents, they begin to form, consciously or unconsciously, some kind of ideal about the child that is coming. The most obvious and conscious of these ideals is, of course, that the child is to be a girl, or a boy, as the case may be.

One needs only to be at the receiving end of a telephone when a new father is first telling the news to discover how important this ideal has become through the long months of waiting. If the father exclaims, "It's a boy!" then the baby has attained the first standard of the ideal. But if the father describes the details of the birth, and what a fine healthy specimen the baby is before he admits, "It's a boy, but he's such a fine little fellow we really aren't disappointed," then trouble may already be brewing for this new individual in his family situation. For no matter how fine the baby, his parents wanted a girl; and the parents continue to wish for her arrival.

Sex, however, is only a small part of the ideal. The whole picture of what is desired in a child is determined by many things. One mother, as the record tells, wanted a "cuddly" baby and was chilled by an undemonstrative one. Parents seem naturally to incline to the youngster who develops "cute tricks" and easy sociability. Even current fashion plays its part in the ideal. In the days of the Puritans, curly hair was a plague, always to be wetted and plastered into strict straightness. Nowadays, when we see a cherubic two-year-old lass wth crackly corkscrews hanging to her shoulders, we can at least be thankful that the machine age has aided the child in upholding her mother's desire for a curly-headed little girl.

As their children grow older, parents make other demands of the ideal. Economic status and community culture exert their influence. Parents who are not too well off financially have wanted children who are helpful around the house, or who have a flashy talent that will earn money quickly. Other parents have wanted a butterfly daughter to outshine those of their neighbors in party popularity, while still others have put a premium on the kind of child who always makes the highest grades in school.

Whatever the most desired pattern, whether Father finds his ideal most nearly in the daughter who is a copy of the girl he courted, or in the son who is a little image of himself, there is in the family a difference in affection, based on a real preference.

There is probably no agony for a child more real than that of being loved by his parents less than a sibling is loved. And he is going to make somebody pay for that agony. The behavior resorted to by children as retribution for such treatment is so varied that it can hardly be described except in individual terms. The converse problem of this situation is the favored child. Nothing can so consistently foster smug over-confidence as the knowledge that one is the shining star of the family's affection. That leads to a calm tyranny which will be extended to every relationship which will endure that tyranny. The determination of the one child to avenge his hurt, and the jealous guarding of the key position by the favored child result in a familiar situation.

Mrs. Weston was frightened nearly into a breakdown because she thought that her six-year-old daughter, Laura, was abnormal sexually. She was a bit of an exhibitionist in her play with the neighborhood boys. But Laura was actually very normal. She adored her father, who had no use for girls, and who completely ignored her in favor of her brother. Laura was not consciously paying her father back. She was trying to earn his love by identifying herself with boys and becoming like them. It happened that she had come upon a rather unconventional way of winning popularity with them. But her family did pay, and might have paid exorbitantly for their discrimination.[17]

And what of the favored child and his relationship to the family? The favorite does not break into case records as often as the frustrated sibling, for his behavior is generally more acceptable to his parents. But all that has been said of the over-indulged child holds true of the favorite. For regardless of actual degree, this child is relatively over-indulged in affection. He always expects more than his due, in relation to others, and harasses his family with every trick at his command when they are unable to fulfill his expectations.

The "Impartial" Home

The family that makes a fetish of impartiality is a close kin to the Favored-Child Home. But while the latter is found again and again in case records, the former is strikingly absent. "Impartial"

[17] Blanche Weill, *Through Children's Eyes*, pp. 83-102.

parents are consciously aware of their preference, and believe that they are solving the problems that might follow. Naturally, they do not consult a psychiatrist when they have faith in their own method, and so do not enter the case record files.

The "Impartial" Home is interpolated here because it has effects distinctly different from the Favored-Child Home, which, for two reasons at least, make it unhealthy. First, a child is not fooled by the superficialities of equality in treatment. Children often give as proof of discrimination the discrepancy between the material goods given to them and those given to their siblings. But that is the only way they know to express in words the thing that they feel exists. They do not, conversely, assume that exactly similar treatment proves their share of affection equal if they feel it to be otherwise. And while the unfavored child who is treated frankly is usually given to understand the reasons for his unpopularity and can believe them or resent them, the one who hears his parents *talk* their "impartiality," and *act* their "impartiality," is baffled. There is nothing specific in his situation, nothing to fight against nor to work on. The second reason is that insincere impartiality usually betrays itself in over-careful and exact identity of treatment. And there are no two children living, not even identical twins, who have the same needs.

An educated man who knew just enough of psychology to face the fact that he much preferred his younger daughter to her year-older sister, thought he had analyzed himself out of his partiality. In conversation, he never praised or blamed one without praising or blaming the other. Wherever he went with one he took the other along. Their mother shared his favoritism and responded similarly. The trouble was that everyone in the family was being penalized by this procedure. For Martha, the younger, was a lively, pretty girl, witty and facile, and full of social graces. She was as destined to shine among crowds of clever people as were her mother and father. But Mildred stood upon "piano legs," and would have liked more than anything else to walk out on her chummy family and rough it in old clothes with a few chosen athletic friends. She did not want money spent on fussy clothes and parties and beauticians. And Martha, who did, was restricted by the budget which was made to spread equally. Always, in their shared activities, Mildred shamed her family. But to have allowed Mildred to go her own wanted way, and let Martha cling to her parents, would have looked like the casting out of an unloved child. And at all costs the mask of impartiality had to be kept. So no one was very happy in family life. Mildred knew that she did not fit, and so did everyone else.[18]

True impartiality is proportional in treatment. It estimates the need of every member of the family, and tries to supply them with equality of effort.

INCONSISTENCY OF AFFECTION

The Bickering Home

The Bickering Home enjoys tremendous popularity nowadays, and not only, or chiefly, in families under economic pressure.

Myra's parents spent every waking moment nagging at each other, though sometimes they took a few minutes off to nag at the children. The children were constantly asked to take sides. Life was a series of minute wars. And when we see what one big war can do to the state of mind of a world, we realize what a series of wars between the people who make the foundations of her world, can do to a sensitive little girl's.[19]

This is only one of hundreds of almost identical case records in current literature on the family

There seem to be four factors which stand out as contributing to the incidence of the Bickering Home at the present time. First, the tempo of modern life is very fast, and its tone loud and strident. It seems remarkable that so many human beings are able to keep steady nerves and calm tempers in the cacophony of it all. Then, the modern world has shrunk. Living is congested and transportation easy. Barriers have broken down, and people meet and marry mates of unlike status and standards and ideals, with whom harmonious living is well-nigh impossible under the best of circumstances. Third, the patriarchal system of family life has been breaking down, but the memory of it is not gone. Mother is "having a go" at using her own theories of child-rearing. But the concept of the patriarch is still

[18] Case record from author's file.

[19] Carmelite Janvier, "Problem Children and Problem Parents," *The Survey*, October 15, 1929, p. 77.

hallowed by Father, and he is not going to allow his ideas of how to raise his own children to be supplanted by any women's theories. And fourth, the new individualism gives the children themselves a voice in family affairs. They no longer simply stand and wait. They serve their own little ultimatums when they see fit.

The jangled nerves, the unlike standards, the jockeying for authority, the individual will, all of them are conducive to a home where moments of friendly tranquility, if they exist, are constantly interrupted by bickering.

Sometimes it is difficult for an adult, however imaginative, to sense the feelings of a child in a certain situation. But a simile used in the case history of Myra helps us to understand the child, and the adults too, in the Bickering Home. All of us, in America, know too well "what one big war can do to the state of mind. . . ." The relative security in the future, in which we were happy and to which we gave little thought, becomes doubtful. There is no certainty, and certainty becomes more important than it ever was. Psychiatrists' offices are filled with new patients. Fatal heart attacks make news every day. But wars have come and wars have gone, and we all know that some day there will be peace again, and that without the disintegration of the world.

For the members of the home, chronically at war with each other, there is all the uncertainty and anxiety, but with less assurance of ultimate peace.

The Unreliable Home

For proof that there are plenty of Unreliable Homes, refer to any high school or college records in which students discuss their relationship with their parents. It will not take a long search to find a confession like this: "I never know what to expect from Mother and Dad. Sometimes we get along fine together, and then all of a sudden they'll start ripping into me for just nothing at all."

No parents can prevent all variations of temperament. But the reliability of their affection becomes more and more important to members of their family as outside relationships grow less and less intimate. The family is one place where a person should know how he is regarded, accepted, and how he will be treated.

Particularly is this important for the children in a family. A man who has been accustomed to having his wife berate him for lateness at dinner may become suspicious if she greets him with a smile. If he has much intelligence, he may be able to find the reason for the change. To the child, however, his parents' behavior toward him is a direct reaction to *him*, to his being good or bad, loved or not loved. If the child feels consistently loved, he does not have to think much about it. If he feels consistently unloved at home, he must, to the best of his ability, find affection elsewhere. But for the child who never can tell if today he will be beaten for accidentally breaking one of his own toys, or if tomorrow he will be called "my precious" all day no matter what he does, there can be nothing but bewilderment.

This kind of situation is a vicious circle breeding unhappiness. For the child treated inconsistently cannot learn to behave according to a consistent pattern. He has never discovered what kind of behavior is good and profitable, because it always brings satisfying results, and what is bad and unprofitable, because it always brings down woe upon his head. He does not develop far beyond the trial-and-error stage of simply seeing how far he can go. And this kind of child cannot gain consistent affection from his parents, his siblings, or from the rest of the world.

DISPLACEMENT OF AFFECTION

The Home with a New Member

Because it is so important to know one's own acknowledged place in the family in relation to the other members, and to be able to rely upon it, the arrival of a new member into the family circle is upsetting. It affects all the inner relationships. Many are the cases of new fathers who are resentful of the shift in their wives' attention from themselves to the baby who demands so much care and love. Lack of tact and thoughtfulness often cause real animosity to grow out of what is actually a temporary unbalancing of old relationships.

If this kind of misunderstanding occurs between adults, how much more serious is the situation for children who are not able to reason out for themselves this uneasiness over being displaced by another. For children seem to regard their parents' love as a deep pond which grows shallow as its limits extend, rather than as a spring which refills to the brim after every draught taken from it.

The arrival of a new baby is, perhaps, the hardest kind of family increase for an ill-prepared child to bear, and most children have been woefully unprepared for such an advent. Parents have seemed to believe that if they instructed their children honestly in the facts of creation and birth, and told them when to expect the new member, then they had done all that was necessary. Unfortunately this does not in any way prepare a youngster for the great change that a new baby will make in his home life. Happier often is the child who believes the stork legend, if his mother has explained how much care and love the family will want to give to this new little baby, because it will be so helpless in comparison with its brothers and sisters who are already so grown up and responsible. To make the older child secure in his older position, to give him a full share in the adult interest in the baby—this is to prepare the child for actuality.

When a child does not realize the change which is to take place, he may react as Margaret did. She had been a happy little girl during all the three years of her life. Then the baby came. Her mother gave to the baby all those little attentions which Margaret had once enjoyed herself and which she had been trained to out-grow. Father cuddled the baby just as Margaret wished to be cuddled, and when he did Margaret would scream and rage. She was punished for this conduct. As a result, whenever the baby was caressed Margaret had even more violent tantrums, which drew her parents' attention away from the baby and toward her, even if the results were not entirely pleasant. Finally, the tantrums grew so bad that Father and Mother had to give in to Margaret in order to stop them. So Margaret won the war, but she had lost what she was fighting for. She wanted to be loved, and no one could love so disturbing a child as she had become. Her father paid no attention to her, except to scold her, for she had become too dis-agreeable to pet. And her mother was nervous, irritable, and in general at her wits' end.

Margaret had an older brother, Paul, who had once been the baby of the family. When his sister was born, he had gone through the same unhappiness. But because he was not so healthy and vigorous as Margaret, he had retreated into himself, and become a painfully shy and reticent little fellow.[20]

In such a family each new baby brings heartbreak to the child he displaces, and a disturbance of family relationships dependent, in intensity, on the reactions of the individuals.

There is another kind of displacement of affection which has high incidence at the present time. In a study of over half a million marriages, one out of five was found to be a remarriage.[21] Adults no longer think it obligatory to endure loneliness because of their children. They now consider that they are free individuals with lives of their own to fulfill, apart from parental responsibilities. Since it can be assumed, then, that a large number of children are involved in this reshuffling of marital relationships, there enters, on a fairly large scale, the stepmother or stepfather problem in the displacement of affection.

From the very start there is a hazard here because of the popular conception of "stepmother" or "stepfather." Too often adult talk, schoolboy taunts, and fairy tales have prejudiced children against the very idea of being a stepchild.

But there are deeper dangers. A newly married couple is apt to be as overly absorbed in each other as is a mother with a new baby, and to the exclusion of the other members of the family. Many children have complained of feeling "shut out" at a time like this. They are being deprived of their usual stint of affection, and they resent the new parent who is no choice of theirs. He has assumed the place of their former loved parent, who was removed by death or divorce; and he has robbed them of the affection of their real parent.

Children believe to be true whatever they feel, and see with their own eyes. If the baby, or new parent, seems to take away the affection he himself received before, the situation causes him an unhappiness which he will communicate in his own way to the entire family.

[20] Blanche Weill, *op. cit.*, pp. 60-75.
[21] James H. S. Bossard, "Previous Conjugal Condition," *Social Forces*, Volume 18, no. 2, December, 1939, p. 243.

LACK OF AFFECTION

The Nagging Home

As a contrast to the Bickering Home, where waves of affection alternate with explosions of rage, there is the Nagging Home, in which chronic complaining reveals a lack of acceptance of some members into the affectional relationship.

There is a good deal of evidence to be found in current advertising alone that children do not have the same status in the family that they formerly had; that homes are planned chiefly with adults in mind, and are to be kept that way in spite of children. The emphasis in any household magazine is on compact, neat, picture-like little dwellings, with pale walls and plenty of mirrors to give the illusion of space, and a built-in cubby hole to keep unsightly things out of sight. Women have become so enamoured of these pleasant pictures that the plans are carried out, in rows upon rows of houses. Then the children come. And one wonders what is to become of them in these homes. The housework is so highly mechanized that children cannot be of much help. Some of them may be pushed into the basement recreation room, if it has not been fitted out as a pine-paneled bar for the adults. But for many children, who are less important to their parents than is the picture house, life becomes a matter of keeping out of the way and not cluttering up the place.

Little Stephen Knapp learned all about this kind of situation at an early age:

When Mother was scrubbing a floor was always a good time for Stephen. She forgot all about you for a while. Oh, what a weight fell off from your shoulders when Mother forgot about you for a while! How perfectly lovely it was just to walk around in the bedroom and know she wouldn't come to the door any minute and look at you hard and say, "What are you doing, Stephen?" and add, "How *did* you get your rompers so dirty?"

Stephen stepped about and about in the room, silently, drawing long breaths. The bed, the floor, the bureau, everything looked different to you in the time when Mother forgot about you for a minute. It occurred to Stephen that maybe it was a rest to them, too, to have Mother forget about them and stop dusting and polishing and pushing them around. They looked sort of peaceful, the way he felt. He nodded his head to the bed and looked with sympathy at the bureau.[22]

And then the rest of the family came home from school. Their mother, spick and span in a fresh house dress, came to the door to greet them:

"Don't wriggle around on one foot that way to take off your rubbers. Sit down on a chair. No, not that one, it's too high. This one. Lay down your schoolbooks. You can't do anything with them under your arm. There are your mittens on the floor. Put them in your pocket and you'll know where to find them. Unless they're damp. Are they damp? If they are, take them into the kitchen and put them on the rack to dry. . . . Not too close to the stove, or they'll burn."[23]

Thus the Knapps lived from sun-up till bedtime and through three meals a day. The children had bad digestive disorders. So did Mr. Knapp. It seemed a clear case of inherited weakness until Mr. Knapp met with a serious accident. Then Mrs. Knapp had to go out to support the family while her husband took charge of the home from a wheel-chair. In time the indigestion disappeared, the problem-child Stephen became quite human, and Mr. and Mrs. Knapp got to be quite good friends. The children prayed, with fearful earnestness, that their father's paralysis might never be cured. . . .

Another current trend is to budget time, as well as living space. If parents are to be people, as well as parents, they have to hurry, since time is short for all the activities offered to adults. But children simply are not geared to parents who are always in a hurry. Neither can they understand the superior importance of the adults' time schedule over their own occupations. A great deal of adjustment to each others' needs is necessary to allow both child and adult to live full, satisfying lives. And though the nagging parent may be trying to be efficient, he is not reasonable. His commands, therefore, are apt to be conflicting, contradictory, and confusing in the extreme to the small child who wishes to please by obeying his parents. They irritate to a frenzy the child who, like Stephen, wants only a little peace and solitude.

[22] Dorothy Canfield, *The Home-Maker*, pp. 15-16.
[23] *Ibid.*, p. 16.

The Frigid Home

Again, in the Frigid Home, we find an example of a family situation which is largely unrepresented in case histories. Its higher economic status or its traditions of impersonality in private life have kept this kind of home from entering the records. It is difficult to maintain a relationship of formality or frigidity with children when one is in close proximity to them and must constantly perform many services for them. Therefore, the really Frigid Home is largely confined to those families which can afford social distance between its members, and to those others which are determined to imitate the behavior of homes financially more successful.

Level of income, above the necessary minimum, never alone determines the relationships within a given family. But certain customs and traditions that spring up among groups of people who move in the same circles because they can afford the same things often have a profound influence upon the family life. Some obstetricians, aspiring to a lucrative career, hesitate to recommend that a mother nurse her baby. The idea is rather shocking to some of the patients he most wants to keep. It is either "not quite nice," or it is an imposition upon personal liberty which is not to be endured. Similar attitudes in parents lead them to avoid what they regard as menial services for their children.

Upon this kind of base may grow a Frigid Home. The demonstrating of affection is strictly taboo in this family, for it is vulgar and plebeian. Current motion pictures of modern domestic life show man and wife communicating warm affection in a kind of caustic, intellectual banter. But this is not the explicit language of childhood; children cannot grasp the subtle implications of affection. They naturally want frank expression and physical contacts with the people they love. When they shy away from them there has been something wrong with former contacts. The baby who is not cuddled, or the youngster who is never allowed a roughhouse with his parents, comes to see affection in an unnatural light. He will either adopt the frigidity which is so appalling in a child, and unfits him for normal romance, or he may become one of those unhealthy personalities who place too great emphasis upon affection and seek for it rabidly.

In the days of Charles Dickens, the self-effacing heroine, who lived only for those she loved, was a popular figure. Dickens drew her portrait in the life of Florence Dombey. Realistically, though, he did not produce her from a family where the affectional ties were robust and hearty. She was starved for the affection of a father who knew only formality in all of his relationships. He did not mean to be unkind to his child. He was very careful about the character of the woman who attended her, and he deprived her of no material thing which he felt to be right and good for her. He simply was incapable of expressing any tenderness for Florence.

As a result, the girl's chief aim in her early life seemed to be to crawl into a corner near her baby brother's crib, and sleep beside him, because she thought, maybe, he loved her a little. She spent her youth in his service for the reward of his affection. And when the boy died, Florence pursued her search for kindness by watching, from her window, her neighbor and his daughter spending companionable hours at the tea table, until she could stand her grievous envy no longer. Then she would creep to her father's door, hoping for some word or gesture of love.

Mr. Dombey sensed that there was something wrong with their relationship, and that he was at fault. He could not guess, though, what it was, and it made him very uncomfortable. Florence's presence became such a reproach to him that in crises he simply denied her presence altogether.[24]

The modern age is impatient of such pathos. We no longer applaud it. But it exists, nevertheless. A more vigorous child than Florence may make his way in this formal atmosphere by adopting its methods and giving back as much coldness as he gets. But there are many Florences who actually grow as pale and wan as any Victorian heroine just from the lack of warmth in their intimate family relationships.

The Neglectful Home

While the Frigid Home fully intends the good of the child, but injudiciously starves his desire for affection, in the Neglectful Home the parents live only for the gratification of their own pleasures.

[24] Charles Dickens, *Dombey and Son*.

They exclude their children from any interference with these pleasures, and fail to exercise adequate physical or psychological supervision.

From the lowest income-level family, with a brood of children, to the wealthiest one-child family, the neglect depends, not on what the parents are able to do for the child, but on whether they are able to deny their own self-pity or self-gratification enough to put the child on at least a proper proportional footing with the rest of the family. Studies of delinquency areas show, as do hundreds of novels of slum life, that some dirty and ragged children are neglected till criminality is their only escape, while the children of the next-door neighbor, just as ragged, are cared for in all that matters to the child. So omnipresent are the cases of physical neglect in the literature of family life that they scarcely need further description. Psychological neglect is more apt to be overlooked. But it is as prevalent, and is less easy to catch and cure.

Mr. and Mrs. Allston seemed to have everything that nature and the civilized world could bestow upon a fortunate couple. They were young, attractive, wealthy, and had had four children close together; a perfect family. The parents were completely companionable, and they had good fun with the children too—that is, whenever they saw them. But life was such a whirl for these two healthy and popular parents. One week out of each month usually took care of Mr. Allston's business, and during that week his wife would prepare the plans for their next trip and for exciting activities to occupy her offspring while their parents were away. When the children were small it was playground equipment, pedigreed cats and dogs. Later, a tennis court and swimming pool were added for their pleasure, as well as memberships to golf and beach clubs. Their diet was scientific; their clothes well tailored. But an interested observer could appreciate their real neglect. As the car, taking their mother and father away on their latest jaunt, drove from the estate, all the vitality and gay boisterousness that had marked the home would die away. All that was left was four listless, lonely children who did not know what to do with themselves, who never went near the pool or tennis court, and who fell to scrapping amongst themselves to while away the time until the next happy interval should occur. As they reached early adolescence, they got into the habit of taking walks, separately, away from home, deliberately seeking out some mature neighboring housewife who would talk, and not play, with them. The need of these growing children for some adult companionship and guidance was acute. If they were to find it at all, it had to be through their own efforts. For in their home, all the essentials that made for growth from adolescence into happy, independent adulthood were utterly neglected. They were at as great a handicap as those children who are pushed out on to the street to learn their lessons where they will.[25]

REJECTION

The Home of the Unwanted Child

Studies analyzing parental attitudes for their effects upon children have one conclusion in common. It is that the home in which there is frank and unyielding rejection of a child is the sort of home which holds out the smallest hope of help from the psychiatric social worker. The possibility of improving personal relationships rests fundamentally on the desire to do so. But in the Home of the Unwanted Child the wish is to deny and not to improve the tie with the child.

A mother brought her little girl to a clinic because everything that the child did annoyed her parents. The woman had not wanted any children and neither had her husband. The two adults were very congenial. Since neither of them was interested in the responsibilities of home and family, they did not nag at each other when these duties were neglected. But the child was spoiling their enjoyed independence. She had copied her parents' pattern of self-love, and was demanding her own rights in her own way. Her parents wanted the social worker to make the child less disagreeable to them in some miraculous way but without infringing upon their time or their habits.[26]

In another family, little Helen was also an unwanted child, whose mother found any services beyond the absolutely unavoidable

---

[25] Case record from the author's files.

[26] Marjorie Stauffer, "Some Aspects of Treatment by Psychiatrist and Psychiatric Social Worker," *American Journal of Orthopsychiatry*, April, 1932, Volume II, p. 159.

ones of child-rearing a bother. At three and a half, Helen was still bottle-fed, because it was so much less trouble than the slow, untidy process of teaching self-feeding. She had no control of her excretions, and had bad temper tantrums. However, placed in a boarding school, she learned in two months self-feeding, proper toilet habits, and good social behavior.[27] There is no follow-up of Helen's case, but it is obvious that unless her mother's whole attitude was changed, Helen would develop other symptoms of neglect upon her return to her home, and ones that might not be cured so easily in a few months at a boarding school.

Fortunately children who are not wanted at all are gradually coming to be found only in homes unequipped with proper contraceptive devices. But even the child looked forward to or actually enjoyed on arrival may turn into an unwanted child. A difficult pregnancy, the advent of twins where one child was prepared for, a child of the wrong sex; financial reverses, or the development of antisocial characteristics in the child: all of these have deprived children who were planned for of their welcome. The great change that a new individual makes in the family is not always anticipated by married couples, and when it is discovered, the cause is often definitely rejected.

All of these factors and others, more subtle and less easily controlled than the mere fact of contraception, are keeping the Home of the Unwanted Child a situation to conjure with in any classification of family life.

SUMMARY

From excess of affection which swallows up the loved object, to complete rejection which thrusts the hated one out of any affectional ties—so runs the gamut of affectional relationships within the family. Between the extremes lie discrimination with its injustice, inconsistency with its bewilderment, and the displacement which stirs up wild resentment. And also, somewhere between, is that normal affectional relationship which, whether the home holds a large family or small, underprivileged or suddenly wealthy, urban or rural, holds the magic that makes all other problems relatively impotent against the unity and security of the family.

[27] Leo Kanner, op. cit., p. 95.

II. SUBJECTUAL RELATIONSHIPS

Quite apart from any ties of affection within a family, there is a subjectual relationship resulting from contending wills and their adjustment to each other. Any baby, regardless of his love for his parents, is going to try to dominate his own little sphere. That is the natural desire of us all. But because it is a universal desire not everyone can achieve it, and unless proper adjustment of wills occurs, the strongest or the cleverest wins out. Domination of that sort in a family predicates subjection in the same family.

REPRESSION

The Mother-Controlled Home

Typical of the subjectual relationships within a goodly number of American homes today is the Mother-Controlled Home. In the city and surrounding suburbs, as far out as commutation extends, father leaves the home, and with it his control over it during most of its active hours. In these homes, where the economic function is gone, the functions remaining fall to the management of the mother who happens to be there.

Since the Mother-Controlled Home is becoming a widely accepted pattern in native white and the better assimilated foreign-born groups, and is causing no real conflict with community ideas, probably the worst feature of it, in its milder forms, is that summed up by Dr. Groves in his article entitled "A Child Needs Two Parents."[28] Parents, he says, are a child's only connecting link with the outside world. And a child needs two views, the mother-view and the father-view. The parents have different interests and different knowledge. The mother looks outward from the home, her center. The father looks inward toward it from his place in the world. The child needs a guide in a companion-father, for the mother's constant proximity, influence, and discipline come to be taken for granted. The father brings a new and different stimulus.

That was just the stimulus lacking to the ten-year-old boy who wanted to run away from his father-eclipsed life situation. He

[28] Ernest R. Groves, *Progressive Education*, Volume III, October-November-December, 1926, no. 4, pp. 300-304.

fought with his brother, was unhappy with both his mother and father, and was getting more and more into conflict with his boy schoolmates.

His mother was intelligent and affectionate, but she was certain she knew how to train and discipline a child, and she never questioned her own methods. When they did not work, it was the fault of the child who had inherited rebellion from his father's family. The boy's father had completely adjusted to his own subordinate position in the home. He admitted laughingly that when he could not win an argument he treated the whole thing as a joke. He nursed, however, a secret admiration for his own son who pugnaciously abhorred his school which he thought was "sissy," his violin lessons, and the friends chosen for him from a "good social group." But his father would not do anything for him that would mean opposing his wife openly. His son was rapidly becoming unfit for male companionship. He could not be like the boys he admired; so he fought them. He could not put his energy to constructive use in solving his problem, for his mother's will held command.[29]

The Mother-Controlled Home in an extreme form has other effects upon the family. A great many deserters' homes and poorly financed homes have this set-up in subjectual relations. A completely repressed and submissive man is not a good economic risk for any home to have as its provider. Economic survival in most cases demands some fight. But the submissive man who has any fight left usually overcompensates. And the world does not take kindly, either, to the man who plays the tyrant in business because his wife plays the tyrant at home. Even this man's children do not have much respect for him. They may pity him at home, but they get no balanced ideal of masculinity, and they despise his methods of compensation if they learn of them.

For all of these homes the accepted pattern is one of the triumph of the stronger over the weaker, and the exploitation of the weak. It is a pattern which makes for undemocratic personal relationships in all spheres of life.

[29] Madeline U. Moore, "The Treatment of Maternal Attitudes in Problems of Guidance," *American Journal of Orthopsychiatry,* Volume III, no. 2, April, 1933, pp. 114-117.

The Father-Dominated Home

Although the harsh patriarchal pattern of Colonial family life is softening into one of greater equality between husband and wife, descriptions of the behavior of fathers in child guidance clinics prove that the pattern is not entirely lost. Furthermore, our large immigrant population, raised by that pattern in its own generation, does not easily give it up in the next. Homes with foreign-born parents form a large proportion, though by no means all, of the cases which naturally fall under the name of the Father-Dominated Home.

The most widely known and highly colorful example of the results of a father's domination is the home life of Elizabeth Barrett and her brothers and sisters. Without delving into the over-emphasized Freudian analysis of this family, certain surface facts show the general configuration.

Edward Moulton-Barrett was not to be crossed in any of his commands as to how family life should be conducted. Certain of his many children submitted, and inspired no story books. But Elizabeth had a mind of her own, and it was a superior mind. A slight figure, she could not stand up to her father's physical strength. Did she find in weakness a weapon which she could employ? We know that she developed a very real illness that caused her in the face of crises to sink into a semiconscious state. When her favorite brother Edward, who had been staying with her in Italy, was summoned home by his father, Elizabeth felt that she needed him, her only companion, to remain. Mr. Barrett insisted in his demand, and Elizabeth's condition became so aggravated that her doctor advised Mr. Barrett that to oppose her will might mean her death. Many times her doctor's words, "Elizabeth must not be agitated," were the only means of winning for her a wish that otherwise would have been sacrified to her father's will.

We know that Elizabeth's doctor prescribed morphine for her pain. We cannot know how much her ultimate dependence on that drug was caused by the constant goading she experienced. It is certain that when Browning remonstrated against her habit, she wrote that he little knew how much she had to bear, that her pain was not all physical.

And last, there remains the fact that when Elizabeth, a woman of forty, determined to marry, she begged Browning not to tell her father, for then he would surely imprison her in her room. Instead, this grown woman had to make careful plans to escape from her home without her father's knowledge.[30]

For two reasons, at least, the Father-Dominated Home is apt to be a more damaging situation that the Mother-Controlled Home. First, it is coming to be a sort of culture lag, a hangover from the patriarchal pattern. In a community where women are accustomed to running their homes and children as they please, the submissive mother is more apt to be marked than is the submissive father, who is able to escape for most of the day. Then, second, even in these homes the children are more often with their mother than with the father. They form their earliest affectional ties with her and take her as their first model. And in this case, the model is an inefficient and docile personality, one who submits necessarily and can compensate only through her children. As the most-present member, she must attempt family discipline, but she is denied her children's respect for her commands through interference and over-ruling by the father. So inconsistency of discipline occurs, and the children can run to mother for protection, yet disregard her when it suits their purpose. For the development of consistent social behavior, the Father-Dominated Home, in an era when father's presence is limited, is not a satisfactory model.

The Overly Demanding Home

There are plenty of homes in which parents dominate their children not just to create a dominating role for themselves, but to force an arbitrarily conceived rôle upon the children. When this rôle runs counter to the wishes and the natural abilities of the child, it acts as a suppression of whatever is natural to that child.

Rarely does a parent have to be overly demanding if the course he sets conforms to the child's own natural bent and desires. For then the child will need little prodding, only some help in over-coming the obstacles and distractions in his path.

Miriam Van Waters, in her experience with parents in juvenile

[30] Jeannette Marks, *The Family of the Barrett.*

court, discovered many of this kind who try to make the child fit the home. Her comment upon this type of situation is that a healthy child cannot survive in a family where adult tastes rule exclusively, but only in a home where the values of each member are recognized and permitted growth.[31]

In the home of William Butler, the values typical of an intelligent, capable "white-collar family" prevailed. All the members lived according to that standard without difficulty until, at fourteen, William began getting into trouble. His father, who held higher education a social necessity, had sent him to a school where he had to take special academic courses. His grades slipped below the approved mark and he started playing hookey. In spite of considerate and kindly treatment and advice, this habit continued until the boy landed in a truancy school. There it was discovered that William was definitely below the mental level required for an academic career. He had known his own limit better than his father, and had attempted to escape before he reached the breaking point. It was a sad blow to his father, when he discovered that it would be impossible to force one member of the family to pursue what he had demanded as essential to the respectability of the family, and very little solace to find that his son had unusual manual ability. Though the father's intelligence and affection made him consent to the suitable program for William, still manual training did not fit into a "white-collar" home.[32]

Children in an Overly Demanding Home often develop a deep sense of inferiority for preferring activities unacceptable to the family, and work themselves into a breakdown in their attempts to conform. Some of them overtly rebel, as did William, but not all of these are as lucky in having flexible parents. And finally, some, by sheer determination, make the desired grade, only to find ultimately that they are dissatisfied with and unsuited to the whole life scheme that their parents have imposed upon them.

---

[31] Miriam Van Waters, *Parents on Probation*, p. 75.

[32] Susan Burlingham, "Casework with Adolescents Who Have Run Afoul of the Law," *American Journal of Orthopsychiatry*, Volume VII, no. 4, October, 1937, p. 497.

ANARCHY

The Child-Dictated Home

Most of the analyses of subjectual relationships in family situations assume that the parents control each situation, and that its content, if unhealthy, is a result of their faulty management. In most cases this is clearly true. But in some, after careful study, it became apparent that not the parents but the child himself was the master of the situation and the dictator of family life.

A married couple who were very much lacking in self-confidence and who were not in good physical health either, gave birth to a determined little girl who, at the age of three, was the self-willed, stubborn controller of the family. Her parents found rest in giving in to Doris' strength. But to plan her own life, at three, was too big a burden for the child. She ate only what and when she pleased. She never slept until she felt like it. Whenever she wanted to play, her mother and father had to stop what they were doing and play with her. Naturally, she could not know that it was her own planned program which made her an undernourished, ill, excitable, and unhappy little wreck of human nature. There was no sane basis for expecting that this baby could work out a constuctive and successful program for health and development and the progress of the family.[33]

The home in which the child dictates may look, to the casual observer, like a plain case of over-indulgence. But there is a great and serious difference between the Over-Indulgent Home and the Child-Dictated Home. In the first, the child is pressed with the things he desires because of his parents' excessive love for him. In the latter, he battles his way to what he wants because he dominates the relatively weaker adults. In the former, the child may be wisely guided in some matters while he is being indulged in others. In the latter, the child does the leading.

A small child is utterly incapable of understanding the adult social world. One grows into that understanding slowly even when

---

[33] Esther Colby Sweet, "Nursery School as a Contributing Factor in Mental Health," *American Journal of Orthopsychiatry*, Volume III, no. 4, October, 1933, pp. 406-407.

properly guided. All overt baby behavior takes the shortest cut toward self-satisfaction, until this directness is socialized out of him. It is through his parents that he gets his first glimpse of the adult world and by them is fitted for participation in it. But the home organized on the basis of a child's undirected will is a center for the nervous instability and ineffectiveness of all its members. The children have no rules fitted to their needs. The adults are not permitted to have a program of their own. The law governing such a home reverts to the survival of the fittest, and children get no idea of the all-pervading cosmic and social authority to which they must be subjected later.

A child in a museum, bewildered by the acres of interesting objects at his eyes' command, said to his adult companion. "You must take me where I ought to go, or I shall miss something I ought to see."[34] It is this kind of wise selection, from the variety of the world, that is lacking in the Child-Dictated Home.

CONFUSION

The Home with Too Many Bosses

Students of the family have come to no agreement on the comparative help to a child of having grandparents and other relatives living with the family or outside of it. Without them, some say, there is the loss of the deep perspective which comes with long experience in living. With them, retort the others, there is too much resistance to the facts of a fast-changing world. Without adopting either point of view, one can see in actual family cases certain results of having the authority of many relatives in one home. Some of these results will be reported here in describing the Home with Too Many Bosses.

The House in Dormer Forest was a very unpleasant place in which to live. There were altogether too many people in it, considering the sort of people they were. Mr. Darke insisted that his children take religion seriously. Mrs. Darke was determined that they conform to the conventions of good family life, and marry "properly." Grandmother was equally fond of convention and religion and added a few appraising words to all Mr. and Mrs.

[34] Miriam Van Waters, *op. cit.*, p. 53.

Darke's commands. The unmarried cousin who was young and very beautiful was vitally interested in making the whole family become slaves to her personal ambitions.

Within this framework lived the four children, Amber, Ruby, Jasper, and Peter. And any remark or activity of any of the children was seized up and tossed like a ball from righteous Father to proper Mother, to sensuous Cousin, and then gathered in by Grandmother before the second round started.

Peter, quite innocently, kissed a servant girl; then rebelling against his family's suspicious warnings, deliberately had an affair with her. Next, confused by a mistaken conventionality, he married her, and finally, more confusedly, paid to send her away to hide his family's disgrace. Jasper, standing out firmly against his father's desired profession in the church, fell, on the rebound, into the clutches of his cousin and developed an almost fatal love for her. Ruby took the easy way. She just slid into the marriage of her mother's choice. Then realizing her mistake, too late, she ran out of her bedroom on her wedding night, only to be forcibly pushed back by her cousin. So Ruby lived with her husband and always hated him. Only Amber, who managed to escape notice in the turmoil, was able to chart her own set course in life. Such were the results to the attractive, thoroughly likable children, of too many bosses in the family.[35]

For the most part, families do not consist of so many adults as they did a generation or two ago. But the records show that even those who live apart and make visits play their rôle in the child's own family situation. Relatives with their own homes to retire to are more at liberty to spoil children since they do not have to bear the results of their actions. Their treatment cannot be based upon so full a knowledge of the child as if they lived with him. How often one hears a grandmother say that she enjoys her grandchildren more than she did her own youngsters. Her reason? "I have all of the fun and pleasure, and none of the responsibility." That has a foreboding sound to the parents who do have the responsibility.

There is another factor which enters into the current problem of

[35] Mary Webb, *The House in Dormer Forest.*

grandparents. The status of their authority is more confusing than it was formerly, for when experience was at a premium the old folks had the last word. Now, when not experience, but the latest theories and techniques in a fast-changing world give the answer to questions, grandparents' ideas are passé. There are cases in which the child, subject to both generations, watches his mother ridiculing or defying her own mother. He has to obey *his* mother because she is older. But his grandmother, who is still older, is just an old fogey.

Life histories disclose two other complications which affect this already confusing relationship. Often the grandparents hold the family money bags. Then parents try to foster courteous respect in their children for definite ends, while still trying to keep independence of action. And second, grandparents are also parents-in-law. There is frequently a great difference to the child in how well he must obey his grandparents, depending upon whether his mother or his father is present.

Children themselves tell us that not only grandparents, but married siblings who live at home, kitchen help, governesses, boarders or lodgers—any adults who, with ideas different from the parents', try to impose their authority—make it just that much more difficult for children to live happily according to one consistent regimen.

APPROACHING BALANCE

The Democratic Home

Many of the recent case histories of family situations show a subjectual relationship which is neither parent-dominated nor child-dictated. Theirs is a relationship of continuous adjustment and readjustment of dominance and submission which results in some families in a near-equality of authority. This pattern of subjectual relationships is coming to be thought of as the ideal one for the modern American family.

Two specific factors have helped to produce this equalitarian alliance. The first is the effect of modern science upon the study of family relationships and child development, which has been to stress the genetic viewpoint and to give clearer insight into causation.[36] We realize now that the personality of the child as it emerges in his first few years in his family is the foundation of the adult that he is to become. The family atmosphere must stimulate him to develop traits both of leadership and of concurrence so that he may become a well-balanced adult.

The second factor is the expansion of social consciousness. The genetic viewpoint extends out beyond the immediate family, into the national group and the next generation. We believe now that we must fit the child at home for something more than his adjustment to his family. We must prepare him to become the kind of adult he should be to fit best into the society he will live in when he grows up.

If this viewpoint is applied consistently, then the most effective set-up in subjectual relationships within the family must depend upon the larger social sphere in which that family happens to live. We pass over the whole issue of whether the child in an authoritarian world should be trained democratically in the home in order to benefit society in the next generation. That has no place here. But for the effectiveness and happiness of the child in his conformance to his own world, what a difference there must be in the methods of the families of democratic and authoritarian societies. It is just that kind of difference which makes us look at the so-called "typical" American college girl, in her careful-careless garb, with her natural comfort and assurance, her freedom of motion and freedom of mind, and know, surely, that such a creature could have been produced only in America, and could fit only into the part of the world she has had the good fortune to be born into.

The Griffins live in Cedar Rapids. Mr. and Mrs. Griffin are in their middle thirties, Jacquie is ten and Benny seven. They are pretty typical of a large slice of American familydom. Mr. Griffin earns about two thousand dollars a year. Mrs. Griffin does all her own housework, and the two youngsters share in the income and and the housework alike. The tradition of democracy, as it has been known in America, is consciously fostered in this home. All matters of concern to the family are decided by debate and vote, whether it is buying some new equipment, solving a household

[36] James H. S. Bossard, *Marriage and the Child*, Chapter I.

problem, or choosing a new activity. No question gets the answer "Mother, or Father, knows best." Jacquie and Benny receive allowances, and get them on their father's payday as their part in the family income. In order that their mother may have time for her own outside activities, the children help with housework and answer telephone calls, writing down messages with accuracy while their father uses his skill at mending household equipment and building efficiency gadgets for his wife. Jacquie and her mother are very good friends. They enjoy going to the movies together. The whole family work and play with their miniature zoo in the back yard. They put on their best clothes and go to church and Sunday school each week. And always there is time reserved for Mother's and Father's social evenings together after the children are in bed, and for their separate hobbies of woodworking and dramatics. Jacquie plays the cornet and is learning to cook. The animals are Benny's particular interest, and there is an accordion waiting for him when he is a little older.

Mrs. Griffin admits that she is surprised at the shrewdness of her small children in matters of family debate. They listen to their parents, they consider where they want to go, they choose methods they think best to get them there. And they are as self-reliant as they are wise, for they are happy and certain in their own home. They are on their way, as members of a Democratic Home, to becoming effective personalities and good democratic citizens.[37]

SUMMARY

This chapter has been concerned with a study of the personal interrelationships of family members as they have been found in the literature of family life. Certain general tendencies have seemed to manifest themselves.

1. The affectional relations within the family tend to influence, more than does any other one thing, the sense of security and "belongingness" of its members, and especially so in the case of the children.

2. Where there is excess of affection, there is an attempt to absorb all of the "belongingness-feeling" so that it is centered in the family to the exclusion of other groups. Often this attempt

[37] "How America Lives," *Ladies' Home Journal*, February, 1940, pp. 47-53.

succeeds, and members feel no security in the outside world. In other cases the revolt against such absorption results in the break of family ties.

3. A lack of affection deprives the child of his first and fundamental source of security. He is forced to seek for it outside of the home. However, the present structure of social organization contains no other group offering such adequate satisfactions for security-feeling as can be found in family life.

4. Discrimination, inconsistency, and displacement in affection are disorganizing forces in the affectional life of the family in that they set no one constant pattern upon which the members may depend and thereby set their own responses and behavior.

5. The subjectual relations within the family influence both qualitatively and quantitatively the growth and development of the members, and set up attitudes toward authority and dependence in later life.

6. Domination by parents is a corollary to repression of children, resulting in a marked dependence or an antipathy to all authority. Domination by the child results in a lack of direction, depriving the child of the stability and guidance which normally come to him through adult transmission of his social heritage.

7. Inconsistency in authority, like inconsistency in affection, affords no set pattern for response. Often it results in a trial-and-error attitude toward all authority.

8. In both affectional and subjectual relations there is in some families an approach to the golden mean, setting the foundations for personal security and an attitude of independence tempered by a respect for the authority of the group.

CHAPTER VII

FAMILY PATTERNS

THE MOTHER of a very impressionable adolescent girl once declared that when her daughter came home to dinner, she could always tell, without asking, in which one of her friends' homes the girl had been spending the afternoon. "She is different after each visit," she noticed, "she brings home the marks of every family with her." So visible are these marks of a family, so pronouncedly do they vary from one household to another, that they serve readily to identify a family's distinctive way of life.

Something akin to this is found in many of the studies of family situations. Over and over again, in our perusal of the literature, a family situation is described in terms of some one outstanding fact or feature, which gives tone or meaning to the entire complex of attitudes, habits, and relationships which cluster about it. This one fact or feature stands out so clearly, and differs in such pronounced fashion, from one family to another, that it gives us the key to the understanding of the pattern of life which is distinctive for a particular family. It is from this feature, too, that the problems and pathologies, if so they may be called, seem chiefly to derive.

In seeking to classify and to summarize the various studies of family situations found in the literature of the period 1926-1940, the term "family patterns" is applied to include that large number which have thus identified or emphasized some distinctive feature of family life or situations as indicated above. Upon further examination, the features which the studies emphasize, and the family patterns they reveal, seem to group themselves into four main subgroups. The first of these have to do with the size of the family. This means primarily the number of persons involved in the situation, with the further implication that the pattern is influenced markedly by this fact of size. The second group of references concern themselves chiefly with the way in which the home life of the family is organized, and three representative types are included in our analysis of this subgroup. Third are those where the basic feature identified has to do with the prevailing activity of the family. This does not necessarily mean the occupations of the members of the family, but rather some form of activity which dominates the family interest, and around which its life is organized. Finally, there are those family situations where the key to the family pattern of living seems to be some outstanding value or goal. Each of these four subgroups will be considered briefly, with illustrative material drawn from various sources.

SIZE

The number of people in a family has a great influence upon the resulting family situation. Often, in family case records, certain kinds of problems are found to represent large families almost exclusively, while quite different ones are typical of the small family. Treatment of the family problems varies also, depending on the numbers of people concerned in them.

Some of the influences of numbers upon the family situation have already been touched upon. We have seen, in the Home with a New Member, that the personal relationships within the family become more complicated for each member by the presence of one more person. In the Family with Too Many Bosses, we caught a glimpse of what numbers can mean in the subjectual relationships. The size of the family also has a bearing upon what activities are open to it, and how heavily external pressures settle down upon it. So size, as a factor by itself, must be considered as an element in the family pattern.

The Large Family

In spite of the generally accepted fact that size is an influencing factor in the family situation, there is almost no case record which could be shown here as representative of the situation arising from the sole fact of the family being large.

There are two reasons for this. In the first place, case records are made primarily with treatment in view. The large family is considered chiefly in the light of the problems intensified by its size. It is those *problems* which are emphasized in case records, for our philosophy in social case work is such that tampering with numbers, or reducing the size of a given family is considered only as a last resort after other methods have failed. The mere number is accepted, then, and its effects studied but little.

A second reason why it is difficult to isolate numbers as a sole factor is that size of family, in our kind of society, is so inextricably tied to other known factors. In general, large families are also families on the low economic, occupational, and educational levels. A large proportion of them are of foreign origin. These conditions, in themselves, have come to be accepted so definitely as causes of certain situations that we cannot easily isolate the one fact of largeness to find its effects.

The study of numbers in the family pattern, then, is still to a great extent in the theoretical stage. There is little of measurement or accurate description. But a survey of the literature, nevertheless, does disclose three different types of Large Families with three different kinds of patterns. First, there are those homes which cannot afford the children and do not want them, but have not been able to prevent their arrival. Here there are real problems: economic, because there are too many; physical, because they cannot be cared for properly; psychological, because they were not wanted and create a complexity of unbalanced affectional and subjectual relationships. Then there are the homes in which, for religious reasons, children cannot be limited. Sometimes, in these homes, the same problems occur. But there is a softening factor even when the income is low. In these homes, children, as children, are valuable in the eyes of the group, and the prestige they give to their parents in the community can take away a lot of psychological sting. And third, there are the homes where children are wanted and planned for, where parents can afford them, or where they are willing to have all members forego certain material advantages for the, to them, higher advantage of an extended family relationship.

There is one other way to get at the effects of a Large Family relationship, discounting all related factors, and that is from the point of view of the satisfaction of the fundamental needs of human beings, and of human beings in a particular kind of society. Dr. Carle Zimmerman, at a conference on Tomorrow's Children, urged patriotic Americans to have larger families lest the nation be hampered by "a weakened and decadent fatalism."[1] What is there in a large family which, in spite of the increased intricacy of family interaction, would prevent this attitude toward the world?

Take away the extremes of physical and mental hardship, and the members of large families are apt to have relatively good mental health and a sound realistic outlook for three reasons. The child who gets his security from his family and identifies his self-assurance with his belonging to it gains more strength in this feeling if there are a lot of these people of his around him both at home and in the community. A child very seldom boasts of being an only. For children are team-choosers, and the more people they have in their family the more they have on their side. There was security in the primitive clan. There is much the same kind for the member of the Large Family. This, then, fills the first basic need for mental health.

Then, these people have to learn to live with a variety of personalities. They must make their own place within the family set-up and still view that place in relation to the rights and demands of others. This leaves little room for illusions, either of fatalism or ungrounded optimism, for they are living in the midst of ever-present, robust reality. Often they must give more to and get more from their family, for numbers of people create numbers of needs, and in the process they develop a group loyalty and a technique for living with people that paves the way to well-balanced participation in the larger social group. And last, the Large Family, all other things being equal, is not so apt to breed introverts as the small family where the child gets too much, or too little attention. There is always a crowd around. There is always something to do and someone to go with. There is a quality of hearty extroversion in a Large Family similar to that in an active, unified crowd. And this quality is not one that tends to "decadent fatalism."

The One-Child Family

In comparison with the Large Family, the One-Child Family has received considerable attention from analysts. Since numbers

[1] *Evening Bulletin*, Philadelphia, July 16, 1941, p. 1, column 4.

are coming into the field of interest, the smallest family is naturally seized upon first as being the least complicated set-up on which to try out new quantitative procedures. Study of the One-Child Family is further simplified by the fact that it is not usually characterized by the other adverse pressures which involve homes with more children. It is possible, though, that the conclusions of such studies are biased because of the very difference in the total situations in which the many-child and the only-child family are found generally.

These conclusions, summed up and considered in the light of the family situation alone, are that the differences between the large and small families are chiefly ones of degree. Whatever the family is like, the only child within it receives the concentrated force of all its influences. If the parents are over-attentive he gets more over-attention that if he had siblings. If they are under-attentive, then he is lonelier. Though he does not have the natural social training for give-and-take relationships that siblingship gives, he still may have the economic resources for wider social experiences that might be deprived him were there brothers and sisters to share the family income. Often, only children seem to be retarded when they set out from the family to other circles, where they have to meet strangers as equals and make their way among them. Frequently, if and when they adjust, they assume a precocity greater than their comrades', for they have had the advantage of special help and special training which their friends have missed.

In William Makepeace Thackeray we see both the advantages and the disadvantages of the only child. All of his genius might have been lost to the world just because he was an only. Yet, when external circumstances drew out his talents, he had a wealth of material and training with which to express them because he had been the center of his parents' attention.

When he was just a little boy, his mother conceived the idea that he drew wonderfully, and was to become an artist. She gave him every help and encouragement she could. But somehow he never was satisfied with this supposed talent and he never kept at it consistently. He never kept at anything consistently. He did not have to. If he did not like a school, he was permitted to change.

When he found it would be difficult for him to get a degree at Cambridge, he and his parents decided that he should not try. After that he drifted around Europe "making contacts," enjoying himself and spending his legacy freely. After his legacy was gone he fell in love and wrote to his parents that if he married they would have to support him. They did.

Once in a while, stung by his conscience, and dissatisfied with his attempts as an artist, he tried his hand at a literary career. But he did not keep at that either. He still did not have to.

And then came family reverses. He was driven by necessity to support his wife and children. Then Thackeray achieved success, and the world gained, because the opportunities and experiences lavished upon this only child provided the wealth of colorful material, trained the artist's creative ability that made the masterpieces of Thackeray.[2]

HOME ORGANIZATION

A phenomenon quite separate from the personal relationship of parent to parent, parent to child, and siblings to each other, is the relationship of the family members to the home as an institution. In each family there is a certain attitude toward the home, a kind of value placed upon it which results in overt behavior. If the value is high, then the thing is worth working for, together. If the value is not so high, the members may use it for what it is worth to them, only as long as it is worth anything. If the family institution becomes destructive of values considered more worthy than its own, then the home may be broken completely.

The Coöperative Family

A survey of stories of family life strips all illusion from the concept of coöperation. It is generally true that there must be something that the individual gains by his coöperative efforts to make his efforts worth while. Therefore, the truly Coöperative Family is characteristic of that great class of society in which life is not too hard and not too easy.

In homes where sheer economic necessity drives its members

[2] Malcolm Elwin, *Thackeray, A Personality.*

together for actual survival alone, what seems to be a coöperative organization lasts only until the members can find a way out that offers something better than just survival. While at the opposite extreme, where advantages are easily attained, the sharing of such opportunities has no powerful drive toward cohesiveness in the necessity of coöperation for the earning of them.

In the homes that lie between these extremes, there is a very real benefit to be gained by coöperation. When the budget is limited, but equal to providing all actual necessities for subsistence, joint effort will free a portion for recreation and luxuries, and it will free the time to enjoy them, as well as the money to secure them. If these homes are coöperative, there is a chance to put on the little show that means keeping up to the Joneses, and of affording special privileges for its members. These things make coöperation worth the effort.

The Griffins (see Chapter VI) are a Coöperative Family. They could have been quite as democratic as they are and simply have had less to be democratic about. Instead, they chose to benefit the whole family by mutual work and help. If Mr. Griffin did not exert himself to build a garage and driveway, a garden pool and all those little gadgets that so endear a house to its owners; if Mrs. Griffin were not willing to do all her own housework and so release the money for materials, then the house would be a bare place and not the attractive home it is. There would not be the zoo in the yard, nice clothes to wear, movies for the family, and the entertaining of good friends. The money spent for these enrichers of family life would have to go into necessities. In turn, Jacquie and Benny, taking care of the dishes each weekday night, win an allowance for themselves. They are too young to realize the greater gain that comes to them from relieving the tension of a mother, at the time of day when she is most tired and craving to rest her back and nerves. As they grow older, there will be more chances for these children to coöperate for their home, and larger benefits to gain for it.[3]

Perhaps the greatest gain of the Coöperative Family is a non-material one, and one which the members learn to take for

---

[3] "How America Lives," *Ladies' Home Journal*, February, 1940, pp. 47-53.

granted. Hard work, shared day by day, creates the appreciation for the contributions of co-workers. Each member, then, earns his own worthy rôle and status in the family, and that leads to happy home membership.

The Independent Family

Out of the older unit, the group, there has appeared today the individual as the unit in society.[4] One of the unfortunate results of this splitting of society's atom is the birth of the Independent Family. In this home, the family is only incidental to the supreme value of individuality, and as such, is merely used and not to be sacrificed for.

Only the services of the modern world have made this possible. Nursery schools take in babies of three, whose mothers want the time to do themselves over and regain the maidenly charm they had before the baby spoiled it. That starts the break, and baby soon becomes an individual who can choose his own outside activities from a growing wealth of choices in which his parents have no share, while Mother gets increasingly greedy for freedom from home chores. Father comes home late from work to have dinner before going to play badminton, only to find that his wife got home late too. So the family climbs into the car and goes off to a restaurant. Even fifteen short years ago Thursday night was "family night" in restaurants, because it was the maid's night out. Now every night is family night, and cafeterias are thronged each morning as well, with business men who snatch a bite on their way to work. It is so much easier and quicker, and probably his daughters are reducing anyway and his wife still in bed. The home has been much criticized as being a place to eat and sleep. Many homes are becoming places to sleep, bathe, and change to go out again.

When the individuals in this sort of family do get together for an hour, what do they have in common? Novels, short stories, and case records hint that they have very little. There is no real interest in the house they share, except that it supply their transient demands, and these become a source of mutual concern only when these needs are not properly supplied. The family members may

[4] James H. S. Bossard, *Social Change and Social Problems*, p. 88.

tell each other where they have been. But they have not shared their activities and have no real insight into what the family has been doing. They have no knowledge of what sorts of "whole persons" their family members are, for they see them only in bits, and seldom find out what sort of picture they make to the outside world. In some instances, mothers, suddenly called to juvenile court, find out for the first time what their children are really like. In other cases, the family has by chance discovered that some member, a parent or older sibling, has formed a more dependent and complete attachment for himself quite outside of the bounds of his Independent Family.

Kimball Young states that "one of the basic problems in a diffuse democratic society is how to retain variability, uniqueness, and flexibility without losing coöperation, sympathy, and certain essential fixities in the social order that are necessary to a complex culture and all that it may mean for individual security and satisfaction."[5] In some cases members of the Independent Family have been able to find security and satisfaction in other attachments and groups outside the home. But it is seldom that young children have found by themselves a place that offers these essentials denied to them by their parents.

Of all kinds of family that exist, this kind best fits the description given by those radicals who believe that the family institution has outworn its usefulness and should be supplanted by some other. For every function which once was the family's own has here been transferred outside the home, except the one biological function of creating children. And one does not even find a large brood of children in the Independent Family.

The Incomplete Family

There are many cases in which the family institution has become so destructive of a value held in superior esteem by one or more members of the family that the home has been broken in an attempt to preserve that value. If the family members lose all contact with each other, then the family, as such, is gone and deserves no consideration here. But if a nucleus remains, then the family remains, incomplete and altered.

[5] Kimball Young, *Personality and Problems of Adjustment*, p. 813.

The home broken by death stands in a different class, for the break is involuntary. But it has the three results which are common to all broken homes: a blow to emotional security, a loss in the effectiveness of the family because of the removal of a member with a specific rôle and duties, and a deviation from the normal pattern of the family as seen by the community.

But here the similarity between all Incomplete Families ends. Each one has its own specific aspect, depending on the other factors entering into that situation. Joanna Colcord has made one classification of broken homes as follows:

1. voluntary breakage.
    a. where removal of a discordant member leaves a more stable family situation, with some possibility of repairing the damage.
    b. where parent who leaves was the control element and whose absence allows the influence which was producing anti-social behavior to proceed unchecked.
2. involuntary breakage.
    a. where security and family loyalty remain intact.
    b. where they do not.[6]

Another classification might be based on the economic aspect, and how well the family can afford the break financially. Still another might consider the pressure of the social milieu, which determines whether desertion or divorce are taken as ordinary occurrences or are frowned upon. And yet another on whether the break was a death, desertion, divorce, or institutionalization.

But however specific the situation of the Incomplete Family, in the great average of broken homes the child loses more than he gains. His parent is disillusioned and upset and is different from his friends' mothers and fathers who have a partner. So his parent is often not a very satisfactory parent because of personal adult problems.

Elmer lived with his mother fairly contentedly, even though she was separated from his father, until the boy was twelve. Then he was sent to his father. The man had been used to getting along

---

[6] Joanna Colcord, "Discussion of 'Are Broken Homes a Factor in Juvenile Delinquency?'" *Social Forces*, Volume X, May, 1932, pp. 525-527.

without his son, and the boy's arrival was a bit upsetting. Elmer felt definitely unwanted, and ran away. He was put into a training school where he did very well until his mother had conscience-pangs and sent for him to come home. Unfortunately, she too had built up a life for herself without Elmer while he was away, though she never admitted it even to herself. Elmer felt the difference acutely. He went to a social worker and explained his situation in these words:

I've been thinking about things a lot. I would just like to have someone I could talk to about anything, someone who will take an interest in me. What I think I need most is a home and family. I want someone to give me a little support for a while until I can stand on my own feet. I need that an awful lot, Miss C., if I don't have it I'm afraid I may get into trouble.[7]

ACTIVITY

The family is not just a static concern in which the members feel certain ways toward each other or assume a certain set position in relation to each other—a concern which has a definite size and a degree of cohesion. The family has motion and activity, and no two move and act in just the same way. However, in the following classification we see that certain families can be classed as conforming to a general kind of activity.

The Nomadic Family

A phenomenon of modern civilization is the large-scale moving of individual families from one place to another in rapid succession. "A recent investigation shows that New Yorkers change homes on an average of every two years and two months. That means that if they survive the repeated ordeal of moving long enough, at seventy years of age they will have lived in thirty different homes."[8] A study in Kansas in 1929 showed that two thousand families, including four thousand children, received aid while passing through the state on their way from one place to another.[9]

[7] Susan Burlingham, "Casework with Adolescents Who Have Run Afoul of the Law," *American Journal of Orthopsychiatry*, October, 1937, Volume VII, no. 4, pp. 491-492.
[8] James H. S. Bossard, *op. cit.*, p. 103.
[9] E. R. Groves, *The American Family*, p. 279.

What do these families that move from house to house and from place to place look like on the inside? An intellectually superior girl made good adjustments at first whenever her family moved, but gradually she became unhappy at the constant breaking of attachments. She wrote letters and sent presents to her old friends in an attempt to keep up with them. But she was away and others were at hand, so they dropped her. She started to shrink from forming new friendships and to withdraw into herself. Her school work suffered because instead of concentrating she indulged in continuous day dreams. Her behavior fluctuated between listlessness and great irritability.[10]

Of those families who drift haphazardly, Groves writes:

The family, once it takes on the habit of moving from place to place, rarely escapes a loss of its normal functioning. It becomes broken by its inability to build permanent ties or to accept definite social responsibilities. The child's attachments are so transitory that he is robbed of much of the emotional meaning of home life. The adults, as a consequence of their drifting program, lose whatever social stability they once had. The family also suffers from the loss of any considerable habit life, and there is a spirit of irresponsibility that shows itself in all the undertakings of the family through failure to develop normal habits, particularly the habit of steady work on the part of the father. Associations are temporary and contribute little to self-discipline and the learning of the art of living with others.

Want of conveniences, lack of privacy—in short, the meagerness of the home—reduces to the smallest proportion the value of family fellowship. Although the migratory family is in a position to do so little for the children, the latter are likely to suffer the added misfortune of meager or no schooling. Not only may the child fail to find in his migratory family the security and character building influences that belong to the home, but also he may be purposely exploited by his parents.[11]

Allen and Walter Beach mitigate this picture a bit while agreeing to most of its statements. They add that there are children who learn to get acquainted quickly and easily, who so enjoy their always new and stimulating experiences that they easily forego

[10] Leo Kanner, *Child Psychiatry*, p. 92.
[11] E. R. Groves, *op. cit.*, p. 280.

firmer ties as long as they do have their family. And also, there is the question how greatly family fellowship is reduced in such situations. The Beaches think it may even be enhanced by being the only permanent, intimate tie.[12]

There is an intangible something that marks a distinct difference between all firmly rooted families and those who are forever being transplanted. In order to have any status as a family, in relation to the rest of the world, there must be a basis for contacts with other families and individuals. The family with a solid footing on a piece of ground finds these contacts in the schools they maintain for their children, the churches they go to, the community chest to which they contribute, the keeping of their homes in good repair, and the trading of recipes and garden seeds over the back fence. This kind of contact has come, through generations, to have a certain value. "Stable," "substantial," "real" are the adjectives we use to describe the value and the kind of personality which emerges out of such contacts.

What takes the place of these contacts which have no meaning for the Nomadic Family? They must be rootless ones such as will be found anywhere in drifting circles. Jane and Lily Bell, who lived on a barge, found out quickly enough what were the ever-acceptable contacts with the kinds of people they were apt to meet. And they prepared themselves with the headlines and the scandal sheet of the *Sunday Gazette*. Anyone could share these things with interest. They learned the popular songs from the radio, for people sang them everywhere. They ran to the movies whenever they had a chance. The same feature plays at theatres hundreds of miles apart, and one may always catch up with someone who has seen the same show. These activities, which we think of as superficial and not the substantial ones with roots in the firm ground, were the only ones they found that they had in common with other folks.[13]

At present, the literature discusses the differences between patterns of stability and mobility in terms of integration and disintegration of personality. Only time and research will approve or dis-

[12] Allen and Walter G. Beach, "Family Migratoriness and Child Behavior," *Sociology and Social Research*, July-August, 1937, pp. 503-523.
[13] A. P. Herbert, *The Water Gipsies*, Chapter II.

prove that theory. But, unfortunately, research into the mobile family is only slowly emerging from the stage at which we found Broken Homes before that concept was broken down into separate categories. There are now hundreds of kinds of Nomadic Families, varying from the sort that moves a relatively short distance every several years, to the kind of family that has no personal possessions and no place that could be regarded as even a temporary home. The fact of mobility has many meanings in these different types of families, and not just one. There is need to study them for their separate meanings.

Nomadism of many types is on the increase. Gradually a new kind of culture is being built up around certain kinds of nomadic groups. The comic cartoon, "Trailer Tintypes," gives a hint of it every so often in the newspapers. Old hierarchies of values are being reshuffled, slowly, into a working order for a new sort of life. It may be a long time, though, before man's heritage of sticking to his land allows him to adjust to this new culture happily and securely.

The Joiner Family

The primary group is losing its potency. In large cities it has grown very feeble. The Joiner Family is sorry about that, and is looking around for face-to-face contacts in an individual-centered world. There are many such families and they do not often live in a large city, for they do not like its anonymity. They are usually found in the suburbs and country with the kind of people who cluster in friendly groups. There is no thrill for them in the wanderlust of the Nomadic Family, for they want to belong to a crowd and one small enough to permit of close and warm association. They know that their crowd will dictate to them, within limits, concerning their morals, their conventions, their very attitudes. But they want that comfort and are perfectly willing to conform for the sake of the association.

The Langners of Wood River find their fun in intimate contacts with the fellow members of their community. They say that they spend more for recreation and social life than a budget-fixer would approve. But, to them, it is worth it. Mrs. Langner is president of the Parent-Teachers Association of the Wood River school to which her two sons go. She not only originated the idea of free lunch boxes for the children who need them, but takes charge of the minstrel show which supports the project financially. She participates in Red Cross activities, and gives and goes to card parties to help raise funds for the community. Her husband has organized water polo teams at the municipal swimming pool. They belong to a group of young married folks who swim and dance, picnic and skate together. Twice a year they give a dinner party at home. And there is an annual spree for the crowd at a large hotel.

Davey and Donnie, their sons, are fortunate children. Their parents like people, and Davey and Donnie are two of the people they like best. They may not be brought up according to the latest tricks of child psychology, but they are well cared for and they have lots of fun with their parents. They have organized a family orchestra in which each participates. Every year they have a motor trip together during their father's vacation. The boy's desire is to grow up to be just like Father. And they probably will. For the larger conflicts of the world enter only slightly into their picture. They are steady, substantial, extroverted, and friendly in their family life. They will grow to Boy Scout age and "dating" age with an appreciation for other people and a knowledge of how to get along with them, as well as of the responsibilities attendant upon belonging to an intimate "face-to-face" society.[14]

The Family of the Intelligentsia

The parents in the Family of the Intelligentsia do not hunt up activities for the purpose of mingling with the horde. They are either trying to raise themselves above it, to devote their talents to raising the horde to them, or are, purely and simply, pursuing a fad.

They are anything rather than just conformist. They range from the elegantly groomed and carefully bred lady of Republican fastidiousness who lectures to her plodding sisters on the beauty of Keats, to the slatternly woman with Pink inclinations who, clad in smock and slippers, subjects her family to life in an attic rather than to change the style of the art she is pursuing into one which

[14] "How America Lives," *Ladies' Home Journal*, May, 1941, pp. 87-90.

would produce earthly gains. Between them lie the parents who, from their platform of higher education, try to use their intelligence to live most constructively and wisely and to guide their children in the same way.

Professor Marshall and his wife were very careful about their children's training. They had their own ideas about it. They steered clear of the "exclusive set." They had neither a smart home nor smart visitors. Instead they met "interesting" people. The children heard not about what was proper to say, but about freedom of speech. They were not taught about good grooming, but how to be fair and tolerant and energetic, and how to avoid, above all things, smugness, inertia and dependence. But little daughter Sylvia grew up to adolescence, and when her mother registered surprise that a girl of Sylvia's training should be interested in a certain boy, Sylvia burst out with, "Oh, you don't know how sick I get of being so everlastingly highbrow! What's the *use* of it? People don't think any more of you! They think less! You don't have any better time—nor so good! And why should you and Father always be so down on anybody that's rich or dresses decently? Jerry's all right—if his clothes *do* fit!"[15]

As a contrast, a picture of the home life of a musical family is found in *The Constant Nymph*. Mr. Sanger was a great musician. His whole family, which was large because his temperament had worn out the lives of two wives and had seduced a third, had been well trained musically too, and music was their god. But however intellectual an interest in music may be, the god of music is a god of the senses, and the Sangers lived according to his dictates alone. They were healthy, vital people, careless and dirty, but as direct and honest as a proper family would never dare to be. They always said exactly what they thought and felt. When they loved they did so sincerely, with abandon and without certificate. No family eyebrows were raised in horror at such frankness, even in a girl of sixteen. The strangers, though, who visited their home, called it "Sanger's Circus."[16]

But the Sanger children, too, like Sylvia Marshall, found the

[15] Dorothy Canfield, *The Bent Twig*, p. 187.
[16] Margaret Kennedy, *The Constant Nymph*.

time when they had to mix with just normal people. And they discovered what is the penalty in living with a family obsessed with a horror of the average. The Sangers did wish that they could fit into the school they were sent to. Sylvia longed for a friendship of pleasant normality. And the young Sycamore girl in the enchanting drama *You Can't Take It with You* would have moved heaven to produce just one proper dinner party for her fiancé's parents.

Nevertheless, the Sangers, the Sycamores, the Marshalls all raised colorful and attractive children. There was a great deal of comradery in all three families, of a stimulating and honest kind. Life can be hectic in a home where everyone is temperamentally pursuing an interest. But for the members of the intelligentsia there is real pleasure and satisfaction in the bringing together of diverse interests, talents and points of view, and a high degree of appreciation for the eccentricities of fellow-intellectuals.

The Cliff-Dweller Family

John Nollen has written, "The cliff-dweller is rapidly becoming the predominant element in our citizenship."[17] He describes this family as one living in small, mechanized tenements and apartments, where there are no small tasks for children, no space for recreation, and a lack of fresh air and sunshine except in summer camps where the parents are absent. And he concludes that if home life is the best life for children, then the children in these homes do not get the best.

What kind of activity characterizes these cliff-dwellers? Obviously they must all go outside of their home for recreation, for social intercourse, for the pursuit of a hobby, for their very privacy. Limited space makes almost any kind of home activity impossible. The youngsters cannot make collections of anything larger than postage stamps, father cannot find relaxation in tinkering at a workbench, Mother cannot escape from housework into the garden. And when anyone wants to be alone and quiet there is no place to go except a dark, air-conditioned moving picture theater.

[17] John S. Nollen, "The Child and His Home," *National Congress of Parents and Teachers, Proceedings of Thirty-Eighth Annual Meeting*, Volume 38, May, 1934, p. 63.

People living together in such a confined space can get on each other's nerves to an extreme degree. Then the essentials of happy family life go out of the window. They can also escape the irritation by keeping away from the home. But in that case the family loses both its authority and its influence. Finally, they may try to keep their family unity by seeking activities which they can enjoy together wherever they find them. Then the family takes on the semblance of the Nomadic Family which travels together from place to place, having as its permanent abode four walls surrounding a table and beds for its comfort in eating and sleeping.

The Community-Benefactor Family

A family which has been popular in American fiction but has escaped the case records is the Community-Benefactor Family, that result of the special circumstances of frontier and free enterprise as they have developed in this country.

Mr. Caxton had once been a pioneer and is now a successful and wealthy man. He practically owns the town he lives in, and he has tried to do his intelligent and kindly best for it, never forgetting that he was at the same time serving the best interests of his own family. Since he established the little town it has boomed, grown in population and in heterogeneity of population, and has been struck down by depression again. He has assumed the rôle of community patriarch and has never let down the people for whom he feels responsible.

His children walk through the civic center and point with pride to "Papa's buildings." They show visitors "Papa's new swimming pool and recreation ground," but they do not swim and play there. They use the pool in their own yard. They take care of their clothes, so that they may be handed down to the poor people who need them, and they help to distribute baskets of food to ones who might go hungry. And the next day they sit in school at the same desk with a little girl who wears the dress they gave away yesterday, and ate her dinner from the basket they supplied.[18]

These children have a mistaken sense of the place of their own family in relation to the rest of the world. The rules which they

[18] Case record from the author's files.

know apply to others do not exist for them. Their father provides
and pays the bills for the others. No one is going to bring his children to account. They have no natural relationships with the other
children, for they meet either bitterness or subservience. The simple generosity with no returns expected, which plays between equals
in advantage, turns here to patronage. It carries over into their
home life, for these children have the idea that they can rule
others by largess, and inversely, that by conforming outwardly to
the whims of their superiors they can gain mercenary ends.

"Poverty in the midst of plenty,—the great paradox of our
day," writes Theodore Dreiser, "We have become so used to living
in a gigantic paradox that paradox is already accepted as the normal
state of affairs."[19] In city, country, and suburb there is the Community-Benefactor Family. The older generation may be living,
as is Mr. Caxton, according to democratic ideals. They know that
the success they have won has given them a responsibility to the
people without whom they could not have won it. But the children
usually do not have the same perspective. To them, their father is
the man who has done it all and is kind enough to share some of
his blessings. They themselves are his rightful heirs to an exalted
position.

VALUES AND GOALS

There is scarcely a family worthy of the name that lives so haphazardly as not to be guided, consciously or unconsciously, by certain values and goals. In general the routes families must traverse
toward similar goals are enough alike to mark these families, in
their progress, as being in the same category. Below are classified
certain families, distinguishable because of the obvious goals that
they are pursuing.

The Social-Climber Family

Almost every American family is a potential Social-Climber
Family. Let those who declare that America has a class system as
rigid as any European pattern dip into some case records and stories
of humble American life. Opportunities may be thinning out, but
the point of view is still thriving. There is not the tradition of awe

[19] Theodore Dreiser, *America Is Worth Saving*, p. 16.

reverence for the upper classes that produces a feeling of unworthiness and prevents aspiration. Most familiees feel and express a confidence that they could make the social climb if they could just get started up the ladder. And many, many of them scale the ladder.

Any goal, possible of attainment and not destructive, gives a family vitality and organized energy, provided the members are united in their evaluation of that goal, and in their strength to pursue it. Then they seem to blossom with each success and find a challenge in each rebuff.

But there are reasons why the vitality in some Social-Climber Families may wear thin. The road to social success is a long and hard road and entails a pretty set program. Yeomans describes it as "dragging with it its class loyalties and fastening them around the neck of each child as a kind of sacrament: prep school, college, university club, business success."[20] And for girls there is private school, a smart debut, social popularity, and a "good" marriage. There are few slack moments in a life like this; it keeps one at high pressure, on one's toes.

Not every individual in the family always takes to it easily. And these members pay heavily for their membership. Mr. Bennet, the father of the famed family of daughters in *Pride and Prejudice*, grew weary, so weary, of the constant prodding of his socially minded wife and those two ambitious younger children of his. He had to pay the bills to get them where they wanted to go, but he did manage to keep pretty well away from the actual clatter of the cherished society itself. But the older daughters, more sensitive to the proprieties of life than their small sisters, had to participate. They heard their own family being laughed at as aspiring country bumpkins. They were embarrassed and outraged time and time again by the obvious connivances of their mother to gain for them the recognition they finally won on the merits of their own sensible and worthy personalities.[21]

And when a member does not make the grade, after being pushed to the breaking point, he not only is an irritation to himself, but

[20] Edward W. Yeomans, "Salvaging the Family," *Progressive Education*, Volume III, no. 4, October-November-December, 1926, pp. 283-288.

[21] Jane Austen, *Pride and Prejudice*.

a disgrace to the family. He becomes the ugly duckling who must be hidden, or have excuses made for him upon every occasion, while the member who is positively antagonistic to his family's goal attains a deep disgust for the whole family set-up and plants the seed of discord in his home.

The Materialistic Family

As a contrast to the Social-Climber Family there is another kind which feels as worthy and as competent, but has a distinctly different goal. Spurning the codes and conventions of the blue-bloods and regarding them as decadent and anemic, the Materialistic Family ploughs its own way through toward the accumulation of the things that money can buy. They want luxury and "show" first, and then comfort, putting everything else subsidiary to the attainment of them.

The activities and services of this family, both in the home and out of it, are performed for material gain. The children come to accept that as the reason for living, for working, for acting something like human beings, and they expect to be rewarded for every service or bit of good behavior. Right and wrong come to be dependent upon rewards and fines. It is an extremely bad pattern for them to learn, for the world is not going to pay them, according to their terms, for fulfilling the obligations they will owe to society as adults.

Sooner or later the Materialistic Family is apt to find out that all their money cannot buy for them something without which their happiness will be destroyed, something which they had overlooked as a real value. Then the whole family philosophy comes crashing down to earth.

That happened to Mr. Dombey. He was a staunch materialist. Everything went into the firm of Dombey and Son in order to produce more from the firm. He had no time to love his children, except to cherish little Paul as the "Son" of his firm. And then his son asked him, "Father, what is money?" His father was aghast. He could not answer what he felt money to be. But Paul explained that he meant, "What is money, after all, what can it do?" That was better. Mr. Dombey patted the child's head and told him it could do anything—anything. Just above a whisper, Paul wondered why, if money could do anything, it had not saved his mother for him, and then, why it did not make him feel well and strong? But Father fell to musing about the future of the firm of Dombey and Son, which was never to be realized, because all his money could not save Paul for him either.[22]

Things material have a way of being destroyed. The Materialistic family is not prepared for this kind of eventuality. They have not become acquainted with the spiritual values that remain through any adversity. In comparing the records of many of the families that came to grief during the depression crisis with those families in like circumstances that struggled through, the effects of materialism as a goal are shown in the attitudes of the family members concerned. In the one, the family itself was a value to fall back upon. In the other, when a cash payment was not forthcoming at the end of each effort, there was no exertion for the family that was worth the attempt.

The Overly-Religious Family

However vague the line between "religious" and "overly-religious" may be in theory, the situations created in the Overly-Religious Family stand out with clarity in a survey of family life. For this reason, it seems wise to try to define that vague line, and to explain what, for our purpose, is meant by "overly-religious."

As the progress of evolution has brought man out of the un-differentiated homogeneity of the tribal group into the heterogeneity of individual-centered modern life, a change has come over the values which belong exclusively to the religious sphere of life. Célestin Bouglé, that great French social theorist, has pointed out that in the world of primitive man, religion was all-inclusive. Art was dedicated to the gods, drama was born from worship, education was largely the learning of the ways to propitiate the gods, economic success or failure was the direct result of the pleasure or anger of the gods. Gradually, as centuries unrolled, the arts became ends in themselves, education received its autonomy, agnostics gave their attention to economic theories rather than to rites and prayers, and managed to succeed financially. All of these systems, set up as

[22] Charles Dickens, *Dombey and Son*.

values differentiated from the once all-inclusive religious domination, gave to religion a relative place in life. It has come to be a value in so far as it gives benefits to men, and not simply pleasure to the gods. It has become more of a human value and less mystical.[23]

In general, it is accepted as such, and is held as a very real value in family life. But there are families which cannot and care not to change the older pattern of religious domination. Religion governs the whole of their family life. Pleasure to God becomes the supreme goal of the Overly-Religious Family, to which the good of the family becomes second, and is not a pursuit but an expected reward.

The modern world is an affront to this family, for the world is bent on establishing cosmic laws which seem to take away the power of the God of their particular conception, and give it into the hands of the men who know, and know how to use the laws. The Overly-Religious Family must take on a holier-than-thou attitude, for the whole realm of science is denying its principles and it must declare itself superior to justify its own set-up.

There are so few places where members of this family can find contacts with the present day. Public gatherings of all kinds—what with the habit of freedom of action and expression—are not to be endured. Only the church is left. And many families there are, who break from one church in anger each year to try to find another fundamental enough to fit the family philosophy.

Thus, pushed to their own resources, the family turns in upon itself more and more. Even there, natural inclinations must be suppressed as wicked. But at length cosmic authority asserts its rights. Aggression does follow frustration. The parents have their children upon whom to work out their aggression and their guilt complexes. Some of the children, often not subject to quite the same social pressure as were their parents, openly rebel and break away from the family, others are forced to cling to the pattern and renew it in future aggression upon their own offspring.

Mary was the victim of such a family:

Her childhood had been spent on a farm, her college work in biology

[23] C. Célestin Bouglé, *The Evolution of Values.*

had been adequate. She did not shrink from men, but found herself at twenty-two with no zest for life.

Her parents had no interest in her achievements. They were both intelligent and kindly. Religion was the dominant motive of her father's life; to him religion was the only door to truth. He took no happiness in his daughter's mental growth; it did not occur to him that mathematics is a search for truth also. Into his religion flowed no streams of modern humanism, science, or culture. His wife busied herself with church organization and membership. Both were stone blind to their daughter's personality.

In her childhood two incidents stood out clearly. When she was five, she danced with delight on receiving a red calico dress and was rebuked by her father for worldliness. When she was eleven, she was talking to a boy cousin in the cellar of her house and was punished by her mother. She did not understand why she was punished. She did not resent it, but could not forget the stern horror on her mother's face. In adolescence, there were family scenes because, although she attended church, it was plain her heart was not there.

Mary's awakening intellectual interests were as unbuttressed by family support as if both parents were non-existent, or spent their lives playing bridge. She had capacity for friendship, but her mental level was higher than that of her contemporaries, and at home she had no training in games, or general conversation. She never felt she belonged to any group. . . .

Mary has been sacrificed on one of the oldest altars in the world: interest in religion which is so absorbing that it sucks out parental feeling.[24]

There is a thing to be said for the family which clings to the older religious pattern. Small children hunger for certainty. A grown woman, wondering what to do about the religious education of her children, admitted that when she was a child, and had discovered that her parents were fallible human beings, she found complete certainty in her faith in a personal Father-God who, if she were a good girl, would pull all the proper strings for her physical safety and happiness. Whenever she found herself in a tight spot, she sang to herself, "Be not dismayed whate'er betide. God will take care of you." And she knew certainty. Now that she is grown, she has taken upon herself the responsibility for her own destiny.

[24] Miriam Van Waters, *Parents on Probation*, pp. 68-69.

She tries to live well and also wisely, but she does not know what to give her children as a substitute for the kind of security she knew. How, she wonders, can she give to her children a religious training with which their own parents' views are incompatible? And how can she possibly deny to her children the comfort of the certainties which kept her own childhood secure and happy?[25]

This conflict does not come to the parents in the Overly-Religious Family. But they may be preparing their own children to face it in the future.

The Scientific Family

One aspect of the Scientific Family has already been touched upon in the preceding classification: the lack of comfort, to children, of cold scientific fact.

William Lyon Phelps, in his autobiography, has commented on that point:

I have been informed that some psychiatrists today urge parents not to teach their children the familiar prayer "Now I lay me down to sleep," because it will suggest to the infant mind the thought of death and thus inspire fear at bedtime. The hard-boiled Puritan babies of New England got out of that prayer agreeable relaxation; they handed the responsibility over to God and went to sleep peacefully.[26]

But there is another aspect of the family which regards every scientific principle as an absolute law in family life and household management. An over-respect for the words in books, and under-respect for "common horse-sense," makes these people forget that, in the social sciences, rules and regulations have been formulated either according to an artificial average, or according to the extremes of deviation from the normal. All of them must be tempered by common sense to individuals and real situations. Even the medical recommendations of diets and preventives of disease are not blankets to be thrown carelessly over a world of people. We read of cases in which it would have been infinitely better for a shy child to get a good case of measles than to have been shut away by himself, as he was, until the school officer caught up with him. In others, wheedling the proper amount of vitamins into baby has done him more

---

[25] Case record from the author's files.
[26] William Lyon Phelps, *Autobiography with Letters*, p. 5.

harm than if he had been allowed to go hungry. Insanitary care-lessness has endangered the health of a whole family, but an ob-sessional fear of germs on the part of any one member has been equally as damaging to its nerves.

Families of this sort lose the sense of carefreeness in daily life. And many of them are exceedingly confused, also. For new ideas come thick and fast, and they are often conflicting. Fifteen years ago, a baby was supposed to sleep at a certain time, eat at a certain time, and never to be stimulated into a disagreeable complex by being cuddled. Now the schedule is to be fitted with reason to the individual's and the family's needs, and the infant's first security is his comfortable and firm position in his mother's arms. Just how can the Scientific Family keep up?

Moreover, it is easier for a family to be coldly scientific than warmly scientific. Facts, rules and regulations about training and discipline are relatively easy to grasp. More elusive is a balanced scientific attitude toward spiritual values, so elusive that they are often lost sight of completely by the Scientific Family afraid of anything but absolutes.

Mr. Gradgrind conducted a model school. All its students were to be model students, patterned after his own progeny, who were to be the supreme models. His program? fact, hard fact, nothing but fact.

The Gradgrinds lived in a logical house, perfectly symmetrical, with straight-ruled lawns and paths with no nonsense about them. Inside was a conchological cabinet, a metallurgical cabinet, a min-eralogical cabinet. The little Gradgrinds knew all the real answers to questions. They never saw the man in the moon, for there is none. They did not know such a silly verse as "Twinkle, twinkle little star; how I wonder what you are." They knew what stars are.

And so the little Gradgrinds lived and grew. Tom found that he needed money. Where does money come from? The bank, of course. With factual directness Tom went to the bank, at night, and took the money, and the sentimental world called him a thief.

Mr. Gradgrind gave to Louisa all the facts of why she should marry Mr. Bounderby. They were reasonable and logical and she accepted. Too late, she found that there was inside her breast an organ which beat furiously to the soft words of another man. She came home, a beaten person, to her father who, because he really did love his children, realized that there is a wisdom of the head and a wisdom of the heart. He had supposed the first to be all-sufficient, but maybe—maybe . . . .[27]

The wisdom of the head, which forms the goal of the Scientific Family, unless complementary to a wisdom of the heart, unfits that family for the tempering of facts to its needs.

The Superstitious Family

Every family has a few pet superstitions. The world is still tolerant of individual vagaries of that sort. If a family chooses to traipse in single file around the edge of a ladder rather than to pursue their course abreast beneath it, they won't be seriously marked nor their family life much affected.

But every tradition which wears out all its use, every theory which explodes into meaninglessness can survive as a superstition. And the family that lives on exploded theories, some harmless and some really harmful physically and psychologically, is marked as a family of "eccentrics."

The mental life of the family is harassed by fear of the unknown; their plan to combat it is a kind of jingoism. As long as one kind of magic seems to work they would not consider trying a new one.

Case records and literary material reveal families whose medical notions are carry-overs from the days of primitive witch-doctoring. Some of the herb concoctions with which the members of the family are dosed, plus the absence of distrusted modern drugs, are enough to ruin the family health. There are families in which the old horror of cousin-marriages clings so tenaciously that a member deprives himself of the partner of his choice for fear of producing such a monstrosity as is known to him to be the inevitable result of such a marriage. Other children living in this family, live till death in lonely sterility because they mistakenly believe that some acquired deformity of their own would be visited upon their children.

Children who are healthy and normal have become definitely afflicted because of the absurd notions of their Superstitious Family.

[27] Charles Dickens, *Hard Times.*

Betty's parents knew that she was "marked" for epilepsy, because her mother witnessed an epileptic fit just before Betty's birth. Every symptom she had was interpreted and treated as epilepsy. Her habit training was completely neglected. She was never allowed to be alone for a moment, even at night, for fear she might have a fit. And she was worn out from being dragged from doctor to doctor. At six she was a nervous, enuretic child, who could not even dress herself, a feeding problem who gagged and vomited and had temper tantrums—but not epilepsy.[28]

These families are closely similar to that designated by Dr. Groves as the backward family. They hold to traditions lagging behind the knowledge and customs of their own era. They fail to keep pace with general progress, their members are maladjusted socially, for they are not well oriented to the world as it works to-day.[29]

The Conventional Family

The Conventional Family does not appear in clinical studies until a crisis occurs, and then it usually comes to be characterized by some other factor than its conventionality. But the writer of fiction seems to find great pleasure in picturing, and then in diabolically tampering with, the Conventional Family.

Thomas Burke found one in Clapham Common. Putting it down on the printed page he caught its look, its values, its people and their relationships.

Here . . . they have a real dining-room, very small, but still . . . a dining-room. They keep a maid, trim and smiling. And after dinner you go into the drawing-room. The drawing-room is a snug little concern, decorated in a commonplace way. . . . There is no attempt at heavy lavishness, nor is there any attempt at breaking away from tradition. The piano is open. The music on the stand is "Little Grey Home in the West," it is smothering Tchaikowsky's "Chant sans Paroles." . . .

After dinner, the children climb all over you, and upset your coffee, and burn themselves on your cigarette. Then Mother asks the rumple-haired baby, eight years old, to recite to the guest, and she declines.

[28] Leo Kanner, *op. cit.*, p. 103.
[29] E. R. Groves, *The American Family*, p. 129.

So Mother goes to the piano, and insists she shall sing. . . . So she stands . . . and sings very prettily, "Sweet and Low."

Then baby goes in care of the maid to bed, and Mother and Father and Helen, who is twelve years old, go to the pictures. There, for sixpence, they have an entertainment which is quite satisfying to their modest temperaments and one, withal, which is quite suitable to Miss Twelve Years Old; for Father and Mother are Proper People, and would not like to take their treasure to the sullying atmosphere of even a suburban music-hall. . . .

Miss Twelve Years Old secretly admires the airy adventures of the debonair Max Linder—she thinks he is a dear, only she daren't tell Mother and Father so, or they would be startled. . . .

After the pictures, they go home, and Miss Twelve goes to bed, while Mother and Father sit up awhile. Father has a nightcap, perhaps, and Mother gives him a little music. She doesn't pretend to play, she will tell her guests, she just amuses herself. . . .

Then, one by one, the lights in their Avenue disappear; the windows close their tired eyes; and in the soft silence of the London night they ascend, hand in hand, to their comfortable little bedroom; and it is all very sweet and sacramental. . . .[30]

And just suppose that baby sang better than just "prettily," or that Miss Twelve started to pursue the "airy adventures" she admired at the cinema. Then, in truth, a psychiatrist might meet the family. For genius is as out of key with the Conventional Family as is the libertine. "Most people" says Miriam Van Waters, "prefer a child who is like their idea of other children. When they begin to suspect that their child is different, they feel the blow intolerable. They try to force the child to do things so antagonistic to his nature that they are likely to destroy him."[31]

The goal of the Conventional Family is to escape conspicuousness, and this standard is equally hard for the handicapped child and the gifted child whose nature it is to be conspicuous.

What of this family when its children set out for college? They are not prepared for new ideas, and different kinds of people. In college records we find that some of these children become completely unbalanced by this strikingly different environment. Others

[30] Thomas Burke, *Nights in London*, pp. 77-79.
[31] Miriam Van Waters, *op. cit.*, p. 43.

adjust themselves gradually to a broader concept of convention. Then their home becomes to them a stuffy place indeed, and their presence highly uncomfortable for their parents.

SUMMARY

By way of summarizing this chapter, its main ideas may be stated in the following brief form:

1. Many studies of family situations identify or emphasize some one distinctive fact or feature of the family's life, which is shown to give tone or meaning to the entire complex of attitudes, habits, and relationships which cluster about it. The term "family patterns" is used to indicate this group of studies.

2. Some family patterns seem to be conditioned markedly by the size of the family. Discussed are the very large and the very small family, serving to illustrate the general proposition that the number of persons in a family has much to do in determining its way of life.

3. Another clue to the life of a family may be found in the ways in which the home life is organized. Illustrative of definitely different forms of such organization are the Coöperative Family, the Independent Family, and the Incomplete Family.

4. The family is not just a static concern in which the members feel certain ways toward each other; it has motion, it is active. Often some aspect of this activity is the chief key to the interpretation of the family life, and selected illustrations of such instances are cited.

5. Finally, as distinctive as any of the features which may be distinguished about a family and dictate the pattern of its life are its values and goals. In general, the routes which families traverse toward similar goals are enough alike to mark these families as following the same general pattern of family life. Any family, for example, with a strong aspiration toward the social register has its way of life definitely determined, and the ways of all such families are strangely similar. Other family values dictate other family patterns.

CHAPTER VIII

EXTERNAL FACTORS

In the two preceding chapters, the situations described have been classed according to some striking feature produced by the personalities of the family members and their behavior within their own group. In the situations thus far studied there has been no one unavoidable influence, coming from outside of the family, which has marked a limit to the range of attitudes, choices, and activities possible to that family and has directly affected the persons within it.

This chapter is devoted to the description of those situations whose marked feature is produced by external factors which come, like a *deus ex machina,* and pull the strings which bend the family's fate in one direction or another. These external factors, we have seen, are far from being the whole story of any family situation. Nevertheless the story is incomplete without the recognition of their pressure and influence. Their name is legion, and they obtrude themselves upon every family. Of them, those which seem most marked and frequent will be discussed under the classifications of Socio-Economic Status, Neighborhood, and Health.

SOCIO-ECONOMIC STATUS

Every family is affected by the extent of its resources. In a discussion of "Income as a Factor in Well-Being,"[1] some of the relationships between income and the family situation are clearly pointed. Even in the formation of the family the income sets limits, for fathers' earnings, as they decreased, were found to coincide with a steady increase in infant mortality. Although nutrition and physical development definitely do not depend entirely on income, nevertheless studies of low-income groups point with fair accuracy to the places where the bulk of undernourished and sickly parents and children is found. In terms of the family situation, income can make the difference between a situation in which, with the aid of medical help and adequate family care, parents bring into

[1] James H. S. Bossard, *op. cit.,* pp. 142-156.

184

their circle babies well-disposed to surviving and growing healthily, bringing joy and confidence to the family; and another in which the babies, with no proper start, either die off before they begin to live, with all that means of distress to parents, or struggle on unhappily, a drag on themselves and a worry to all those who want to keep them.

The same discussion reveals the relationship between income and the way the family regards itself. The family which views itself with esteem is constructive. Little is so damaging to the success of a family as a discouraged feeling of inadequacy in its own capabilities. Meager resources cut down the potential family capability, and color the members' mental estimate of themselves and their importance in relation to others.

Money and material are only one part of a family's resources. There are also its social resources. Too often these two factors vary directly with each other. It is not always the case, for we read of families which, on a minimum income, live in adequate ease by the use of their social contacts, and inversely, of those families whose large incomes are nothing of satisfaction or health for them because they are social outcasts. But these are the exceptions. Usually poverty goes hand in hand with a lack of social resources, and wealth with an abundance of them. The two factors tend to re-create and strengthen each other and, in extremes, get the family situation tightly within their grip. Some of the most noticeable of these extremes will form the following classification.

The Inadequately Financed Home[2]

Superficially, most families in the United States consider themselves to be inadequately financed. The possibility of ever-increasing incomes for the whole population, which dwindled with the closing of the physical frontier days of our country, has not yet noticeably diminished as a goal in American family life. For this reason, it is difficult to define the inadequately financed family except in very general terms. Obviously, it cannot be restricted to those families whose incomes are insufficient for their minimum physical

[2] Title suggested by classification label in Louella C. Pressey, "Some Serious Family Maladjustments among College Students," *Social Forces*, December, 1931, Volume X, no. 2, pp. 236-242.

needs. For according to present democratic and humanitarian philosophy mere physical survival is not adequate for family life. There
must be that extra which makes the difference between surviving
and living.

A grouping of families according to planes of living[3] includes the
Poverty Level, the Minimum Subsistence Level, the Minimum
Health and Decency Level, and the Comfort Level. The last class
is unconditionally excluded from our present category. But the first
two are inadequately financed according to humanitarian ideology,
and the Minimum Health and Decency Level is in that unhappy
position where any crisis or emergency sucks it down into the ranks
of the lower levels until such time as its equilibrium may be re-
stored.

Because the economic status of a family is more easily measurable than other potently influencing factors in family life, a great
number of tests of its effects have been made. Two of them have
special significance for results to the intra-family relationships.

In a study of fifty special class graduates,[4] Blackey found that
in rating the children's success from A, high, to D, low, and their
parents' attitudes in terms of constructiveness by the same scale
of A to D, the highest frequencies occurred consistently where constructiveness of parental attitudes and degree of success coincided
in the scale. This suggested that the relative success of children
was closely allied to their parents' attitudes. An attempt was then
made to find the relation between economic status and parental
attitudes. Here healthy attitudes in parents varied directly in frequency with a rise in economic status.

A second study[5] tackled intra-family relationships from the
opposite angle, that of children's attitudes toward their parents.
Meltzer found that children living on the lowest economic level
had the least pleasantly toned attitudes toward their parents; that
they had more repressive attitudes and hostility than did the chil-

[3] James H. S. Bossard, *op. cit.*, pp. 164-165.
[4] Eileen Blackey, "The Social and Economic Adjustment of a Group of
Special Class Graduates," *Smith College Studies in Social Work*, December, 1930,
Volume I, no. 2, pp. 160-179.
[5] H. Meltzer, "Economic Security and Children's Attitudes to Parents," *American Journal of Orthopsychiatry*, October, 1936, Volume VI, no. 4, pp. 590-608.

dren of the middle level, but less than those of the high economic level; that they enjoyed a healthier degree of dependence or attachment than the other income groups. In general it was the middle income group which showed the healthiest attitudes toward their parents, the lower level clinging to a middle course and the higher level faring badly.

These two studies, taken at face value and summarized, hint that economic insufficiency and destructive parental attitudes go hand in hand and affect adversely the successful adjustment of the children, but may lead to more constructive relations between the child and his parent than does economic abundance.

It is interesting to note that the conclusions of these tests parallel the assumption made for the Frigid Home: that dependence upon parents, plus the social distance made possible by economic ease does not tend to so hearty a relationship as does a good degree of independence bound around by necessary close association. They also add credence to the belief that the great middle level escapes many of the adverse influences of both extremes and yet leaves benefits from both that can result in the sincerely Coöperative Family.

Rudi and Ada, aged nine and twelve, lived in a home characterized by Dr. Bühler as one in which the struggle for existence constituted the central interest.[6] The children had to contribute a great deal to the work of the home and were fully aware of the state of things and the necessity for their help. They held no visible resentment, they were stern realists in the actuality of keeping the family head above the stream. The usual kind of child play was not indulged in by Rudi and his sister, nor did they assume a position inferior to their mother. They were adult-minded people accepting together the inevitable, and they were succeeding. In their few moments of leisure, the penalties to the family for this kind of existence cropped up. Ada and Rudi discussed abstractions at great length as their way of escape. Their mother, who could not, indulged in card playing which Rudi had to share with her. He could win and did and exulted in his taunts, for he had no respect for her or anyone as just an adult. Success was the thing, success by any means he could get away with. Attempts at cheating by both

---

[6] Charlotte Bühler, *The Child and His Family*, pp. 163-167.

mother and son resulted in family rages. The mother tried to put her son in his proper place in relation to her, and her son refused, in play, to be reduced to the subordinate position he had not been allowed to assume in work. His mother, thwarted in reaching superiority in this, her only recreational outlet, nagged at Rudi and nursed her resentment against him even when they were not playing. Rudi was hungry for affection, but he was denied it. It was a time-luxury in this family and they had not learned the spirit of it. The children seldom quarreled. They simply had respect for each other.

Adding some small confirmation to the Meltzer test, the attitudes of these children in their family relationship were constructive. But the relationship was not rich. They paid for their success in survival with the lack of all sorts of relationships of affection and position which are considered normal in a family to which survival need not be the first thought.

The case of Rudi and Ada is not one of extremes in poverty and other related adverse factors. It is, therefore, cited as representative of what is the family situation in a great many Inadequately Financed Homes. There are others in which the specter of failure constantly hovers closer. Ceaseless worry and hard work bring mental and physical illness. Bills further cut down on income and reserves. Greater worry is added over the money and health problems, tensions become acute, and the circle of misfortune closes more and more tightly around the family which is choked within it.

The act of living together successfully in family life is analogous to that which doctors like to describe as the act of living together successfully in sex life. It does not come about as an end result of marriage, or of affection in marriage. It is an art, to be learned, to be striven for, and never to be accomplished with finality. In one, as in the other, education, good health, calm nerves, inner peace, and leisure time are factors which are effective aids to giving the opportunity and ability to pursue the art. In the Inadequately Financed Home it is the gaining of these factors which must absorb the family energies before any energy can be expended for the luxury of pursuing the art of living together.

The Suddenly Wealthy Home

One of the results of the churning waves of social change that have surged back and forth over our country for the past century is the sudden rise and fall in economic status of individual families. Actually, two factors have joined to affect the family in these cases; their position in relation to wealth or poverty, and the suddenness and extent of the change to the family.

Some of the effects of the first factor, that of position in relation to wealth or poverty, were discussed in the preceding situation. The suddenness and extent of the change is, therefore, the factor of greatest interest here as affecting the Suddenly Wealthy Home.

The fortune-making period of American history holds pictures a-plenty of this kind of family. None is perhaps more pathetically convincing of the adverse affects upon a family of the sudden transplanting from one economic sphere to another than is that of the Dryfoos family in Howells' novel of rapidly changing fortunes.[7]

Jacob Dryfoos had been a substantial farmer. His stout and generous-natured wife was a good mate for him and brought up three children in a haphazard but wholesome way. The two girls were pretty, normal, country girls, healthy and active. They had been away to school and had come home with just a little hankering to see more of the world than they were seeing. Son Conrad was a farmer with a touch of missionary zeal. He wanted to help his less fortunate fellow men. It was, altogether, a normally happy family.

Then oil was discovered in the Dryfoss' country. Offers were made for the land, but Jacob was unimpressed. Farming was his life, and why should he sell his life to gain money? One by one, his neighbors left for the city, and oil wells sprang up where tilled fields had been. They soiled Dryfoos' clean countryside, and the greedy fellows who had bought the land began to excite Conrad with new ideas. His daughters too saw glimpses of the glamorous life money could buy for them. Finally the pressure of his children's demands was more than he could withstand, and Jacob parted with his farm at an unbelievable price.

The family moved to the city, where the girls could launch

[7] William D. Howells, *A Hazard of New Fortunes*, 1889.

themselves into the social life fitting to girls of their new economic status, and the family situation began to change. Almost at once Jacob grew restless. There was nothing for him to do that really interested him. He felt that he would go crazy from sheer inactivity. And because he was an intelligent man he found work for himself. The purpose of it was to keep him occupied and to provide his son with a firm business setting. The result was that everything Dryfoos touched turned into money and the family grew, for them, fabulously wealthy.

Before long, Conrad felt stifled. Furthermore, he began to see what a city is like and how most of its people have to live. With time and money at his command and a germ of social idealism in his heart, he fell prey to fanaticism and radicalism. For the first time violent bursts of antagonism developed between the father, who had built up an important career for his son, and the boy who neglected it and scorned the money it made, to give his services to the masses.

The girls, too, discovered problems. In the country they had been direct and spontaneous. In New York, unchanged except in financial circumstances, they were vulgar and common. They were largely ignored. When a social governess was employed to help them out they became so dependent upon her that they were afraid to speak a word without first seeing her approving nod. It did not increase their happiness to see that the men they admired and wished they could marry considered them hilarious diversions with an influential father—and after being sufficiently diverted returned to the circles to which they were accustomed.

Slow and heavy Mrs. Dryfoos just could not keep up. Her health began to fail and she lost her incentive. Almost everything she said and did evoked an "Oh, Mamma!" from her children, and she, who had been used to a loving family and cordial informal friendships, was bewildered and heartbroken in the cold loneliness of her wealthy life.

So father and son became strange to each other. The girls were annoyed with the brother who could have helped them and did not care to. They were ashamed of their mother, who, in turn, could not even understand the language they spoke. And there fell, even, a shadow between the wife who pleaded, "Jacob, let us go back to where we were happy," and her baited husband who, in anger at her and at circumstances, because such was his wish too, cried, "Stop saying things like that. We *can't* go back. There's nothing to go back to!"

Adaptability is one of the properties of human nature that has given it survival. But those individuals whose habits of life and ways of action and thought adjust satisfactorily to revolutionary changes are figures against the sky of history. For the most of us, adaptation must be a slow process, like growth. In a family, a unit of individuals, the process is even slower, and its pace uneven among the members. In sudden great changes of circumstance, tensions which change inner relationships seem unavoidable.

The Large-Inheritance Home

In all of the classifications of family situations one kind of family has been ignored, that one which is in the upper economic brackets whose children expect to be assured a large sufficiency even after the break-up of their present family. Our philosophy may have accepted this family as the ultimate in success and promptly disregarded it as one not to be tampered with in scientific analysis. But those few people who have attempted to describe it have brought to attention some of the ways this family may look in its inner situation.

Two descriptions of the Large-Inheritance Family, by people of widely different interests, note the same feature of it. William Healy,[8] the scientist, believes that the pressures of business and social life which go along with the accruing of a large fortune often outweigh concern over the personality formation of the children. Further, the prospect of inheriting prevents the growth of ambition to make one's own way in the world, and of the necessity for becoming a good citizen. And Isadora Duncan, the artist and dancer, whose worldly wisdom sprang from full living with open eyes, wrote:

When I hear fathers of families saying they are working to leave a lot of money for their children, I wonder if they realize that by doing so they are taking all the spirit of adventure from the lives of those

[8] William Healy, *Personality in Formation and Action*, 1938.

children. For every dollar they have makes them so much the weaker. The finest inheritance you can give to a child is to allow it to make its own way, completely on its own feet. Our teaching has led my sister and me into the richest houses in San Francisco. I did not envy those rich children, on the contrary, I pitied them. I am amazed at the smallness of their lives, and, in comparison to these children of millionaires, I seemed to be a thousand times richer in everything that made life worth while.[9]

These ideas are worth serious observation as to their accuracy and the extent of the phenomena they describe. For in the present topsy-turvy scramble of world affairs the words "decadence of the upper classes" and "vitality of the masses" sound in the ear with increasing frequency. The truth of these concepts has never been proved. But until found to be true or false they are too meaningful to be ignored by old and prosperous civilizations. If any evidence were to be found in such a trend, then causes too must be found, for the causes will not lie in just age or just prosperity. The hints given by Dr. Healy and Isadora Duncan must have some meaning, for we can be assured that neither wrote these bits of description for any purposes of propaganda.

A more commonly recognized feature of the Large-Inheritance Family is the power the parents have over the lives of their children because of the inheritance. This is no trifling power. Normally the physical and psychological sway that parents hold over their families gives way slowly before the adolescence and adulthood of the children. In other cases, we have seen already what the continuing of this power, against the will of growing children, does to the whole family.

Usually the true meaning of an inheritance dawns upon the younger generation at just about that time in its life when it should be growing into real independence and allowed to do it unhindered. A large inheritance is often the deciding factor in the hampering of that process, for it reacts both on the parents and on the children. For the parents it is a tool with which to keep command. For the children it is something so important as to be worth denying themselves freedom, while at the same time their natural urge for freedom bubbles fiercely beneath the surface. When children are grown,

[9] Isadora Duncan, *My Life*.

such situations range in intensity from the unpleasantly hypocritical to the mentally and morally dangerous. And frequently they do extend into the adulthood of the children.

This happened in the Coryston family.[10] Lord Coryston, at his death, left all his property to his wife to manage as she chose. He assumed, since she was a woman of good intelligence and strong principle, that the bulk of it would one day go to the elder son, James, that the younger, Arthur, would receive a sufficiency, and that the daughter, Marion, would be married to a wealthy man. His wife concurred in this traditional arrangement.

But to Lady Coryston politics was life, and politics meant only the Tory party. No doubts ever came to her. Toryism was white, all else black. Her whole family was to be devoted to the maintaining and strengthening of the party, under the direction of her clever leadership.

James caused the first disaster. He refused to be a Tory, or to affiliate himself with any party that would prevent him from fighting injustice as he saw it and where he saw it. His mother reached for the weapon of the will and, after a fiery scene with James, changed it in favor of Arthur, the boy who had already launched his career in the House of Commons, with a speech carefully prepared and rehearsed by his mother. James took his medicine but not quietly. The bitterness he felt he put into his campaign against his family's party and even into public drives against conditions on his mother's estates. Arthur and James were pulled as far apart as strangers, with much more hatred between them than if they had been.

Then Arthur, as susceptible to other strong-minded women as he was to his mother, fell in love with the daughter of a famous Liberal leader, a girl who shared her father's views with intensity and seemed to have no other vices. Lady Coryston, who had no son left now to entrust with her estate, tried to extract a promise from the girl that she would not marry her son, under the threat of cutting him off, penniless. This interference with his love affair roused a strength in Arthur which he had not seemed to possess. His counter-attack was a threat to quit all political life.

[10] Mrs. Humphrey Ward, *The Coryston Family.*

In the lulls between the storms with her sons, Lady Coryston had managed to engage Marion to young Newbury, the approved man. Unfortunately there was no humanism in Newbury's Toryism and there was a great deal of it in Marion's generous heart. Torn between her mother's strength, her elder brother's attempts to break the engagement for his sister's own sake, and actual evidences of her finance's hardness of principle, Marion withdrew from the approaching marriage. The last child of the three had struggled to prevent her life from being ruined by the power of a will, and had finally risked it, and her family happiness, to secure her own freedom.

Not until Lady Coryston was dying was there a rebirth of unity and affection in this family. And then it came because Lady Coryston finally had broken before the knowledge that these children would never again be subdued before her legal weapon.

Not all families of children are so strong, even in their adulthood. Many of them live abjectly and unhappily in their family, foregoing their own choice in life for the unsure promise of what the far future may bring to them. Subconsciously, if not consciously, they are only bearing with their family in the exciting anticipation of its break-up.

The Mother-Supported Family

In a classification of family situations created by external factors, the Mother-Supported Family is, exclusively, that family in which the mother must unavoidably give her efforts as a wage earner. If she simply chooses to pursue a career, or decides to raise the living standard of the family and keep a balanced budget sheet, then it is a matter of relatively free choice of action, influenced by values, family organization and activities.

All other things being equal, and the mother being a normally well-meaning person, those children whose mothers choose to leave home are in a position to be fairly well cared for without them, or the choice would not be thus made. It would seem, then, that the situations resulting from this kind of working-mother home are sufficiently touched upon in such families as the Independent Family, the Joiner Family and the Family of the Intelligentsia.

Quite another situation embraces that family whose mother is taken from it by necessary employment regardless of the condition of the family at the moment and of how the home can be cared for. The two situations seem so widely different as to deserve no place within one narrow category. As was the case with the broken home, once considered as an over-all detrimental situation, and finally re-analyzed into many degrees of harmfulness and helpfulness, so, obviously, must the home of the working mother be re-analyzed, for there is an even less constant detrimental factor in this case.

Well known is the usual type of clinical case record on the Mother-Supported Home. The family has too many children for its own welfare. It has been managing just to sustain itself with the mother overworking at home to make ends meet. Then something has happened, the father has fallen ill, or lost his job, had a reduction in wages, or has been laid off for a while. The children are not old enough to support the family, so the mother must. She is needed at home because the children are young, the wages she makes are apt to be less than her husband made, but the cost of running the home goes up because she is not there to supervise. The children, then, are less well fed and clothed, they run wild and defy discipline. And their mother, when they do see her, is physically fatigued and mentally harassed by what she sees. The usual result is that she nags at the children, and comes to see the father as the cause of all her troubles. The father's damaged self-respect is not mended by her attitude, and he too becomes more worried and irritable. Finally, the family reaches the breaking point and seeks the help that results in its becoming a "case."

There are many, though, who because their circumstances have been different at the start do not become "cases" and do not fit so well into the recognized picture.

Mr. Ennis was sales manager for a substantial firm.[11] His five-thousand-dollar salary, plus the expense account extended to him when he traveled, kept his wife and two children rather lavishly, compared to most of their intimate friends. Mrs. Ennis enjoyed her position in the community. She was young, college educated, and

[11] Case record from author's files.

on a better financial plane than most of the maturer women she knew. She felt that all eyes turned to her, and she was determined there would be plenty for them to see. Always her bills just slightly exceeded her husband's income, and always the expense account had to be stretched to cover the difference. Then the inconceivable occurred. The firm, quite well aware of the common practice of "expense account juggling," decided to bring it into the open and make an example of someone. The short straw fell to Mr. Ennis, and the job was done thoroughly and publicly. Though in their community there was no disgrace to the Ennises, whose friends considered them as Christian martyrs, Mr. Ennis could get no new position as far away as his firm reached out. In the crisis, the school board opened its arms to charming Mrs. Ennis, who had taught before she was married, and she entered, with her head proudly high.

Within a year practically every aspect of their family life had changed. The youngsters, tenderly cared for and carefully guarded, had to be taken from their private school and sent to the public school which in that town had no high reputation as to student body. These little story-book aristocrats came home with grammatical errors, unpleasant habits, and filthy language. To their mother, even the texture of their fine fair hair and ivory skins seemed to be coarsened. Their playmates she could not tolerate, nor could she be at hand often enough to be decisive in their choices. The pretty home, through which the little ruffians romped, grew very shabby, for the payments were so high as to leave nothing for repairs and replacements from the present salary. Mrs. Ennis' pretty mouth became set in a grim line of disappointment with her life, her children, her home, and with her husband too. For Mr. Ennis, the "wronged man," had retired to the cellar to become an inventor, who would some day show the world. His wife knew that only some circumstances as unforeseen as the one which had already befallen them would ever stir her husband into any successful venture again, and that, as time went on, where she had been envied she would be pitied as being the head of a Mother-Supported Family.

No matter what the economic level of the family, it usually goes downward when the mother takes over as a wage earner—such is the double standard of wages at the present time. Furthermore, a married woman who has been "idle" loses that much more value to the business market. And even in those exceptional cases where the mother's earnings can maintain the old standard, there is the problem of the reversal of rôles of supporter and supported, a serious psychological disturbance when continued for any length of time.

The Family Marked by Peculiar Occupational Characteristics

In a large part of the families of America, the routine of the father runs to a fairly standardized schedule. He leaves home in the early morning, and comes home just before dinner time. On Saturday he works half time, or not at all, and on Sundays he is free. He can celebrate the few national holidays with his family, and usually has a bit of a vacation with them in the summer time.

This sort of schedule is considered normal by all the many families who live by it. It often causes a shock to wives and mothers when they suddenly discover how differently others have to live. How can any kind of routine be kept when the family clock does not run in this sensible fashion?

Those whose schedule is different often succeed admirably in adjusting to another, despite the sympathy they arouse. But in many cases the family is marked, nevertheless, by the peculiar aspects of the occupation of the father.

Such occupations are far too numerous to be even listed in the space permitted. But a few may be touched upon.

The following conversation took place at a bridge table, between two out-of-town guests from the same city, while their partners who knew them just slightly listened in as if to a foreign language.[12]

Mrs. Young, "Does your little Gretchen know her father?"

Mrs. Drew, in surprise, "Yes, of course. Gretchen is six years old now, you know. But Toddy doesn't, not very well, he's only two. And naturally, the baby doesn't know him from the grocery man. . . . How about your little girl?"

Mrs. Young, excitedly, "She's really beginning to recognize her Dad! A few months ago he was just a man to her. But she sees him every other week-end now and she is beginning to call him 'Dada.' "

[12] Case record from author's files.

The other two commonplace young women, whose husbands rushed home at five every day to toss their babies in the air, had to have this lingo explained to them. The eccentricities of the family situation in which the father is a traveling salesman were then unfolded.

My husband comes home with such high ideas [one confided]. He has lived at the best and biggest hotels, eaten all kinds of exotic food, and been served the best drinks. Then he complains about the meals at home. He wants his suits pressed every time he wears them and changes his shirts twice a day. I can't keep up to that. We have to *pay* for the bills we run up at home. Then the babies cry when he rushes at them, because they aren't used to him and that makes him cross. I've been lonely and looking forward to grown-up company, and when he starts to complain about how meager the life is that I've been living right along, why, I get angry myself. It's a jolly life!

How little thought is given, by those folks who travel home at night after the movies by trolley or taxi, who rise the next morning to take in the milk from the porch and to read their newspapers at breakfast, to the families of the men who have piloted their taxis, brought the milk, and put to print and delivered that early morning paper. A whole army of fathers is working all night, every night, in order that the normal routine of others' lives may run pleasantly.

The man who has worked all night comes home, tired, for his "dinner" at just the time when his youngsters, full of the energy of the new day, are finishing their breakfasts and rushing boisterously off to school. Their mother's duty is a double one; to prepare for the wide-awake day, and for the atmosphere of rest and quiet which her husband now needs. The time for the companionable conversations and planning which come to other couples when the children are in bed and all work is finished, must come to these people in the morning hours so precious to the housewife for the ordering of her business, or not at all. When the children run home from school, their father is sleeping. He must not be wakened, but neither can children be eternally hushed. And at the end of the day, when the children sleep, it is time again for the wife to prepare her husband's meal, pack up his lunch and send him off, while she spends her evening and goes to bed alone. Where is the time, in a life like this, for the family members to get together with anything of common interest, when one part of it is always withdrawing from its activities, the other part just starting forth upon them, and the mother and wife standing forever between the two?

All of those great office and administrative buildings which are emptied of their workers at the end of the day must be repaired of the evidence of each day's work. Then there arrive the scrubwomen with their pails. They have been painted, in fiction, as pathetic but romantic characters who live vicariously the important lives of the folk who have left before they came. But they are family people, too.

. National emergency has brought more clearly to attention those families which cannot hope for a permanent home. From camp to camp, port to port, and industry to industry they are being transported back and forth like shuttles. In a short time of crisis, this life can be popular and exciting. But the glory wears thin for solid citizens when it continues and their situation becomes analogous to that of the Nomadic Family.

There are the families always haunted by the possibilities of disaster, families of coal miners, scaffold riveters, munitions workers, acrobats, and race-track drivers; the families of seasonal workers continually facing the interval of unemployment; families whose home is a workshop and who must try to find some space and time for ordinary family life uninterrupted by the eternal bell-ringing of customers.

What is the inside picture of the home life of the domestic servant who works and carefully tends the youngsters of her mistress and goes home to look upon her own underprivileged little brood? What does it mean to the children of the creative artist who, at home all day, with or without the proverbial temperament, must nevertheless have a degree of peace for creation? How do school teachers, psychologists, and doctors, continuously confronted by the problems of other peoples' children, react to their own when they find time for them? One doctor's wife could get no help at all on her health problems until she set out to find a good doctor for herself. So weary of illness was her husband that he simply refused to face the possibility of it in his own family. Every complaint was pushed aside by, "You are just imagining it."

Ad infinitum, the Families Marked by Peculiar Occupational Characteristics stretch out in number and kind. Perhaps the occupation of every family has some feature which marks its situation. But there is an open field for research into just those family situations most strikingly marked by occupational characteristics.

The Home of Culture Conflict

Every home is a Home of Culture Conflict, and most of them survive it successfully. This does not deny the truth of the fact that in some homes the cultures are so divergent as to make any blending very difficult, and that in many of these homes the individuals are sensitive to the divergencies to such a degree that culture conflict becomes the dominating fact of their family situation.

As has been frequently stated, no one factor is here construed as being the cause or cure of unsatisfactory family life. Rather, adverse factors stack up against the propitious ones and create some kind of ratio which determines the situation. It is not, moreover, a simple mathematical balancing of the helpful against the hurtful. Again and again it has been shown that a family beset by seemingly unsurmountable obstacles succeeds through an unanalyzable strength in the personalities of its members, while the opposite occurs as often.

But culture conflict is one cause of family tension. In homes already unstable, a very minor cultural divergence may determine the set of the scale. In others, a wide divergence can make adjustment well-nigh impossible between the most stable personalities.

A watchful if superficial glance at a cross-section of American citizenry today can show why this is so. Only a chosen few have, at the same time, enough factual knowledge and enough sympathetic imagination to put themselves emotionally into another's place. Radio debates, in days of crisis, between people selected especially for their knowledge of factual data and of the background of their opponents, reveal, time and time again, how very vulnerable, emotionally, are the most gifted of our citizens. The honest factual trend of the exposition is lost, the debaters' voices thicken with emotion as they try to browbeat each other, personally, into adopting their own points of view. The opponents become, in each others' eyes, merely unreasonably stubborn folk who refuse to see the plain truth. Each one forgets that the other's philosophy is not arbitrarily chosen for the purpose of opposing someone, but that it too is a product of background. It is not enough to *know* that people are different. It is more important to *feel* how they feel in their own special situation, to believe, not just to know, that all truth and right is relative to each individual as his life has made him see it.

This, of course, is asking too much of human nature, when its very feelings are conditioned and limited by its environments. And if these emotional blocks show up in the relatively cold surroundings of radiodom, it takes little imagination to conceive of their importance to the intimate family group, where emotionalism is born.

One case seems to show how a very simple act, which is interpreted differently by two members of the family because of their dissimilar cultures, can create a severe family tension. It is the story of a boy who grew very nervous over his father's habit of sitting alone in the dark, far into the night, smoking and staring into the blackness.[13] The boy was certain that something was wrong, it was such a strange kind of behavior. Was his father ill? Was he lonely, or worried over money? Night after night the boy got up out of bed, came down to the dark room where his father was sitting and asked him what was wrong. Always the reply came, "Nothing. Just resting." Finally the fear of things he did not know about became too great for the boy. He was determined to share his father's troubles. Into the dark room he walked, turned on the light and demanded to know what was the matter. "Nothing," his father snapped, "only turn out that light. There were no lights at home when I was a boy." Then his son leaned against the door looking at him, while relief relaxed his tension. To his mind there came a picture of the room his parent had often described, that large, quiet, dark room in the old country, where he had spent his childhood's evenings before the dying embers in the huge fireplace, until he finally slipped into secure boyhood sleep. Now his son understood. His father was not tuned to noise and traffic and bright lights. This was not his way of expressing worry, it was comfort. He was just resting in the only way and place he could find familiar in an unfamiliar life.

[13] Jerome Weidman, "My Father Sits in the Dark," *Story Magazine*, November, 1934.

How, though, can an American boy thus imaginatively put himself in the place of the father whose own foreign upbringing has taught him to believe that to have children is to own them, to determine the kind of work they shall do, to take away all their wages, and supervise their clothing and activities? Case records are filled with such situations. How can the eternal rightness of the religious fanatic feel anything like sympathy for the ways of other religions when they are manifested by a member of his own family? We read of many families split apart because of their religious differences.

This kind of extreme cultural conflict may breed animosity far deeper than the radio debaters', for it causes shame in one's own group and frustration to one's own desires. Differences in the family which run at cross purposes to its members' wills come to seem like completely irrational, personal affronts.

The Disgraced Home

A survey of disgraced homes proves that immorality does not go hand-in-hand with ill treatment of children, nor even with teaching them immorality. Many a parent has become criminal for the sake of the children whom he holds in tender regard. Children accept the ways of their parents with little moralizing, and many live happily unaware of a frowning society's codes. But public disgrace injects into the family a factor which is far from helpful. Even when the family members cling loyally together a sense of isolation occurs. A family against the world does not have an atmosphere of assurance and contentment within. It loses caste, and that is a blow to the self-respect of any family or individual.

Mrs. Carmichael's husband was not a good provider.[14] His frequent drinking bouts not only decreased the family budget but were making him ineffective in his work. His wife nagged at him about it, particularly when she saw that he had been drinking and that she would be given no money with which to feed the youngsters. And he, pugnacious under the influence of drink and goaded by the nagging, would become threatening and dangerous. Nevertheless they were both fond of their children ánd very friendly and affectionate with them—until little Norman started repeating to a neigh-

[14] Nora Hoult, *Time Gentlemen! Time!*

bor scraps of conversation he had heard at home. His mother had said that if his father spent his money for liquor there would be none for food. And the friendly neighbor offered to feed the child. This was more than Mrs. Carmichael could bear. As long as she could keep her family troubles hidden she could struggle with them and maintain her pride. But to have her neighbors know was to disgrace her home and bring pity upon the family. She struck out at Norman, slapped him viciously and called him a little beast. Norman was surprised and very frightened. He could not understand what he had done, and became cross and sulky. This little incident marked the turning point in the family struggle. Disgrace broke Mrs. Carmichael's will to keep up an acceptable family structure. Once the news was out it was out, and she indulged in complaining to everyone about her sad state instead of combating it. The children suffered and so did her husband, until conditions at home became so unbearable to him that he brought upon his family a final and public disgrace.

The most frequent kind of family disgrace is the imprisonment of a member. When the imprisoned member is a parent and a wage earner the results to the family are very tangible. A study of prisoners' families in Kentucky[15] showed that no matter what the plane of living had been before the family's disgrace, it went lower during the imprisonment. The costs of the trial, the loss of the wage earner, illness from worry were some of the depressors of the family level. Some of the families were broken entirely. Many found it necessary to move from the scene of their disgrace, with all the expense that entails.

Sometimes the removal brought about a loss of identity and a solution to that part of the problem. But usually the disgraced member comes home again. Then the children must be readjusted to the parent who has failed them once. What will be their attitude toward this adult who broke the law and was punished and now comes home to be an authority over them once more, who is himself in a precariously unadjusted condition? Removal from a neighborhood will not solve the psychological problems facing its members as a result of its former situation as a Disgraced Family.

[15] Ruth S. Bloodgood, *Welfare of Prisoner's Families in Kentucky*, U. S. Dept. of Labor, Children's Bureau, Publication No. 82, 1928.

The Family in the Public Eye

A study of great interest could be made, were it possible, of the families of prominent men who have erred from the dictates of the legal code and been caught at it. Here prominence itself is a factor which changes the situation.

In the absence of such a study, one must turn to fiction and biography for the meaning of this situation. They suggest three things. First, although the physical handicaps are less than for the poor and obscure family, the rebuilding of family respect is more difficult because of the impossibility of moving to where it is not known, and starting over again. This family is known too widely. The most personal activities of the members have been enlarged upon in the newspapers, and wherever a member may go fresh interest will be stirred up. The shock of the change from popularity in publicity to suspicion and adverse criticism will follow and encroach upon the family efforts to readjust. Second, the general public sometimes makes it harder for this family because of an unconscious desire to get even with them for their superior position and their misuse of it. The rationalization of this vengeful behavior is that prominent people are expected to live right, for they have all the advantages—wealth, power, status, education—which are believed to prevent the necessity or provocation to wrongdoing. Not much is expected from the underprivileged, it is assumed that they will resort to crime. They must be helped a great deal and punished a bit too. But the privileged citizen who fails in his responsibilities must be made an example. And third, there is the suggestion that the members of the prominent family expect more of each other and in a different way than do their more lowly brethren. Sometimes children brought up to hardship learn a tolerance and wisdom beyond their years. They may well see eye to eye with their convicted father, when they are sharing his drab existence and longing for some escape themselves. Those other children, though, see their parents as outstanding and successful people. If they have been successful parents too, there is double disillusion. If they have been overbearing parents, the children may be utterly repelled by the hypocrisy of the situation. It seems entirely possible that readjustment is more difficult in the family where children have been carefully brought up to high social standards, than in the family where they are coached in the classroom of hard realism.

The Family in the Public Eye feels the burden of prominence in circumstances other than those of disgrace. All of the normal little functions of family life, which in the average home have meaning only to its members, are thrown under a klieg light for the prominent ones.

How does one relax into easy family relationships when surrounded by reporters eager for sensational details? Servants are susceptible to pressure for "inside stories" and leave few really unguarded moments even in the home. Most of us can and do reserve a rôle for ourselves with which our families are not familiar, which would be quite startling to the family were it to be revealed. We resort to inconsistencies because we do not even want to regard ourselves as one persistently set person whose reactions we cannot escape. No doubt we save our families considerable nervous strain by thus indulging ourselves in their absence. But this relief of escape from a set rôle is dangerous for the members of the Family in the Public Eye. Inconsistencies look unpleasant in print, and people in a prominent family are bound to be found out.

The recent wave of biographies aimed at the tearing down of national idols, and succeeding admirably, points up realistically what publicity can do to a family's ideas about itself. There is probably no family, however upright and normal, which would not be put to the test of great strain by the recording and interpreting of every speech and action of its members in public and private, and the summing up of them into a description of their group life. To reveal it would be surprising, if not disorganizing to the family itself. This, to a lesser degree, is the sort of tension under which the Family in the Public Eye must live continuously.

NEIGHBORHOOD

Current ecological studies which deal with the family in one community show a close tie-up between the community situation, institutions, and customs, and the kind of family which is average to that community. There is no simple straight line of causation. The site may have been chosen for a special kind of family life, and the institutions grown to fit it accordingly. But a pattern becomes set. It not only draws similar families to it by the process of selection; it changes the families within it by the process of socialization. Just as truly as each family is different because of its own unique combination of life factors, so are families similar because they come from the same street, community, town, or nation.

Even in these days of standardization of clothing and coiffure, it is possible to detect, in the enveloping environment of a great metropolis, some of the families which have come from the country to the big city to do their shopping, other suburban families indulging in luncheon and the movies, and those city folks who are eating their accustomed lunch at their chosen near-by restaurant. Thrown all together, something of the communities from which they come still sets them apart in different groups.

This community culture is one of the external pressures on the family. It beats its way into the home and becomes one of the elements of the family culture. In all cases it affects the family situation to some degree. In cases of extreme conflict between family and community it can overshadow all other effects to the situation.

The Farm Family

Many of the features of modern industrial life which are considered to have a disorganizing effect upon the family have not as yet penetrated the rural community. The absence of those influences keeps the country family in closer conformity to the older established pattern of family life from which urban families are deviating. Nostalgia for the past brings forth descriptions of the rural pattern as being "stable," "wholesome," and based on real, as opposed to artificial, values. To a great extent these qualities do mark the country family, not because they are sounder people with better values, but because the culture of the country shapes the family pattern to its own ways.

The Handevidts,[16] a family of five, sometimes make a thousand dollars a year from their farm. To the city family of five this is hardship. But the Handevidts live well. Their family economy is not based on cash, but on direct production from the soil by family labor. Because they are dependent, not upon money, but upon their

[16] "How America Lives," *The Ladies' Home Journal*, September, 1940, pp. 55-58.

own work, the value placed upon these two things is almost directly opposite to a city family's values. Money is not an end but a means. The ability to work well is rated so high as to have become almost an end in itself. A description of their home life shows what this means in terms of activity:

The Handevidts are not great moviegoers—breakfast at 5:30 A.M. in summer and 6:30 A.M. in winter makes late hours inadvisable the night before. They also pay relatively little attention to the entertainment aspect of the shiny new radio. . . . Farm-and-home programs and news broadcasts get most of the play. . . .

Even their recreation is largely self-sustaining. Sunday-picnic drives to one of the local lakes, church festivals and sociables. Table tennis, Chinese checkers, old-fashioned checkers, horseshoe pitching in the yard on summer evenings. Or an hour or two of singing at the piano in the evening. . . .

Both the boys are heart and soul in the job of making those fat black acres produce more and more per acre. They have every respect for this hardy, full and thrifty life. . . .

The Handevidt youngsters are outstanding achievers in the 4-H. Last year at the country fair Harold and Lewis won first and second with their baby beeves. Lewis also won second in the hog-feeding contest. Margarieth took first in meal planning and room furnishing, in pineapple, spinach and pear canning, and in cake baking. . . . Margarieth's resultant skill in dietetics and cooking and decorating make her not only an invaluable assistant to her mother in running a top-notch household, but also a remarkably eligible wife.[17]

This family is independent and interdependent, its functions so simply and naturally realistic that the family budget is kept by the fifteen-year-old son. It is a stable and close unity in which all its interests come from within the group and work themselves out for the benefit of the group. No one has a hobby or career antagonistic to the all-enveloping family institution, nor do they take vacations away from home, except to display their products at the country fair. As the Handevidts put it, "They don't have jobs— they have a way of living. And you don't need or desire vacations from living."[18]

[17] *Ibid.*, p. 58.
[18] *Ibid.*, p. 59.

This is the successful Farm Family situation, the unimpeded result of its own environment. But the Handevidt family shows the influence of a "pure" type of country culture. If a conflicting culture surrounds them, it has not entered their home. For many Farm Families conflict comes when bits of city culture become mixed with their own. Then the picture changes.

Galpin says of rural life:

The farm family is cut off more or less by distance, climate and topography from people of its own sort, and thrown back upon its own household resources and its own family type for a fundamental knowledge of human kind. This is the generally perceived restriction of farm life. Perhaps, however, it has not often enough been pointed out just what the apex of this tragic circumstance is; is it not that the family type of thinking becomes for this family somewhat fixedly the norm of human thinking in general? Is not the legitimacy of other attitudes, of other temperaments, of other fundamental judgements, ideals, philosophies, religions, which have become fixed just as solidly . . . certain to be questioned, if not outlawed, by this family?[19]

Because of this inflexibility, the cause of which Galpin attributes to the farm neighborhood itself, many family situations of acute conflict are produced when children are touched by an infiltration of city ideas. The parents resist, or are utterly unable to understand, the changing values of their country children, as country culture becomes adulterated by the spread of the forces which have made cities.

One farm-father writes:

We have one son and would have been glad to have him be a farmer as we have several farms and have to rent them, and it is not always possible to have desirable tenants. This son has a B.S. from the University. He is now teaching in a junior high school at a salary probably less than the income he would get from operating one of the farms.[20]

Another letter, written by the city wife of a farmer, reveals another situation:

Our farm, which is a good one, has been in the family for three generations. My husband is quite insistent that our son, an only child, shall

[19] Charles Josiah Galpin, *Rural Life*, p. 40.
[20] Roy H. Holmes, "The Modifying Influence of the Family-Farm upon Choice of Occupation," *Rural Sociology*, Volume 2, no. 1, March, 1937, p. 61.

keep the farm in the family for another generation. The boy, who has graduated from high school, is not interested in the farm and wishes to become a chemical engineer. I can say nothing—just watch and wait.[21]

These cases reveal the habits of living and thinking that limit the family situation in one kind of community, and of how the habits resist and conflict with a changing culture.

The Small-Town Family

A small town is rather uncertain of definition when great metropolitan areas are spreading their tentacles out toward the most remote countryside. In a broad classification such as this, the definition must loosely compare to that happy medium between farm and city with which H. Paul Douglass describes the small town.

The farmer, he says, wakes silently, works all day often at a distance from the other working members of his family, sees few outsiders in the course of a day or a week. The city man, at the other extreme, rises to noise and the pressure of people to whom he has become insensitive because of their numbers and their ubiquity. He goes to bed with the city shouting at him. But

The little townsman has already greeted his fellows this morning as he splits the kindling or feeds his chickens in the back yard. His wife has called a "good morning" to her neighbors during domestic processes, or compared notes on infant diseases over the fence. As the man starts "down town" he is sure to find and fall in step with another man, breathing friendliness—and possibly the diverse interests of another calling. All day the incidental contacts of life continue, varied and shifting. There is leisure for humour, for human intercourse for its own sake. . . . There is pause in the day's work; noon with the school children trooping home; the return of the business man to dinner; the comings and goings of women to market or club; the daily exodus of half the inhabitants when the train comes in; the equal interest in the base ball club; the concourse of the whole town at fight or fire. This is social richness and complexity as compared with farm environment; on the other hand, it is an open formation of life and informality in contrast with the city's regimentation. These make the little townsman what he is. . . .[22]

[21] *Ibid.*, p. 62.
[22] H. Paul Douglas, *The Little Town.*

This community is conducive to the kind of family which Charlotte Bühler describes as having the child, as a child, its chief interest (see Chapter V). Children are not, here, as important economically as in the Farm Family, nor as burdensome as they are in the limited physical surroundings of the city. Therefore they can be both welcomed cordially and permitted of more freedom in development. Parents are subjected to many varying stimuli without yet being completely harried by them, and have time to give youngsters the advantage of their complex experiences. Surrounded by neighbors whose homes are similar, but whose interests and occupations differ, both sociality and sympathy are encouraged, and spread into the relationships of family life. Having lost the isolation of the farm, protected from many tensions of the city, the Small Town Family gains the characteristics of democracy of opportunity and attitude, with an overtone of "the child's the thing,"—not for any special family need, nor yet as an intellectual experiment, but as the central interest of family life.

The City Family

Dr. Douglass has said that the small town has two centers, the home and "down town"; the farm only one center, the home.[23] To extend this thought, it could be said that the city, too, has only one center, the city. For the unchecked growth of the metropolis has so relentlessly overrun the physical limits of the city home and chiseled it down to the minimum in space that the former functions of the home have necessarily been split off from it and given over to the city itself. Along with this encroachment upon the space allotted to the city family has come the intensifying of economic and social competition which absorbs as well the time formerly spent in the home. As a result, occupation, education, and recreation are sought in the city itself, for they are largely impossible in the shell of a home that is left where few people are able to spend many consecutive hours. What remains is the intimate personal relationships between people whose lives strike out at different tangents, but who choose to keep the same starting point.

The hundreds of case records coming out of the city show that those relationships vary greatly from family to family. Some are

[23] *Ibid.*, p. 78.

as firm when based on free will as they are in the Farm Family when tied by necessity. Some are even more sympathetic, because the members of the City Family are accustomed to regarding many different kinds of people as good and useful citizens. But regardless of the kind of relationship which exists, the primary group power of the family is weakened. Physical and psychological control over its members is diluted by the very facts of city life. The lack of compulsion, then, and the aspect of individuality, mark the City Family.

One evening in the uneventful life of Louise Dickson,[24] and contrasted with the story of the Handevidts, may serve to show typical city family relations. At six, Louise came home from work, just in time for the dinner her mother had ready. Mr. Dickson had returned a little before her and seconded her mother's welcoming "Hello! That you?" There was no discussion of what had occurred during the day because Louise was preoccupied. She wanted to think out a problem of her own. So, right after dinner she withdrew to her room and carefully calculated her budget. Soon she was to have a sixteen-day vacation, and though formerly she had spent her vacations with her family at the seashore, this year she was determined on something more diverting. If Jack, her brother, paid her the two pounds he had borrowed, maybe she could make it.

Just then Jack stuck his head in through the doorway. "I was just wondering," he asked, "if you could lend me another pound?" Quite some discussion ensued as to terms. Louise made no enquiries about why her brother needed so much more than he made, nor did her brother ask why she stipulated that he must return the money before her vacation time. But when he agreed to that condition Louise very amiably handed over the pound. It is true, she thought to herself, that boys need a lot more money than girls if they are to have any social life.

To prevent being disturbed again Louise went out into the park, to plan her trip alone. On her way back home, as she passed the "Three Crowns" a man came out. It was her father. "Hello, Dad," she called, "What are you doing out here?" "Getting some fresh air," he answered, "And you?" "Just sitting in the park thinking." Mr. Dickson thought that a funny thing to do, and said no more.

[24] George C. Foster, *Louise of Leadenhall Street.*

But Louise had made up her mind about her vacation and thought she might as well break the news right now. She did so directly but warily. Her father showed neither surprise nor disappointment. That is what he would have wanted to do if he were younger— have some fun. Would twenty pounds help? "Twenty pounds!" cried Louise, and then, "It's not because I don't want to be with you and Mother, you know." "Yes, I understand," her father replied. And they walked home silently.

No one of the Dicksons was familiar with the lives and thoughts of any of the others. They went their own ways so completely that only critical decisions were mentioned. And yet it was a friendly, happy family, each one adopting an attitude of helpfulness and affection toward the others, and a respect for the privacy of each personality.

Unfortunately the parent generation in the city is not usually so urbanized as its children. Family control is still full of virtue to them. Conflict enters the city community just as it does the farm neighborhood. But where, in the country, the external pressure of the surroundings lines itself with the parents, in the city everything works to the advantage of the children. The Farm Family still has its power given to it by its own milieu. The city parents are fighting for something which the city has already taken away from them.

The Seashore Resort Family

Literature has dealt with the seashore resort rather blindly. The glamour of the resort is in its frolicking vacationists, its season of excitement. The family at the seashore, found in story form, is the one which whirlwinds in, plays out its little drama, and then leaves for home. The real Seashore Resort Family is the one which remains behind after the gay folk have left.

In an ecological study of Ocean City, New Jersey, Dr. Voss has pointed up the meaning of its peculiar milieu to the year-round residents of the resort. The most striking characteristic of the community is its chameleon-like change. In the winter time it is sparsely populated, with two dwellings to every individual. Its people, Dr. Voss explains, are almost entirely family people, and there is little of the bustle of work. For the town has no industry except for utilities, and a minimum of business which is not directly related to the summer functions. Then suddenly this quiet town, where mothers and fathers and children have had time to be together and to share in the small-town educational, recreational, and religious institutions, turns, with the arrival of summer, into a maelstrom of activity. For every room in Ocean City, there are now two people. Many of the year-round residents move out of their homes and rent them. Most of the others are crowded by boarders. Nearly 39% of the Ocean City mothers are now employed outside of their homes, and in 90% of the families both parents are employed in some way other than the care of their own immediate family. A complete change has taken place in the family set-up and does take place, thus, twice every year.

This community "is neither urban nor rural but alternatingly takes on the nature of both."[25] Instead of being a happy medium between the two, this community offers to its families a winter of small-town family relationships and a summer of disorganization, during which the children are relatively free to care for themselves in the time when festivity is at its height and their parents' work is at its greatest pressure. Crowded out at home, where discipline must be modified to the tastes of the guests, they have the run of the beaches and boardwalks, and the antics of the vacationists to watch and copy. Then, after this taste of freedom, school time comes again. The town quiets down with a great exodus of people, and the frolic is over. Parents now have the leisure winter months to concentrate upon the home, and to make up for the neglect of the summer.

How does this family react to its inevitably recurring change from the near-rural group to the near-city group, to its sudden taking up and dropping of close personal relations? How readily does the mother adjust to domesticity and the pinching of pennies, after the busy and flourishing season? Her attentions may be focused with double keenness on the youngsters who come into sight again as emancipated individuals. It would be no cause for wonder if these children do not gladly accept their reëntry into the center of disciplinary attention from which, through no will of their own, they had formerly been so rudely thrust out.

[25] J. Ellis Voss, *Ocean City: An Ecological Analysis of a Satellite Community.*

The resort has not been studied for its effects upon the family situation. But it is obvious that these Seashore Resort Families have within them a special kind of relationship which grows out of the exigencies of their own particular kind of community.

The Misfit-in-the-Neighborhood Family

Although the neighborhood tends to bring its families into conformance with its own general plan, there are those families which cannot adjust, or firmly resist adaptation to it. Struggle between the insistence of the community and the resistance of the family has its own effect, in these cases, upon the Misfit-in-the-Neighborhood Family.

Jean lived in a small community of retired business people.[26] She was the only child in her family and the only child in the neighborhood. She craved young companionship, but whenever she did find a playmate she was too handicapped to know how to play and to get along with other children, and became increasingly unhappy. She kept begging her parents to move, for she herself realized the unnaturalness of her position. She was part of a family, and she did not live in a family neighborhood. Its culture was adult and there was no place in it for a little girl.

In the Jago, the presence of the Roper Family was resented.[27] Mr. Roper did not beat his wife nor drink. Mrs. Roper was neatly clad and used a great deal of soap and water. The two children were quiet and could not fight. When some of their attractive furnishings were stolen, they did not go out to knock down the invader and get back their possessions. Instead, they called the neighbors "thieves." The children were always frightened and cringing, their mother tormented and their father abased by his own helplessness to protect his family. Their only solution was to leave their home and at length they were driven from it.

The family of bohemian tastes which was forced by necessity to settle in a conventional middle-class district was harassed by the pressure of the community which it consciously resisted with all its might.[28] The neighbors tripped over the milk bottles on the porch

---

[26] Leo Kanner, op. cit., p. 106.
[27] Arthur Morrison, A Child of the Jago.
[28] Case record from author's files.

at ten in the morning, when they dropped in with a friendly offer
to help with the marketing, and found Mrs. Crane in a housecoat
obviously just roused from sleep. They came in to call at the proper
hour, expecting tea, to find her engaged in household chores they
had long since finished. An invitation for the Cranes to join the
weekly informal bridge club revealed a polite but decided hostility
toward bridge gatherings and all that they stood for. The neighbors felt sorry for the Crane children, and opened their homes to
them. Then the boys, who had been completely adjusted to their
own ways of living, began to see the advantages of a "motherly"
routine. They criticized and nagged at their mother, while she grew
more than ever determined that her life would not be spoiled, or
her sons and home become humdrum little copies of every other
son and home in the community. The family that had been happy-
go-lucky but secure in one pattern became tense and divided when
its pattern did not fit the community.

These are some scattered examples of family situations which
occur when the external factor of neighborhood does not settle down
over a family in a friendly manner. There are many more such
phenomena, for the ecological processes of invasion and succession
go on ceaselessly, and those who take the first steps of invasion as
families are in conflict with the community culture. Though their
ardent desire may be to adopt it, the settled community itself keeps
them as Misfit-in-the-Neighborhood Families as long as it is able
to hold back the modifying forces of the infiltration.

The Family in a Sub-Standard Neighborhood

A house-to-house enquiry in a Manchester ward[29] produced some
detailed descriptions of the physical family situations in one community. The following are representative reports:

Visit No. 6.

1 bedroom. Father (unemployed), Mother, son of 14 (just left
school) ill; two daughters of school age, two children under five;
7 persons in all. . . . House in very bad condition, reeking with damp, the
one bedroom (occupied during the day by the sick son and two small
children) so ill-ventilated as to be difficult to remain in. Practically no
furniture. Wife worn and harassed; all signs of extreme poverty.[30]

[29] John Inman, *Poverty and Housing Conditions in a Manchester Ward.*
[30] *Ibid.*, p. 9.

Visit No. 60.

2 bedrooms. Father (unemployed), Mother, three sons and daughters between 5 and 14; eight persons in all. . . . Would move if father could get work so as to be able to afford rent. House one of the oldest and smallest type, and in very bad condition; no paint, windows broken, roof leaking, and stone floor very damp.[31]

Case after case in the same neighborhood reads similarly. The author comments:

There is another aspect of its life which deserves mention, though it is not among those which are susceptible to precise measurement. This is what has come to be known as "moral deterioration"—the loss of energy and self-respect . . . indifference as to dress, to the condition of the house, to the sort of reception given to a visitor, and so forth. These things are all representative of an attitude in which it has come to be accepted, in some degree, that the effort to maintain self-respect is hopeless, and one which is not worth while continuing to make.[32]

In a modern city, right between the shadows of a large private estate and a university, there lies a block of houses without water or toilet facilities. In the courtyard, hemmed in by the houses, is a pump and several outhouses. The settlement house near-by, equipped with adequate modern tools, teaches the mothers from these houses the proper methods of housekeeping, and their sons and daughters the virtues of cleanliness and modesty. All of the pupils look at the products of the university and the large city house and listen greedily to the advice that will make them more like other people. Then they go home. One glance at the neighborhood becomes an excuse to each family for its own lack of care—a proof that keeping up to the mark is impossible. None of them wants to live in a sub-standard neighborhood. They are there because they must be, and they come to accept its inevitability.

Social workers concerned with these families complain of one constant common characteristic—the lack of sustained energy to carry through with any plans and ideas. A burst of energy starts them off on an attempt to better their family life. For a time the mother will concentrate on a balanced diet—if she can get the money for it—on cleanliness and consistent discipline. She will de-

[31] *Ibid.*, p. 10.
[32] *Ibid.*, p. 27.

termine to make no unreasonable demands on her children and thereby win their confidence. Then, under the tiring ordeal of feeding her family in shifts because the house is too small for them, of lugging in water from the pump and heating it on a leaky stove, of having many children underfoot and cluttering up the house, her energy and temper give way. Often her efforts to keep a tidy house are defeated by the weather, which *will* come through a paper-thin roof, and her attempts at sanitation nullified by an army marching in from her neighbor's carelessly kept kitchen. Someone is almost always ill at home, and health, which is a relative matter, is none too good anywhere in these dark, damp homes.

Because the houses are so inefficient to work in, most of the children are delicatessen-fed. Since the streets are healthier than the houses, and roomier, the mothers often hand the children's "dinner" to them out of the window and they eat it on the run. Home is so uninviting that none of the children ever goes there when it is avoidable, and the life of the community becomes street life and not home life. Even the parents' chief joy in life is the anticipation of those moments when they can be free to go to their "class" at the warm, clean, settlement house.

The sub-standard community makes the Sub-Standard Neighborhood Family what it is for two reasons. The community pattern is one of defeatism. The actual physical living conditions forbid the building up of sufficient sustained energy to combat that pattern.

HEALTH

Poverty and unemployment, inadequate housing and ill-health run together in such a close circle that it is difficult to separate them to find the effects of each upon the family. In order to attempt some such separation, physical and mental health will here be considered in situations where the other factors are absent. Though they may have less dire effects when standing alone, physical and mental illnesses are external forces which change the situation of a family at whatever level that family may happen to live.

The Home of the Invalid

Many are the examples of stoic invalids whose spirit of unselfishness brings sweetness and light to the lives of those around them.

Fiction has romanticized these people and their families along with them. Most normal children from reading families are well acquainted with Dickens' Tiny Tim of "God bless us every one" fame, and with Kate Douglass Wiggin's little heroine of "The Birds' Christmas Carol," who devoted her Christmas selflessly to her less fortunate townsmen and died from the strenuousness of her sacrifice. Imaginative little readers have wished that they too might be such heroic figures, and have pretended incapacities in order to show their own nobility.

This imaginative play in itself gives some insight into the psychology of the invalid and of what he means to the family. No matter how severe and torturing an affliction may be, there is satisfaction and power on the pedestal where these other worldly ones are placed by an unrealistic society. The whole home looks up to that pedestal, and it casts a shadow of repression back upon the others.

Elin Atlee is a chronic invalid.[33] She has never been strong enough to learn to walk and never will be, though she is a grown woman and shows all signs of living to an unhealthy old age. Since she could not be actively of this world, she chose instead the opposite extreme. Her every action has been modeled by the example of the Nazarene, and her life devoted to the spread of His ideals. Elin has always been smiling and happy and has brought much happiness to others.

Her two brothers and two sisters have never had a taste of what life could be like without Elin. For she was the first-born and commander of the family pattern before they became a part of it. But they are all healthy citizens, eligible for the carrying out of the normal earthy business of life. Any worldly urges, however, that have come to them quite naturally have resulted only in pangs of conscience and renunciation. Their sister, who is thought of as having so little, is their self-imposed monitor over what they, as more fortunate people, should do and be. They engage only in the activities of Elin's choice, for she cannot tend to them alone and it takes more than one strong person to manage her heavy chair. The money which might bring healthy enjoyments into the home is

[33] Case record from the author's files.

given over to Elin's projects to compensate her further for her deprivations. The mother and father have both completely lost sight of the fact that Elin is the only one in the family who is, in her restricted way, living fully and heartily the life of her own choosing. The others, who have made it for her, have denied their own.

This is an exceptional case only in intensity. It serves to show, magnified, some of the subtle forces that enter those many homes on record in which there is illness, of long or short duration, and in which the ill person is a hero or of that category described as "just plain ornery." These records themselves show that illness makes demands upon healthy persons. The routines for an invalid interfere with normal routines. Resentment arises naturally in the healthy members because of interference with the accustomed ways and activities, the encroachments upon the budget and upon the family's time and energy. Then, because of a sentimental attitude toward illness, they feel guilt stirring beneath the resentment and resort to over-compensation: a deliberate, unnecessary self-sacrifice which does nothing to reduce the very real antagonism. This behavior toward the invalid serves to give to his situation a significance deeper than just ill health alone would have for him. It often creates a new problem, a personality problem, which works itself out on the family, and in a turn-about play defends itself from solution behind the cloak of illness.

The Home of the Mentally Defective

In the Home of the Mentally Defective, the normal members are subject to the same psychological stresses that occur in the Home of the Invalid. But cases show that there is an added strain which can make the situation even more detrimental to the whole family. The unfortunate culture lag between our present knowledge of the causes of mental unbalance, and our attitudes toward it, adopted in the times when the insane were thought to be possessed by the devil, adds the factor of suspicion and disgrace to the home harboring the mentally defective.

An examination of two different situations[34] shows the meaning of this culture lag to the family. In both homes there are two chil-

[34] Case records from author's files.

dren. In both, one of the childr, n is an incurable mental case. And there the similarity ends.

Mrs. Case has accepted society's attitude toward her maternal duty. Her unfortunate offspring is in her constant care, and no restrictions upon him that would subtract from his full participation in the family life are permitted. No one can tell what this privilege means to the distorted mind of the boy. He is always unresponsive, neither happy nor unhappy. But to his brother it has meant shame, subterfuge, and solitude. He cannot bear to be known as the brother of someone who looks and acts like an imbecile. So he has never allowed his playmates to enter his home. Furthermore, he will not enter theirs, for he knows the obligations that come with being entertained, and he will not fulfill them. He cannot even explain his peculiar position for he would be disgraced. As a result he is considered an undependable teller of tall tales, and is growing up with a strengthening desire to break away from his intolerable home situation, yet with a fear that intimacy with any one else will bring disclosure and denunciation. His solution has been to fasten his affection fiercely upon any available stranger just so long as affection alone is the tie. As soon as the relationship grows to the point where questions are inevitable, the tie is broken and the search for a new stranger begins. It takes little imagination to see what this habit, once formed, will mean when this child reaches adolescence and adulthood.

Mrs. Brown, in spite of constant needling criticism, has ruthlessly resisted society's interpretation of her duty. Her handicapped child goes to a school where such children receive considerate and helpful treatment. The girl boards there and comes home at vacation time just as many normal boys and girls do. Robin, the son, is encouraged to have his friends at home during his sister's absence. Then the parents take it upon themselves, at the proper moments, to talk about their daughter and to discuss her school and the marvelously interesting things that are being taught there to people who are mentally sick. Robin, who has often visited his sister at her school, adds items of interest without the slightest embarrassment. When vacation time comes, Robin's habit of inviting friends home continues, and his sister, who is as happy in her own room as anywhere, is entertained there. Frequently though, Robin himself takes his friends to visit her. He is not suspicious of his friends' curiosity, because to him there is no stigma attached to his situation. So far his wisely prepared friends have not disillusioned him. When one does, Mr. and Mrs. Brown are well equipped to tackle that problem too, and solve it to the family's advantage.

The Brown family situation is abnormal, made so by the inescapable factor of a mentally defective member. But it is not unbearable, for they have refused to let popular prejudices add to their burden. It is the construction society has put upon illness and mental troubles, added to the problems themselves, that created such deplorable situations as those of the Atlees' and the Case's.

SUMMARY

A discussion of certain external factors has shown that the family situation is not simply a net result of the relationships within the home and the complexes built therein. Contributors to the family situation are the social problems and social patterns of the larger group to which each family belongs.

The economic and social status of the family sets definite limits upon the form the situation may take. It determines, in general, the range of what a family can procure for itself and in what spheres it may function. Sudden changes in status disturb the balance of the old situation and create a new one.

The neighborhood too sets its limitation upon the family situation, changing it as the primary group control of the agricultural life thins out toward the suburbs and city, and as the stimuli of the city filter out toward the country. Resistance to the influence of the neighborhood affects the situation as potently, for it brings the conflict which sets the family against its surrounding society.

Finally, the invasion of physical and mental illness into the home tends to contribute to poverty, unemployment, and dependency. But it changes the inner relationships even when it stands alone, because of the demands of illness upon family routine, and the attitudes society expects of its members toward the person who is ill.

Part III

DIVISION OF LABOR

CHAPTER IX

SOCIOLOGY AND THE SITUATIONAL APPROACH TO BEHAVIOR

Two MAIN purposes have dominated the preceding pages of this book, and to each of them a separate part of this volume has been devoted. The first purpose was to state the case for a situational approach to the study of behavior, with the implication that such an approach is a separate and distinctive one, commensurate in importance to the approach in terms of the behaving agent. It was emphasized that social situations need to be studied with the same detached objectivity which we seek to apply to other aspects of behavior problems, and that this can be done perhaps most readily and effectively in the case of family situations. The second main purpose in the foregoing pages has been to present in summary form the studies of family situations which have already been made, and to do so in such a manner that the main divisions of the forest, so to speak, may be discernible despite the number and variety of the individual trees.

There remains now to be considered a final problem: that of the division of scientific labor. Granted that the situational approach to behavior problems be developed to its utmost possibilities, what science or sciences should undertake this responsibility as peculiarly its own? The various sciences which have laid the foundations for the situational approach have been identified. Similarly, the scientific groups which have appropriated the study of the behaving human agent are well known and now fairly well entrenched. What science or sciences are the appropriately responsible ones to assume the leadership in and the responsibility for the further study of the situational approach? What scientific groups have been conscious of and active in the fields directly involved in such an approach? It is the purpose of this final chapter to present an answer to these questions.

Stated in the briefest form, three answers are proposed to the questions just propounded. First and foremost, the contention is made that the one appropriate and available science to do so is sociology. Included in this statement is the assumption that social psychology is a part properly speaking of the science of sociology. The second proposition advanced in this chapter is that if sociologists were to conceive of themselves as concerned primarily with the scientific study of social situations, they would find at long last the distinctive field of work for which they have been groping. The situational approach constitutes, in other words, the sociologists' opportunity to achieve their own distinctive niche in the sisterhood of the sciences. This does not mean to imply that sociologists have made no important scientific advances thus far: the reference is intended to emphasize their future opportunities and prestige. Third is the claim that sociologists are in a position to make distinctive contributions to the developing understanding of human behavior. In other words, there are gaps in our present materials on human behavior which would seem to call for insights which sociological analysis can give. Each of these three propositions will be given more extended consideration.

SOCIOLOGY IS THE APPROPRIATE SCIENCE

Sociology is the appropriate science above all others to undertake the scientific analysis of social situations in general, and of family situations in particular. This statement is based upon the obvious fact that all the requirements for such analysis consist of the materials with which sociologists deal customarily. To begin with, sociologists have been concerned with social structure. Every social institution is a structure, and the general study of social institutions has been a basic part of sociological material. The analysis of the structure of social situations is therefore but a specific application of the sociologists' generalized interest. In other words, to structurize a given social situation is but to particularize the sociologists' traditional approach. Furthermore, as the lines and relationships between the varying social sciences have taken form, the family is the one social institution which has been left almost wholly to sociologists for scientific study. The analysis of the structure of family situations is the application of the sociologists' approach to specific tasks within their own most distinctive field of interest. To put the matter as tersely as possible, both social structure and family are two of the peculiar and distinctive provinces of sociological analysis.

All this is equally true of the study of process in social situations. The sociologists' emphasis upon process has been marked for at least two decades, sometimes almost to the exclusion of other interests. Most definitions of sociology in recent years have been expressed in terms of process: a substantial portion of current research projects fall within this general category. The whole tendency to conceive of sociology in terms of social interaction involves an approach in terms of processes of interpersonal relations. It is in this field that the sociometricians and social psychologists have done such notable work in the past two decades. Particularly have sociologists concerned themselves in recent years with these processes within the family, making this field of investigation peculiarly their own. The analysis of specific social situations in terms of process, and of family situations particularly, is already under way, so that our contention, so far as this phase of sociological work is concerned, involves largely the acceptance of a developing process.

The rôle of the sociologist in the study of the cultural content of family situations brings us at once to the most obvious yet most undeveloped phase of their study. The sociologist's primary concern with culture is now well accepted by sociologists, as well as by other social science guilds. So also is his responsibility, as we have noted, for the field of the family. Yet in the analysis of family cultural patterns and their relationships to cultural patterns of other families, the neighborhood, the larger community, and social classes, the sociological literature is to date rather incomplete. Our contention of the appropriateness of the sociologist's study of this phase of culture and of the family, and of family situations in particular, seems then as imperative as it is natural. It involves the logical extension of the sociologist's concerns with culture and the family to the analysis of their combination in specific family situations.

In summary, it has been pointed out that the analysis of the structure, process, and cultural content of social situations in general, and of family situations in particular, is the peculiarly appropriate province of the sociologist. It marks, in its fundamental essence, the inevitable application of the sociologist's approach to the fields and materials which have been distinctly his own. The situational approach is the sociological approach becoming specific.

A DISTINCTIVE FIELD FOR SOCIOLOGISTS

Sociology has been the last of the social sciences to develop, and many of its problems are such as would follow naturally from this fact. One of the most outstanding of these problems is the determination of the province of sociology. What is its particular field especially in relation to other sciences which deal with human phenomena? Where does it fit into the social science field? What is its distinctive material? Some of the other social sciences, older in development and point of time, with more firmly entrenched positions, have been skeptical or jealous at times of the newcomer, and have insisted that sociology has no field or material of its own. Sociology is to them therefore a sort of scientific poacher.

There is, it must be admitted, some justification for this charge, inasmuch as there is a great deal of duplication and overlapping in all of the social sciences. This is not important, when it is remembered that the distinguishing thing about any science is its objective and viewpoint, not its material. Some of the critics of the new science unfortunately tend to overlook this fact. Again, in many academic institutions, this problem is complicated by the history of the establishment of departments of sociology, with all the resulting emphases and avoidances. Now here, now there, sociology has appeared as a sprout from economics, or ethics, or anthropology, or psychology, or philosophy, or even religion. A third complicating factor is the effort of certain scholars to be very logical in the matter, by drawing clear-cut lines dividing the sciences and their materials from each other, and to defend these lines on logical bases. When, upon subsequent analysis, these supposed logical lines do not coincide with the vagaries of historical reality or academic exigency, there is much mental travail. One is tempted to suspect that here, as in the world at large, much mental distress follows from the operations of logical-minded persons in a world that is, at least, somewhat illogical.

Perhaps the most important consequences of all this has been the effects which it has had upon the sociologists themselves. These effects have varied naturally from one sociologist or group to another. Speaking in general terms, it may be said to have made most sociologists conscious of the need for a distinctive material and a separate field of operation. This consciousness again has varied between a slight academic interest on the one hand and a rather marked sensitiveness to the jibes of related social scientists, on the other. Between these two extremes, several types of response would seem to have been quite persistent, and to have influenced to a considerable degree singly and in combination, the past development of the science of sociology.

In some cases, the excitation of the challenge has been uppermost, leading its victims to mount the fiery steed of sociological activity, and dash off madly in all directions. It is under the stimulus of this restless drive that so many sociologists have been led to wander about in blind alleys, becoming through the years accessory psychologists, psychiatrists, psychoanalysts, anthropologists, and the like. These successive emphases have been discussed elsewhere under the title of sociological fashions.[1]

In a second type of response, the sensitiveness referred to has led sociologists to a marked leaning over backwards as to what constitutes sociology. Such sociologists have pursued a constructive policy, rejecting one field after another as being "not sociology," until only a bit of "pure theory" and a somewhat restricted study of social processes is all that is left. These are the Brahmin sociologists, who turn up their noses at a good deal of scientific work in the societal field and say: "How very interesting, but this is not sociology."

Still another type of response is that which takes the form of a fervent devotion to terminology, and its combination into a guild patter and a conceptual framework. One evidence of this type of response is the current insistence of these sociologists that everything that is done or said or written in sociology shall be put into the proper frame of reference. An analysis of recent book reviews and comments on research projects shows that much of the consideration given them is devoted to determine whether they are placed properly in the appropriate frame of reference, and only incidentally to the question whether a new methodology has been tested or new insight tentatively arrived at, which would seem to be the primary purpose of research. A framework of reference is a

[1] James H. S. Bossard, "Sociological Fashions and Societal Planning," *Social Forces*, December, 1935, pp. 1-8.

scientific essential: comment is made here to a degree of emphasis which imposes it upon every detailed research project. Thus to do would seem to constitute a new type of eclecticism.

The main body of sociologists, however, continue to work eagerly and experimentally toward the development of a distinctive field of operation, and to them the thesis is presented that the situational approach to behavior offers a fulfillment of their hopes. Let the biologists, psychologists, psychiatrists, and psychoanalysts study the individual's behavior: it is the sociologist who studies the social situations to which they react. Here is a separate and distinctive field not preëmpted by other scientific disciplines. Other sciences, as has been emphasized on previous pages, have concerned themselves with social situations only incidentally, and without appreciation of their rôle, range, or complexity. Here is a distinctive approach which is, as popular parlance goes, a "natural" for the sociologist.

To some sociologists this may seem to be a radical proposal which by implication would rule out of sociology a good deal of work which sociologists have done. This implication would then place us in the ranks of the Brahmin sociologists, advocating a particular brand of scientific orthodoxy. The proposal submitted has no such intent nor implication. It regards what sociologists have done by way of supplementing the work of the psychologists, psychiatrists, etc., as so many foundation stones preparing sociologists for their next and logical step: the analysis of the situations which elicit behavior.

POSSIBLE CONTRIBUTIONS BY THE SOCIOLOGIST

Assuming that sociologists accept primary responsibility for the scientific development of the situational approach to the study of behavior, what are the possible lines of inquiry and contributions which they may make? A selected number of suggestions are here made as points of departure for further discussion.

1. In accordance with the natural history of other and older sciences, sociologists should make it a fundamental part of their procedure to *describe* social situations. Such description should be made in simple objective, realistic manner, with a minimum of

interpretation, evaluation and the like. This is a rigorous discipline. It is treacherously easy to slide from description of a situation to the describer's definition of the situation, and while the latter has its function, the primary step in scientific procedure should be complete and objective description.

It would seem proper to begin such analyses with the description of family situations: first, because the family is the sociologists' most distinctive scientific domain; second, because family situations are relatively the most simple to analyze and describe: and third, because of their fundamental importance in the formation of behavior. We agree entirely with Dollard[2] and Mowrer[3] that sociologists must begin the study of personality with a most searching analysis of the family situations into which the child is born. Sociologists have lagged in their analyses of family situations from this standpoint, yet it is obvious, both from the standpoint of the sociological emphasis upon the family and the sociological conception of personality that this is one of their special provinces of inquiry.

2. It would seem helpful if these analyses were made within some adequate conceptual framework. This volume proposes the threefold division of structure, process, and content as such a framework, not by way of dogmatic insistence but rather of scientific suggestion. It is at this point that the reader is asked to compare this conceptual framework, as proposed in the earlier chapters of this volume by one author, with the synthesis of actual studies of family situations and parent child relationships made by various groups of investigators and summarized by the second author of this volume. To a considerable extent, the summary of existing studies, inductively arrived at, points in the direction of our tripartite proposal. The intra-family relationships of Chapter VI represent so many "slides," as it were, of the generic field of process. The patterns of family life, as described in Chapter VII, fall partly within the sociologists' field of family structure and partly in the realm of cultural content. Chapter VIII, which summarizes the

[2] John Dollard, "A Method for the Sociological Study of Infancy and Preschool Children," *Journal of Educational Sociology,* 1935, 9, pp. 88-97.

[3] H. R. Mowrer, "The Study of Marital Adjustment as a Background for Research in Child Behavior," *Journal of Educational Sociology,* 1937, 10, pp. 487-492.

external factors of family life, groups them under the subheadings of status, neighborhood, and health, and gropes toward the all-important field of the cultural content of the family. In other words, the summary of past studies seems to indicate a development not very unlike our proposal and tending to fit into its outline.

While a comparison between the frame of reference proposed for the study of family situations and the summary of past studies of such situations reveals substantial similarities, perhaps its chief value lies in the deficiencies in our past and present research coverage which it reveals. Thinking of these as future research problems, the more outstanding of them will receive brief consideration.

3. A systematic approach to the structure of family situations in relation to the behavior of children would seem to us to lead directly to a reëxamination of existing family structures. It is our opinion that some very significant changes in the structure of family life have occurred within the last quarter of a century, particularly in our larger urban centers. This would seem to be true in regard to the family of procreation, the larger kinship group, and their relationship to each other. Radical changes seem to be occurring also in the relationship between all types of families and the child. These are matters which would vary tremendously between the metropolitan city child, the village child, the farm child, and the suburban child. What kind of changes in continuing relationships, which are the essence of structure, are taking place between the members of urban families where both parents are gainfully employed outside of the home? Between members of equalitarian families? Of unconventional families? These are family problems which have been studied, to be sure, but not primarily in relation to their meaning for family structure. Is the rôle of family traditions declining in the welter of American life, especially urban life, and if so, what is its meaning for family structure? To what extent are the relationships between the members of the family changing? Two decades ago, Thomas and Znaniecki pointed out that the "we-attitudes" characteristic of the family group in other millieus have definitely became "I-attitudes."[4] What is the meaning of this tendency, which has become much more pronounced in the years since, upon the structure of family situations?

⁴ Thomas and Znaniecki, *The Polish Peasant*, Volume II, pp. 1167-1168.

4. In analyzing family structure, there are a number of rather obvious facts which must be noted. The first of these is the mere number of the persons involved in the situation. Studies of delinquency emphasize the significance of the size of the family: we are here referring to it chiefly as an index of the relative range and complexity of the polar points of continuing relationships which are involved. Next, what are the ages of the persons in the family? What is the sex distribution in the family group? Here is an eight-year-old girl living with six older brothers: there is a five-year-old boy living with his divorced mother, a widowed grandmother, and three maiden aunts. What is the effect upon the continuing relationship within these groups of such sex distribution? What is the age differential between the persons included in the family situation? The importance of these factors have been recognized by anthropologists and sociologists in the study of status. Social workers specializing in child placement have long attached great importance to such facts. We are emphasizing here their possible meaning in the structure of family situations.

5. Much emphasis has been given in the study of parent-child relationships to the importance of dominance and submission, but there has been but slight reference to the rôle of prestige. Prestige is one of the undeveloped fields in social interaction. The influence of prestige is pervasive; its operation may vary from silent subtlety to open adoration. "My daddy says" is a phrase with which a seven-year-old girl begins many sentences, and there is no domination-submission in their relationships. "I've always sort of held dad in awe because of something very fine I saw him do when I was a boy," speaks a seventeen-year-old university student. Here is a late adolescent girl who has realized for some years that her domineering mother is not socially acceptable. What is the prestige pattern of the family? How does it operate? What is the specific prestige of the individual members of family situations for each other? How does the prestige of the individual parent change in the eyes of the child with the passage of time? There is need for much more information about this type of relationship within the family.

6. It is the ultimate essence of the modern sociological approach that personality is the product of cultural conditioning, yet contemporary students of behavior, including the sociologists, have been

very slow to proceed forthwith on this basis. To a very large extent, past studies of behavior, regardless of the words they have used, have been conceived in terms of physiological, psychological, and psychiatric processes. It is our belief that the outstanding need in the study of behavior at this time is an approach in cultural terms and processes. Since the concern of the present volume is that of the family and family situations, this is specifically a plea for the study of the cultural content of family situations, and their relationship to the larger cultural setting in which they find themselves. Some of the particularly important aspects of this need will be described briefly.

(a) What is the cultural content of the family situation? Each family has its own distinctive culture, compounded out of the contributions of the individual members of the family and involving a specific and particular combination of these contributed elements. Can an outline be devised for the description and study of a family culture? Can this be done with sufficient objectivity so that a family's culture can be "mounted" just as a botanist mounts his specimens? This would seem to be the first step in the scientific analysis of family culture, and in turn preliminary to the cultural approach to the study of behavior.

(b) The next step involves inevitably the relationships of the cultural elements in the family situation to each other. What cultural conflicts exist within the family situation? How important are these conflicts? Do they exist in regard to fundamental matters, such as religion, nationality, etc., or are they of minor importance? How much tension is involved in these conflicts? Are the tensions sufficient to create a situation fraught with cultural insecurity? Are the conflicts resolved with a sweeping air of tolerance or not? Isaacs, for example, has written penetratingly of the possible meaning to the child of the contrast between family situations in which there is complete freedom and in which there is a stable and ordered world of values.[5]

These questions concerning the cultural harmony or conflicts of family situations are particularly important in the light of numerous facts in the life of the larger society. Among these are the recent

[5] S. Isaacs, *The Social Development of Young Children.*

trends toward progressive education and liberalism in family discipline, and the inevitable large number of "mixed marriages" among a population with so many diverse cultural elements as there are in the United States with its many races, creeds, nationalities, nativities, and isms. The rôle of culture conflict within the family situation in relation to behavior is something which sociologists have recognized, but which neither they nor other students of behavior have adequately explored.

(c) Conflicts between the elements of the family culture are but a part of the larger field of culture conflict. This brings us to the relations of the family culture to that of the larger society. Is the specific family culture that of the nation in which the family lives? Or, is this a Persian, Nazi German, Chilean, or Icelandic family culture, placed, let us say, in rural Arkansas? If the family pattern is different from the national pattern, is the difference complicated by antagonism, and what is the emotional degree of antagonism? These questions are always important: they are doubly so in these times.

What is the relationship between the family culture and that of the region in which it lives? Is this old South Carolina family living in South Carolina, or is it living in an Irish city in Massachusetts? This will have great meaning to the children in this particular family. The rôle of the regional culture, and its relation to family culture, is of very great importance in a country so large and populous as the United States, where history, tradition, and differences in population and language have accentuated so greatly regional culture differentials. The rôle of family-regional culture conflicts in the study of behavior is an almost unexplored field of study in this country.

There are the possible conflicts between the culture of the family and that of the neighborhood and community in which the family live. This is a particularly important field for study in the second-generation group in this country. What reader of the sociological literature is not familiar with the case of Angelo, son of Greek-born parents, with the family now living in a second and third generation Irish and German neighborhood?[6] One-fifth of the chil-

[6] Clifford R. Shaw, *Case Study Methods*, Publications of the American Sociological Society, Volume XXI, pp. 149-157.

dren of the United States fall into this transitional group of native-born of foreign-born parentage, and about three-fourths of them are concentrated in our urban centers of population. This indicates problems of tremendous proportions, but the possibility of conflicts between the culture of the family and the community are by no means confined to this one group. It may be found everywhere, and in all degrees. Recognizing its widespread extent, and its importance in the causation of behavior, it is obvious that this divergence between family and community culture needs continued and more intensive scientific exploration.

Differentials in class culture prevail in every contemporary society. They are deep and broad and persistent. They are tinged often with considerable emotion. Their importance has scarcely been recognized in the sociological literature, dominated as it is so largely by middle-class conceptions and interests. Each family has its class culture, and from the earliest days of its extra-family life, the child comes to sense and to know these class-culture differentials. They run through every group activity in which the child engages, and many of the culture conflicts which incite the child's behavior would seem to be those involving the relationship of the class culture of the family situation and the culture of other classes.[7]

Finally, there must be considered the number and range of these conflicts between the culture of the family and that of other groups in whose life the family members, and particularly the children, participate. Some children live in a world in which there is substantial harmony between the culture of their family situations and that of all or most of the other social situations in which they find themselves; in the case of other children, these cultures are openly, completely, and aggressively perhaps, in conflict with each other. Koshuk has done some interesting work on this at the pre-school level, showing how some children must adapt to groups whose codes and methods of social control are divergent, and possibly contradictory, while others live in a world all of whose groups function harmoniously.[8] In other words, the range of culture con-

[7] Lloyd N. Warner and Paul S. Lunt, *The Social Life of a Modern Community;* Allison Davis, B. B. Gardner, and Mary Gardner, *Deep South.*

[8] Ruth Pearson Koshuk, "Problems for Sociological Research in Personality Development," *The Journal of Educational Sociology,* 1937, 10, pp. 464-469.

flict between family and other social situations runs the gamut from zero to one hundred.

(d) There is a noticeable dearth of reference to possible culture conflicts within the family resulting from cultural change. This is all the more remarkable when viewed in the light of the sociologists' emphasis upon cultural change and the measurable fact of its recent rapidity. The significant question here is this: How does rapid cultural change affect the relations between successive generations? How early are these consequences operative? What is the meaning of this in the analysis of family situations, particularly from the aspect of their cultural content? This problem of parent-child culture conflict obtains in every generation: our query here is directed toward its rôle in a period of very rapid cultural change.

It would be exceedingly interesting, and possibly highly profitable, to examine the significance of the culture-lag theory for family situations. In a rapidly changing culture, children may learn very early how their material culture differs from that of their parents' material culture when they were children. This directs attention to the parents' non-material culture. Has this changed accordingly? How well do the adaptations of the cultures of the members of the family group synchronize in a period of rapid cultural change? There is a curious lack of studies of "old-fashioned" family situations in the literature on the family and parent-child relationships.

Cultural cleavage within the family situation is particularly involved with the rapidity of changes in the field of education. Two changes in particular seem highly important in this connection. One of these is the rapid change in the scope and availability of education. Education for women was an achievement of the two decades marking the turn of the century; higher education for women is a product primarily of the past quarter of a century. A second change significant in this respect has been in the content and method of education, as a result of which children learn at an early age of certain inabilities of their elders in their family situation.

(e) How does the family interpret the culture differentials and conflicts that have been identified in this part of our discussion? What attitudes come to obtain in family situations toward them? What ways of resolving the conflict come to be emphasized? Do the members of the family agree on these methods or not? What are the ways advocated by the dominant member? By the member with the highest prestige? Anderson points out[9] that children accept the way of some one among the personnel in the family situation. Sociologists have developed quite a technique for the analysis of conflict situations. Why should this not be applied specifically in the analysis of culture conflict situations in the family?

(f) Family situations need to be analyzed with reference to the induction of the child into the culture of the family. It is our contention that sociologists need to pay a great deal more attention than they have done to the early social development of the person. This must not be interpreted to mean that a substantial body of sociological theory on the early development of the personality does not already exist. What is emphasized here is that this needs to be tested out and amplified, with particular reference to the operation of the family at the pre-school level.

What aspects of family situations concern themselves with the fixing of cultural values? What phases of family life are of particular significance in this connection? What, for example, is the rôle of family table talk? Here is a phase of family life that may be of very great importance for the purposes of sociological analysis. The family talking at the table may be: (a) the family at ease, speaking its mind; or, (b) the family in haste, operating with blunt directness. Table talk is the clearing house for much of the family information, comments, choices, decisions, gossip, selections, evaluations and the like. It is important both because of the things which are talked about, and the views which are expressed. These views find expression in words, silences, facial expressions, and all other ways in which ideas, emotions, and evaluations may be conveyed. Its repetitious nature means that its rôle is continuous. Social workers have pointed out for many years that one of the conspicuous deficiencies in institutional life for children is the lack of training in life's values which result from table talk in normal family life. Other than this, there is almost no recognition in the sociological literature of its importance. The failure of students of family life to exploit this as an area for investigation and analysis is difficult to understand. It reveals an amazing lack of what might be called scientific alertness.

[9] John B. Anderson, *The Development of Social Behavior*, p. 849.

A second possible way in which families operate to fix cultural values is in the kinds of persons who are brought habitually into the home, and the way in which they are regarded. To illustrate this point concretely, the seven most frequent contacts with male non-family members made in the home by two neighboring boys before they were ten years old will be contrasted. Boy A's contacts, in order of frequency, were with an attorney, a judge, an attorney, vice-president of a large corporation, a university professor, an attorney, and a gentleman farmer. Boy B's contacts, in the order of frequency, were realtor, salesman, advertising solicitor, sales manager, owner of electrical supplies store, automobile salesman, and newspaper reporter. In both instances, the boys have been in the habit of sitting about, listening to the conversation in the home with these visitors. To a large extent, the adults involved in home entertainment or visiting are oblivious to children or largely indifferent to their presence. It is at times like these that children tend to see their parents and their guests off their guard. Not simply in the language used, but in the whole complex of values involved, lies the importance of these situations for the child. Then, after the guests leave, there may be frank appraisals which the children hear. "Daddy, why do you think Mr. Blank's job is a racket?" Some persons, together with their occupation, behavior, and way of life will be spoken of approvingly; others, with varying degrees of disapproval. Children are alert to such expressions.

Perhaps it should be emphasized at this point that the whole study of family situations and their rôle in the development of child behavior may be recast in light of the recent prolongation of the period of preparation for life. Time was when the child's preparation for life was relatively short. Both the questions and answers of life were comparatively few and simple, and were fixed at an early age. Time now is when the questions are numerous, the answers are complex and in a high state of flux, and the period of preparation for life is obviously and necessarily much longer. There is common agreement that today the person continues to develop psychologically and socially long after the years of physical maturity have been reached. In our contemporary society, the fixation of personality comes to be considerably delayed, and is attained, not at one's majority but with old age. Here is a change of the first order in the formation of the personality. It would seem obvious that it calls for corresponding changes in the study of the processes of personality formation.

(g) Finally, attention must be directed to the study of cultural content of family situations which is not expressed but is repressed. The two terms just used would seem to serve aptly to distinguish between the two cultures which obtain in a family. There is an *expressed* culture, which operates on the surface, with activities and words to be taken relatively at their face value. In addition to this, there is a *repressed* culture which exists and operates beneath the level of awareness, in the mental hinterland of the persons involved. As a rule, all that has been artificially repressed in the parents tends to be transmitted to the children in a perverted form. In other words, there are subtle but persistent pressures in family situations to force the children into lines of activity that are compensatory for what was left unfulfilled in the lives of the parents. This may explain why overly-moral parents have so-called immoral children; why an irresponsible and idle father exerts every influence to develop ambition in his son; why a gangster parent encourages his son to enter the priesthood; why an unhappily married mother develops a morbid interest in her son's romantic adventures.

All this is, of course, a commonplace to students who have been steeped in the psychoanalytic literature of recent years, and some use has been made of the idea involved in the technique of sociological analysis. On the whole, however, such recognition has been occasional and isolated. It is our contention that the principle involved should be utilized as basic in the analysis of family situations. Every family has its repressed as well as its expressed culture; every child is submitted to the operation of both cultures. If the statement be not taken too literally, one might say that most persons fall into one of two main categories: (a) those who adjust wholly or largely to the prevailing mores, and tend secretly to feel somewhat sorry for themselves; and, (b) those who do not adjust so completely and are inclined to worry about it. To the extent that this is true, there would follow two prevailing emphases on cultural values in all family situations. At any rate, this repressed phase of the culture situation in family life needs to be explored much more comprehensively than has thus far been the case.

7. Reference has been made thus far in the discussion of possible contributions to the need for descriptions of social situations, and particularly family situations, and to some of the areas for further scientific exploration. One other contention remains to be made, and that has to do with the classification of concrete family situations as they are being studied. This entire subject has been explored in Chapter IV, and there is no intention to repeat the previous discussion in any part, other than to point out the comparative ease and inductive value of classification of studies suggested for the sociologist in this chapter. Already the social psychologists are moving in this direction in their studies in the field of process; for some time, the anthropologists have acted upon the principle of the classification of social structures; it will be the sociologists' peculiar responsibility to facilitate the classification of culture situations.

The classification of social situations will not be a simple or easy task. The student of classificatory systems in the biological field, with its phylum, class, order, family, genus, and species division, will come to realize what is involved in a science whose specimens are as relatively simple as are plant specimens, for example. Social situations would seem to be more complex by far than plants, and the classification of the former must recognize this fact, and the intellectual capacities of the classifiers must be equal to this task. It is hoped that sociology is ready to enter the classification stage of its history, and that its devotees be disposed to impose the required discipline upon themselves. It would seem their inevitable rendezvous with the history of their science.

SUMMARY

This final chapter has been devoted to a discussion of four points, which may be restated in summary form as follows:

1. In considering the academic division of labor involved in the development of the situational approach to the study of behavior, sociology appears as the one appropriate and available science to do so. The structure, process, and cultural content of social situations

invoke the emphases and materials peculiar to sociology.

2. The study of family situations lies most distinctively within the province of the sociologists because this is the one social institution generally assigned to them for scientific study.

3. The analysis of social situations would seem to offer to sociologists a field of investigation and an approach to behavior which would be distinctively their own, and with very little duplication of the work of other scientific groups dealing with behavior.

4. Sociologists are in a position, by accepting the responsibility for the development of the situational approach, to make distinctive contributions to the developing understanding of human behavior. This would be particularly true in the study of the cultural content of social situations, and again, most clearly in the case of family situations.

BIBLIOGRAPHY

BOOKS

Adler, Alfred, *The Neurotic Constitution*, Dodd, Mead and Co., New York, 1917.

———, *Understanding Human Nature*, Garden City Publishing Co., Greenburg, Publisher, New York, 1927.

Adrian, Edgar Douglas, in the Harvard Tercentenary Publications, *Factors Determining Human Behavior*, Harvard University Press, Cambridge, 1937.

Aichhorn, August, *Wayward Youth*, The Viking Press, New York, 1939.

Allport, F. H., *Social Psychology*, Houghton, Mifflin and Company, Boston, 1924.

Anderson, Christopher, *Parent's Book*, S. W. Benedict, New York, 1847.

Anderson, John E., *The Young Child in the Home*, White House Conference Publications, D. Appleton-Century Company, New York, 1936.

Angyal, Andras, *Foundations for a Science of Personality*, The Commonwealth Fund, New York, 1941.

Anderson, John P., *A Study of the Relationships between Certain Aspects of Parental Behavior and Attitudes and the Behavior of Junior High School Pupils*, Bureau of Publications, Teachers College, Columbia University, New York, 1940.

Anderson, Nels, *The Hobo*, University of Chicago Press, Chicago, 1923.

Austen, Jane, *Pride and Prejudice.*

Baber, Ray, *Marriage and the Family*, McGraw-Hill Book Company, New York, 1939.

Bernard, L. L., *Instinct: A Study in Social Psychology*, Henry Holt and Company, New York, 1924.

Blatz, William E., and Bott, Helen, *The Management of Young Children*, William Morrow and Company, New York, 1930.

———, and Griffin, J. D. M., *An Evaluation of the Case Histories of a Group of Pre-School Children*, University of Toronto Press, Toronto, 1936.

Bloodgood, Ruth S., *Welfare of Prisoners' Families in Kentucky*,

U. S. Department of Labor, Children's Bureau, Washington, D.C. Publication Number 182, 1928.

Bossard, James H. S., *Marriage and the Child*, University of Pennsylvania Press, Philadelphia, 1940.

———, *Social Change and Social Problems*, Harper and Brothers, New York, 1938.

Bott, Helen, *Adult Attitudes to Children's Misdemeanors*, University of Toronto Press, Toronto, 1937.

Bouglé, C. Céléstin, *The Evolution of Values*, Henry Holt and Company, New York, 1926.

Brandt, Lilian, *Five Hundred and Seventy-Four Deserters and Their Families*, The Charity Organization Society, New York, 1905.

Bühler, Charlotte, *The Child and His Family*, Harper and Brothers, New York, 1939.

Burgess, Ernest W., *The Adolescent in the Family*, White House Conference on Child Health and Protection, D. Appleton-Century Company, New York, 1934.

Burke, Thomas, *Nights in London*, Henry Holt and Company, New York, 1918.

Canfield, Dorothy, *The Bent Twig*, Henry Holt and Company, New York, 1917.

———, *The Home Maker*, Harcourt, Brace and Company, New York, 1924.

Collip, James B., in the Harvard Tercentenary Publications, *Factors Determining Human Behavior*, Harvard University Press, Cambridge, Mass., 1937.

Conklin, Edwin G., *Heredity and Environment in the Development of Man*, Princeton University Press, Princeton, New Jersey, Fifth Edition Revised, 1923.

Cooley, Charles H., *Human Nature and the Social Order*, Charles Scribner's Sons, New York, 1902.

Cottrell, Leonard S., *The Case Study Method in Prediction*, Sociometry Monograph No. 1, Beacon House, New York, 1941.

———, and Gallagher, Ruth, *Important Developments in Social Psychology, 1930-1940*, Sociometry Monograph, No. 1, Beacon House, New York, 1941.

Crichton-Miller, Hugh, *The New Psychology and the Parent*, Jarrolds, London. (from lectures given in 1921-1922.)

Dashiell, J. F., "Experimental Studies of the Influence of Social Situations on the Behavior of Individual Human Adults," in Murchison, Carl, *A Handbook in Social Psychology*, Clark University Press, Worcester, Mass., 1935, Chapter 23.

Davis, Allison, Gardner, B. B., and Gardner, Mary, *Deep South*, University of Chicago Press, Chicago, 1941.

Dealey, James Q., *The Family in Its Sociological Aspects*, Houghton Mifflin Company, New York, 1912.

Dickens, Charles, *Dombey and Son.*

————, *Hard Times.*

Dollard, John F., *Criteria for the Life History*, Yale University Press, New Haven, 1935.

————, *Frustration and Aggression*, Yale University Press, New Haven, 1939.

Dummer, W. F., *The Unconscious*, Alfred A. Knopf, Inc., New York, 1927.

Douglass, H. Paul, *The Little Town*, The Macmillan Co., New York, 1927.

Dreiser, Theodore, *America Is Worth Saving*, Modern Age Books, New York, 1941.

Duncan, Isadora, *My Life*, Boni and Liveright, New York, 1927.

Elliot, Mable A., and Merrill, Francis E., *Social Disorganization*, Harper and Brothers, New York, 1934.

Elwin, Malcolm, *Thackeray, A Personality*, Jonathan Cape, London, 1932.

Flügel, J. C., *Psycho-Analytic Study of the Family*, Hogarth Press, London, 1926.

Foster, George C., *Louise of Leadenhall Street*, Ivor Nicholson and Watson, Limited, London, 1935.

Foster, J. C., and Anderson, J. E., *The Young Child and His Parents*, University of Minnesota Press, Minneapolis, 1930.

Francis, Kenneth V., and Fillmore, Eva A., *The Influence of Environment upon the Personalities of Children*, University of Iowa Studies, Iowa City. Vol. IX, No. 2, 1934.

Galpin, Charles Josiah, *Rural Life*, The Century Company, New York, 1920.

Gardner, Murphy, and Jensen, Friedrich, *Approaches to Personality*, Coward-McCann, Inc., New York, 1932.

Gillin, J. L., and J. P., *An Introduction to Sociology*, The Macmillan Co., New York, 1942.

Grant, E. I., *The Effect of Certain Factors in the Home Environment upon Child Behavior*, University of Iowa Studies in Child Welfare, 1939, Iowa City, 17, 61-94.

Groves, Ernest R., *The American Family*, J. B. Lippincott Co., Philadelphia, 1934.

————, *Personality and Social Adjustment*, Longmans, Green and Company, New York, revised edition, 1936.

————, and Brooks, Lee M., *Readings in the Family*, J. B. Lippincott Co., Philadelphia, 1934.

————, Skinner, Edna L., and Swenson, Sadie J., *The Family and Its Relationships*, J. B. Lippincott Co., Philadelphia, 1932.

Hayner, Norman, "Hotel Life and Personality," in *Personality and the Social Group*, The University of Chicago Press, Chicago, 1930.

Healy, William, *Personality in Formation and Action*, W. W. Norton and Company, New York, 1938.

————, and Bronner, Augusta F., *New Light on Delinquency and Its Treatment*, Yale University Press, New Haven, 1936.

Hendrick, Ives, *Facts and Theories of Psychoanalysis*, A. A. Knopf, Inc., New York, revised edition, 1939.

Herbert, A. P., *The Water Gipsies*, Doubleday, Doran and Company, Garden City, New York, 1930.

Hollingsworth, L. S., *The Psychology of the Adolescent*, D. Appleton and Company, New York, 1928.

Horney, Karen, *New Ways in Psychoanalysis*, W. W. Norton and Company, New York, 1939.

Hoskins, R. G., *The Tides of Life*, W. W. Norton and Company, New York, 1933.

Hoult, Nora, *Time Gentlemen! Time!*, William Heineman, Limited, London, 1930.

Howard, Sidney, "The Silver Cord," in *Representative American Plays*, edited by Arthur Hobson Quinn, The Century Company, New York, 1930.

Howell, William D., *A Hazard of New Fortunes*, Harper and Brothers, New York, 1889.

Inman, John, *Poverty and Housing Conditions in a Manchester Ward*, Manchester University Press, Manchester, England, 1934.

Isaacs, Susan, *The Social Development of Young Children*, Harcourt Brace and Company, New York, 1933.

Jones, Arthur Hoskin, *Cheltenham Township*, University of Pennsylvania Press, Philadelphia, 1940.

Kanner, Leo, *Child Psychiatry*, Charles C Thomas, Baltimore, 1937.

Kawin, Ethel, *Children of Pre-School Age*, University of Chicago Press, Chicago, 1934.

Kempf, E. J., *The Autonomic Functions and the Personality*, Nervous and Mental Disease Monograph Series, Washington, 1918.

Kennedy, Margaret, *The Constant Nymph*, Doubleday, Page and Company, New York, 1925.

Koshuk, Ruth Pearson, *Social Influences Affecting the Behavior of Young Children,* Publications, The National Research Council, Washington, 1941.

Koster, Donald Nelson, "The Theme of Marriage in the American Drama," Dissertation, manuscript.

Kretschmer, E., *Physique and Character,* Harcourt, Brace and Co., New York, 1925.

Krueger, E. T., and Reckless, W. C., *Social Psychology,* Longmans, Green and Company, New York, 1931.

Laws, Gertrude, *Parent-Child Relationships,* Bureau of Publications, Teachers College Columbia University, New York, 1927.

Leahy, A. M., *The Measurement of Urban Home Environment,* University of Minnesota Press, Minneapolis, 1936.

Lindquist, Ruth, *The Family in the Present Social Order,* University of North Carolina Press, Chapel Hill, 1931.

Lindsay, Howard and Crouse, Russel, *Clarence Day's Life with Father,* A. Knopf & Co., New York, 1940.

Linton, Ralph, *The Study of Man,* D. Appleton-Century Company, New York, 1936.

Locy, William A., *The Growth of Biology,* Henry Holt and Company, New York, 1925.

Lundberg, George, *Foundations of Sociology,* The Macmillan Company, New York, 1939.

MacCarthy, Mary, *Handicaps,* Longmans, Green and Company, London, 1936.

Marks, Jeanette, *The Family of the Barrett,* The Macmillan Company, New York, 1938.

Mead, George H., *Mind, Self and Society,* University of Chicago Press, Chicago, 1934.

Milnes, Nora, *Child Welfare from the Social Point of View,* E. P. Dutton and Co., New York, 1921.

Morrison, Arthur, *A Child of the Jago,* Herbert S. Stone and Company, Chicago, 1896.

Murphy, Lois B., *Social Behavior and Child Personality,* Columbia University Press, New York, 1937.

————, and Murphy, Gardner, *Experimental Social Psychology,* Harper and Brothers, New York, 1931.

————, and Murphy, Gardner, "The Influence of Social Situations Upon the Behavior of Children," In Murchison, Carl, *A Handbook in Social Psychiatry,* Clark University Press, Worcester, Mass., 1935, Chapter 22.

Myers, Theodore R., *Intra-Family Relationships and Pupil Adjustment*, Bureau of Publications, Teachers College, Columbia University Press, New York, 1935.

National Resources Committee, *Regional Factors in National Planning and Development*, U. S. Gov. Printing Office, Washington, 1935.

Nimkoff, M. F., *The Family*, Houghton Mifflin Co., Boston, 1934.

Nordenskiold, Erik, *The History of Biology*, Tudor Publishing Company, New York, 1935.

North, C. C., *Social Differentiation*, University of North Carolina Press, Chapel Hill, 1926.

Odum, Howard, *Southern Regions of the United States*, University of North Carolina Press, Chapel Hill, 1936.

————, and Moore, H. E., *American Regionalism*, Henry Holt and Company, New York, 1938.

Park, Robert, and Burgess, E. W., *Introduction to the Science of Sociology*, University of Chicago Press, Chicago, Revised edition, 1925.

Parmelee, Maurice, *The Science of Human Behavior*, The Macmillan Company, New York, 1913.

Pavlov, I. P., *Conditioned Reflexes*, Translated and edited by Aurep, G. V., Oxford University Press, London, 1927.

Phelps, William Lyon, *Autobiography with Letters*, Oxford University Press, New York, 1939.

Phillips, H. A., *Universal Plot Catalog*, Stanhope-Dodge Publishing Company, Larchmont, New York, 1916.

Plant, James S., *Personality and the Cultural Pattern*, The Commonwealth Fund, New York, 1937.

Polti, Georges, *The Thirty-Six Dramatic Situations*, translated by Lucille Ray, James Knapp Reeve, Franklin, Ohio, 1921.

Pool, Raymond J., *Flowers and Flowering Plants*, McGraw-Hill Book Co., Inc., New York, 1929.

Reuter, Edward B., and Runner, Jessie R., *The Family*, McGraw-Hill Book Co., New York, 1931.

Rice, Stuart A., *Methods in Social Science*, University of Chicago Press, Chicago, 1931.

Richards, Esther Loring, *Social Work Year Book, 1935*, Russell Sage Foundation Publications, New York, 1935.

Sachs, Julius Von, *History of Botany*, Clarendon Press, Oxford, 1906.

Sellin, Thorsten, *Culture Conflict and Crime*, Bulletin of the Social Science Research Council, New York, no. 41, 1938.

Shaw, Clifford, editor, *Brothers in Crime*, University of Chicago Press, Chicago, 1938.

————, *Delinquency Areas,* University of Chicago Press, Chicago, 1929.

————, and others, *The Natural History of a Delinquent Career,* University of Chicago Press, Chicago, 1931.

Sheldon, W. H., Stevens, S. S., and Tucker, W. B., *The Varieties of Human Physique,* Harper and Brothers, New York, 1940.

Shryock, Richard H., *The Development of Modern Medicine,* University of Pennsylvania Press, Philadelphia, 1936.

Simpson, M., *Parent Preferences of Young Children,* Bureau of Publications, Teachers College, Columbia University, New York, No. 652, 1935.

Singer, Edgar A., *Mind as Behavior,* R. G. Adams and Company, Columbus, Ohio, 1924.

Strecker, Eduard A., and Appel, Kenneth, *Discovering Ourselves,* The Macmillan Company, New York, 1931.

Sullenger, Earl T., *Social Determinants in Juvenile Delinquency,* John S. Wiley and Sons, Inc., New York, 1936.

Sumner, William G., *Folkways,* Ginn and Company, Boston, 1911.

Swingle, Deane B., *A Textbook of Systematic Botany,* McGraw-Hill Book Company, Inc., New York, 1928.

Symonds, Percival M., *The Psychology of Parent-Child Relations,* D. Appleton-Century Company, New York, 1939.

Tarde, Gabriel, *Penal Philosophy,* translated by Rapelje Howell, Little, Brown and Co., Boston, 1912.

Thomas, W. I., and Thomas, Dorothy S., *The Child in America,* A. A. Knopf, Inc., New York, 1928.

————, and Znaniecki, Florian, *The Polish Peasant,* Richard G. Badger, Boston, 1919.

Tuckwell, Gertrude M., *The State and Its Children,* Methuen and Company, London, 1894.

Van Waters, Miriam, *Parents on Probation,* New Republic, Inc., New York, 1931.

Voss, J. Ellis, *Ocean City, An Ecological Analysis of a Satellite Community,* Dissertation, University of Pennsylvania, 1941.

Ward, Mrs. Humphrey, *The Coryston Family,* Harper and Brothers, New York, 1913.

Warner, Lloyd N., and Lunt, Paul S., *The Social Life of a Modern Community,* Yale University Press, New Haven, 1941.

Watson, John B., *Psychology from the Standpoint of a Behaviorist,* J. B. Lippincott Co., Philadelphia, 1919.

————, *Behaviorism,* The People's Institute Publishing Company, New York, 1924.

Webb, Mary, *The House in Dormer Forest*, E. P. Dutton and Co., Inc., New York, 1929.

Weill, Blanche C., *The Behavior of Young Children of the Same Family*, Harvard University Press, Cambridge, 1928.

———, *Through Children's Eyes*, Island Workshop Press, New York, 1940.

White, William A., *Mechanisms of Character Formation*, The Macmillan Company, New York, 1924.

———, *The Mental Hygiene of Childhood*, Little, Brown and Company, Boston, 1924.

Wirth, Louis, *The Ghetto*, University of Chicago Press, Chicago, 1928.

Wolfe, A. B., *Conservatism, Radicalism, and the Scientific Method*, The Macmillan Company, New York, 1923.

Young, Donald, *American Minority Peoples*, Harper and Brothers, New York, 1932.

Young, Kimball, *An Introductory Sociology*, The American Book Company, New York, 1934.

———, *Personality and Problems of Adjustment*, F. S. Crofts and Company, New York, 1940.

Zorbaugh, H., *The Gold Coast and the Slum*, University of Chicago Press, Chicago, 1929.

PERIODICALS

Adler, Alfred, "The Cause and Prevention of Neuroses," *The Journal of Abnormal and Social Psychology*, April-June, 1928, pp. 4-11.

———, "Character and Talent," *Harpers Magazine*, June, 1927.

Anderson, John E., "The Development of Social Behavior," *The American Journal of Sociology*, May, 1939, pp. 839-858.

———, "The Motivation of the Young Child," *Proceedings of the Mid-West Conference on Parent Education*, University of Chicago Press, March, 1926, pp. 98-112.

Baruch, Dorothy W., "A Study of Reported Tension in Interparental Relationships as Co-Existant with the Behavior Adjustment in Young Children," *Journal of Experimental Education*, December, 1927, pp. 187-205.

Beach, Allen W., and Beach, Walter G., "Family Migratoriness and Child Behavior," *Sociology and Social Research*, July-August, 1937, pp. 503-523.

Bernard, L. L., "A Classification of Environments," *The American Journal of Sociology*, November, 1925, pp. 318-322.

————, "The Significance of Environment as a Social Factor," *Publications of the American Sociological Society*, Vol. XVI, 1921, pp. 84-112.

Blackey, Eileen, "The Social and Economic Adjustment of a Group of Special Class Graduates," *Smith College Studies in Social Work*, December, 1930, pp. 160-179.

Blanchard, Phyllis, "The Family Situation and Personality Development," *Mental Hygiene*, January, 1927, pp. 15-22.

Blanton, Margaret G., "Mobilizing the Home for Mental Health," *Proceedings of the Mid-West Conference on Parent Education*, University of Chicago Press, March, 1926, pp. 33-43.

Blumer, Herbert, "Science Without Concepts," *The American Journal of Sociology*, January, 1931, pp. 515-534.

Boggess, Virginia, "Some Factors Accounting for the Variation in the Social Adjustment of Children Living in Tenement Area," *Smith College Studies in Social Work*, June, 1936, pp. 324-359.

Bossard, James H. S., "Child Welfare," *The Annals of the American Academy of Political and Social Science*, Philadelphia, November, 1921.

————, "Previous Conjugal Conditions," Social Forces, Vol. XVIII, No. 2, December 1939, p. 243.

————, "Sociological Fashions and Societal Planning," *Social Forces*, December, 1935, pp. 1-8.

————, and Dillon, Thelma, "The Spatial Distribution of Divorced Women," *The American Journal of Sociology*, January, 1935, pp. 503-507.

Bridges, Katharine M., "A Study of Special Development in Infancy," *Child Development*, Vol. 4, 1933, pp. 36-49.

Bronner, Eva Belkin, "Can Parents' Attitudes Toward Their Problem Children Be Modified by Child Guidance Treatment," *Smith College Studies in Social Work*, September, 1936, pp. 1-16.

Brown, Guy L., "The Development of Diverse Patterns of Behavior Among Children of the Same Family," *The Family*, April, 1928, pp. 35-39.

Brunk, Christine, "The Effects of Maternal Over-Protection on the Early Development and Habits of Children," *Smith College Studies in Social Work*, March, 1932, pp. 261-273.

Bruno, Frank J., "The Situational Approach—A Reaction to Individualism," *Social Forces*, June, 1931, pp. 482-483.

Burdick, E. M., "A Group Test of Home Environment," *Archives of Psychology*, No. 189, Columbia University Press, 1935.

Burgess, Ernest W., "The Cultural Approach to the Study of Personality," *Mental Hygiene*, April, 1930, pp. 307-325.

———, "The Family and the Person," *Publications of the American Sociological Society*, 1928, pp. 133-143.

———, "The Family as a Unit of Interacting Personalities," *The Family*, Vol. III.

———, "Family Tradition and the Personality Development," *National Conference of Social Work*, 1928, pp. 322-330.

Burlingham, Susan, "Casework with Adolescents Who Have Run Afoul of the Law," *American Journal of Orthopsychiatry*, October, 1937, pp. 489-499.

Carpenter, June, and Eisenberg, Philip, "Some Relations Between Family Background and Personality," Journal of Psychology, Vol. VI, 1938, pp. 115-136.

Chapin, F. Stuart, "The Advantages of Experimental Sociology in the Study of Family Group Patterns," *Social Forces*, December, 1932, pp. 200-207.

Childers, A. T., "Hyper-Activity in Children Having Behavior Disorders," *American Journal of Orthopsychiatry*, July, 1935, pp. 227-243.

Clothier, Florence, "The Social Development of the Young Child," *Child Development*, September, 1938, pp. 285-291.

Cohen, Marion, and Davis, Ellen, "Patients of the Treatment Division of the Judge Baker Guidance Center," *Smith College Studies in Social Work*, September 1935, pp. 9-24.

Colcord, Joanna C., "Discussion of 'Are Broken Homes a Causative Factor in Juvenile Delinquency?'" *Social Forces*, May 1932, pp. 525-527.

Cottrell, Leonard S. Jr., "Analysis of Situational Fields—Theoretical Orientation for Social Psychology," The American Sociological Review, June, 1942, pp. 370-383.

———, and Gallagher, Ruth, "Important Developments in American Social Psychology During the Past Decade," *Sociometry*, Vol. IV, Nos. 2-3, May-August, 1941.

Crichton-Miller, Hugh, "The Home Background of the Pupil," Mental Hygiene, January, 1932, pp. 23-25.

———, "The Significance of Parental Responsibility," Mental Hygiene, January, 1937, pp. 8-17.

Davis, Allison, "American Status Systems and the Socialization of the Child," *The Sociological Review*, June, 1941, pp. 345-356.

Davis, Kingsley, "The Child and the Social Structure," *The Journal of Educational Sociology*, Dec., 1940, pp. 217-230.

Dollard, John F., "A Method for the Sociological Study of Infancy and Preschool Childhood," *Journal of Educational Sociology*, 1935, 9, pp. 88-97.

———, "The Psychotic Person Seen Culturally," *The American Journal of Sociology*, March, 1934, pp. 637-648.

DuVall, Everett W., "Child-Parent Social Distance," *Sociology and Social Research*, May-June, 1937, pp. 458-463.

Eliot, Thomas D., "Why Family Harmony?" *Mental Hygiene*, January, 1932, pp. 85-100.

Faris, Ellsworth, "Are Instincts Data or Hypotheses?" *American Journal of Medical Science*, Vol. 27, September, 1921, pp. 184-196.

———, "The Nature of Human Nature," *Publications of the American Sociological Society*, University of Chicago Press, Vol. XX, Chicago, 1926, p. 29.

Faris, Robert E. L., "Cultural Isolation and the Schizophrenic Personality," *The American Journal of Sociology*, September, 1934, pp. 155-165.

Figge, Margaret, "Some Factors in the Etiology of Maternal Rejection," *Smith College Studies in Social Work*, March 1932, pp. 237-260.

Fisher, D. C., "How Children Educate Their Parents," *Progressive Education*, October, 1926, pp. 279-282.

Fitz-Simons, Marian J., "Some Parent-Child Relationships, As Shown in Clinical Case Studies," *Journal of Experimental Education*, December, 1933, pp. 170-196.

Foster, Sybil, "A Study of the Personality Make-Up and Social Setting of Fifty Jealous Children," *Mental Hygiene*, January, 1927, pp. 53-77.

Frank, L. K., "The Fundamental Needs of the Child," *Mental Hygiene*, 1928, 22, 353-379.

Ginsburg, Ethel L., "The Relation of Parental Attitudes to Variations in Hyperactivity," *Smith College Studies in Social Work*, September, 1933, pp. 27-53.

Glueck, Bernard, "The Significance of Parental Attitudes for the Destiny of the Individual," *Mental Hygiene*, October 1928, pp. 722-741.

Goodenough, F. F., and Leahy, A. M., "The Effect of Certain Family Relationships upon the Development of Personality," *Journal of Genetic Psychology*, 1927, 34, 45-72.

Gottemoller, R., "The Influence of Certain Aspects of the Home Environment in the Adjustment of Children to Kindergarten," *Smith College Studies in Social Work*, 1939, 9, 303-359.

Groves, Ernest R., "A Child Needs Two Parents," *Progressive Education*, October-November-December, 1926, pp. 300-304.

Gruenberg, Sidonie Matsner, "The Significance of the Home in the Personality and Character Development of the Adolescent," *Proceedings of the First International Congress on Mental Hygiene*, 1932, pp. 172-174.

———, and Gruenberg, Benjamin C., "Education of Children for Family Life," *Annals of the American Academy of Political and Social Science*, March, 1932, pp. 205-215.

Hart, Hornell, "Family Life and the Fulfillment of Personality," *Mental Hygiene*, July, 1930, pp. 580-591.

Hartshorne, H., and May, M. A., "Testing the Knowledge of Right and Wrong," *Religious Education*, October, 1926, pp. 539-554.

Hartwell, Samuel W., "Adult Adjustment and Non-Adjustment in Relation to Their Effects Upon Children, *Mental Hygiene*, October, 1932, pp. 598-609.

Hattwick, Bertha W., "Interrelations Between the Pre-School Child's Behavior and Certain Factors in the Home," *Child Development*, Vol. 7, 1936, pp. 200-226.

Hay, Louise and Paulsen, Pearl, "Bright and Dull Problem Children: Minneapolis Child Guidance Clinic," *Smith College Studies in Social Work*, September, 1935, pp. 31-36.

Herskovits, M. J., and Wiley, M. M., "The Cultural Approach to Sociology," *American Journal of Sociology*, September, 1923, pp. 188-199.

Hertzler, J. O., "Some Notes on the Social Psychology of Regionalism," *Social Forces*, March, 1940, pp. 331-332.

Hill, Patty Smith, "The Home and the School as Centers of Child Life," *Progressive Education*, July-August-September, 1928, pp. 211-217.

Hohman, Leslie, "The Formation of Life Patterns," *Mental Hygiene*, January, 1927, pp. 23-37.

Holmes, Roy H., "The Modifying Influence of the Family Farm upon Choice of Occupation," *Rural Sociology*, March, 1937, p. 61.

Hopkins, Cornelia D., and Haines, Alice R., "A Study of One Hundred Problem Children for Whom Foster Care Was Advised," *American Journal of Orthopsychiatry*, January, 1931, pp. 107-128.

Horowitz, E. L., "Child-Adult Relationships in the Preschool Years," *Journal of Social Psychology*, 1940, 11, 41-58.

Hough, Elizabeth, "Some Factors in the Etiology of Maternal Over-Protection," *Smith College Studies in Social Work*, March, 1932, pp. 188-208.

"How America Lives," *The Ladies Home Journal*, February 1940, September 1940, May 1941.

Irgens, Effie Martin, "Must Parents' Attitudes Become Modified in Order to Bring About Adjustment in Problem Children?" *Smith College Studies in Social Work*, September 1936, pp. 17-45.

Isaacs, Susan, "Some Notes in the Incidence of Neurotic Difficulties in Young Children," *British Journal of Educational Psychology*, February, 1932, pp. 71-91.

Jameson, Samuel H., "Adjustment Problems of University Girls Because of Parental Patterns," *Sociology and Social Research*, January-February 1940.

Janvier, Carmelite, "Problem Children and Problem Parents," *The Survey*, October 15, 1929, pp. 75-77.

Karlin, Edith, and Markus, Lauretta, "Neurotic Children: Mandel Clinic, Michael Reese Hospital," *Smith College Studies in Social Work*, September, 1935, pp. 78-83.

Koshuk, Ruth Pearson, "Problems for Sociological Research in Personality Development," *The Journal of Educational Sociology*, New York, 1937, 10, pp. 464-469.

Krout, Maurice H., "The Social Setting in Children's Lives," *Sociology and Social Research*, May-June, 1931, pp. 437-450.

Levy, David, "Maternal Overprotection," *Psychiatry*, November, 1938, pp. 561-591.

————, "Maternal and Paternal Factors: Theories of Maternal Love," *Psychiatry*, November, 1939, pp. 571-597.

Levy, John, "Conflicts of Culture and Children's Maladjustments," *Mental Hygiene*, January 1933, pp. 41-50.

————, "The Impact of Cultural Forms upon Children's Behavior," *Mental Hygiene*, 1932, 16, 208-220.

Lewenberg, Martha, "Marital Disharmony as a Factor in the Etiology of Maternal Over Protection," *Smith College Studies in Social Work*, March 1932, pp. 224-236.

Logden, George E., "Some Criteria for the Treatability of Mothers and Children by a Child Guidance Clinic," *Smith College Studies in Social Work*, June, 1937, pp. 302-324.

Lowrey, Lawson G., "The Family as a Builder of Personality," *American Journal of Orthopsychiatry*, January 1936, pp. 117-124.

————, "Environmental Factors in the Behavior of Children," *American Journal of Psychiatry*, October 1926, pp. 227-237.

Lumpkin, Katharine Du Pré, "Parental Conditions of Wisconsin Girl

Delinquents," *American Journal of Sociology*, September 1932, pp. 232-240.

McFarland, Margaret B., "Relationships Between Young Sisters as Revealed in Their Overt Responses," *Journal of Experimental Education*, December 1937, pp. 173-179.

MacFarlane, J. W., "Family Influences on Children's Personality Development," *Childhood Education*, 1938, 15, 55-59.

May, M. A. and Hartshorne, H., "Personality and Character Tests," *The Psychological Bulletin*, 23: 395-411, 1926.

Meltzer, H., "Children's Attitudes to Parents," *American Journal of Orthopsychiatry*, July 1935, pp. 244-265.

————, "Economic Security and Children's Attitudes to Parents," *American Journal of Orthopsychiatry*, October 1936, pp. 590-608.

Menninger, Karl A., "Adaptation Difficulties in College Students," *Mental Hygiene*, July 1927, pp. 519-535.

Moore, Madeline U., "The Treatment of Maternal Attitudes in Problems of Guidance," *American Journal of Orthopsychiatry*, April 1933, pp. 113-127.

Moulton, Bryant E., "Some Causes of Delinquency in Relation to Family Attitudes," *American Journal of Orthopsychiatry*, January, 1931, pp. 173-177.

Mowrer, H. R., "The Study of Marital Adjustment as a Background for Research in Child Behavior," *Journal of Educational Sociology*, 1937, 10, 487-492.

Myers, Garry C., "Parents Who Disagree Before Their Children," *Child Welfare*, April 1929, pp. 409-413.

————, "Our Children and Their Parents," *Parent Education*, Third Yearbook, May 1932, pp. 27-60.

Needham, J., "Lucretius Redivivus," *Psyche*, 7:10-13, (1927).

Neumann, Frederika, "The Effects on the Child of an Unstable Home Situation," *Mental Hygiene*, October 1928, pp. 742-751.

Neumann, Henry, "The Father's Responsibility in the Training of his Children," *Proceedings of the Mid-West Conference on Parent Education*, University of Chicago Press, March, 1926, pp. 222-233.

Newell, H. W., "A Further Study of Maternal Rejection," *American Journal of Orthopsychiatry*, October, 1936, pp. 576-589.

Nimkoff, M. F., "Parent-Child Intimacy: An Introductory Study," *Social Forces*, December, 1928, pp. 244-249.

————, "The Relation of Parental Dominance to Parent-Child Conflict," *Social Forces*, June 1931.

Nollen, John S., "The Child and His Home," *National Congress of Parents and Teachers, Proceedings of the Thirty-Eighth Annual Meeting,* May 1934, pp. 62-69.

Olin, Ida, "A Follow-Up Study of Twenty-Six Dull-Normal Problem Children," *Smith College Studies in Social Work,* December 1930, pp. 107-159.

Oxnam, G. B., "The Character-Forming Home," *National Congress of Parents and Teachers,* Proceedings of the Fortieth Annual Meeting, May 1936, pp. 20-24.

Parsons, Alice Beal, "How Changing Conditions Change Mothers," *Progressive Education,* October-November-December 1926, pp. 295-330.

Pisula, Cecilia, "Behavior Problems of Children from High and Low Socio-Economic Groups," *Mental Hygiene,* September 1937, pp. 452-456.

Plaut, James, "The Child as a Member of the Family," *Annals of the American Academy of Political and Social Sciences,* March, 1932, pp. 66-74.

Popenoe, Paul, "The Changing Family in a Changing World" *National Congress of Parents and Teachers,* Vol. 42, 1938, pp. 22-29.

Pressey, Luella C., "Some Serious Family Maladjustments among College Students," *Social Forces,* December 1931, pp. 236-242.

Preston, George H., "Mental-Hygiene Factors in Parenthood and Parental Relationships," *Mental Hygiene,* October 1928, pp. 751-761.

Prichett, Henry Lucien, "The Adjustment of College Students: Family Problems," *Social Forces,* October 1931, pp. 84-89.

Queen, Stuart A., "Some Problems of the Situational Approach," *Social Forces,* June 1931, pp. 480-481.

Rasey, Mabel, and Witmer, Helen, "Case Studies of Eight Well-Adjusted Families with Special Reference to the Childhood of the Parents," *Smith College Studies in Social Work,* September 1936, pp. 46-91.

Rice, Stuart A., "Units and Their Definition in Social Science," *Social Forces,* June 1931, pp. 475-479.

Ross, Bertha M., "Some Traits Associated with Sibling Jealousy in Problem Children," *Smith College Studies in Social Work,* June 1931, pp. 364-376.

Schwartz, Louis A., "Intra-Family Relationships and Resulting Trends," *Annals of the American Academy of Political and Social Science,* March 1932, pp. 45-48.

Sears, Florence and Witmer, Helen, "Some Possible Motives in the Sexual Delinquency of Children of Adequate Intelligence," *Smith College Studies in Social Work,* September 1931, pp. 1-45.

Sewall, Mabel, "Some Cause of Jealousy in Young Children," *Smith College Studies in Social Work,* September 1930, pp. 6-22.

Shalloo, J. P., "Understanding Behavior Problems of Children," in the *Annals of the American Academy of Political and Social Science,* November, 1940, pp. 194-202.

Shaw, Clifford R., "Case Study Method," *Publications of the American Sociological Society,* Vol. XXI, University of Chicago Press, 1927, pp. 149-157.

Sheffield, Ada E., "Conditioning Patterns in the Family Circle," *Social Forces,* June 1930, pp. 533-535.

———, "The 'Situation' as the Unit of Family Case Study," *Social Forces,* June 1931, pp. 465-475.

Sheldon, Sybil, "Bright Children Failing in School: St. Paul Child Guidance Clinic," *Smith College Studies in Social Work,* September 1935, pp. 75-77.

Silverman, Baruch, "The Behavior of Children from Broken Homes," *American Journal of Orthopsychiatry,* January 1935, pp. 11-18.

Singer, Edgar A., "Sensation on the Datum of Science," *The Philosophical Review,* Vol. VII, No. 5, pp. 487.

Slayter, Mary R., "Cases Treated by the Social Worker Only: Hartley-Salmon Clinic for Child Guidance," *Smith College Studies in Social Work,* September 1935, pp. 61-68.

Sletto, Raymond F., "Sibling Position and Juvenile Delinquency," *American Journal of Sociology,* March 1934, pp. 657-669.

Smalley, Ruth E., "The Influence of Differences in Age, Sex, and Intelligence in Determining the Attitudes of Siblings Toward Each Other," *Smith College Studies in Social Work,* September 1930, pp. 23-40.

Smith, H. L., "What My Father Means to Me," *Child Welfare Magazine,* September 1930, pp. 16-19.

Sowers, Alice, "Parent-Child Relationships from the Child's Point of View," *Journal of Experimental Education,* December 1937, pp. 203-231.

Stagner, Ross, "The Role of the Parent in the Development of Emotional Instability," *American Journal of Orthopsychiatry,* January 1938, pp. 122-129.

Stauffer, Marjorie, "Some Aspects of Treatment by Psychiatrist and

Psychiatric Social Worker," *American Journal of Orthopsychiatry*, April, 1932, pp. 152-161.

Stevens, George C., "Autobiographical Material Concerning the Childhood Environments and the Effects on the After-Adjustment of One Hundred Recidivists and One Hundred College Freshmen," *American Journal of Orthopsychiatry*, July 1932, pp. 279-303.

Stodgill, R. M., "The Measurement of Attitudes toward Parental Control and the Social Adjustment of Children," *Journal of Applied Psychology*, 1936, 20, 359-367.

―――, "Parental Attitudes and Mental Hygiene Standards," *Mental Hygiene*, October 1931, pp. 813-827.

Stonequist, Everett, "The Problem of the Marginal Man," *The American Journal of Sociology*, July 1935, pp. 1-13.

Sullivan, Harry Stack, "Conceptions of Modern Psychiatry, "*Psychiatry*, February 1940, pp. 1-13.

Sweet, Esther C., "Nursery School As a Contributing Factor in Mental Health," *American Journal of Orthopsychiatry*, October 1933, pp. 406-407.

Thom, Douglas A., "Environmental Factors and Their Relation to Social Adjustment," *Mental Hygiene*, July 1939, pp. 379-414.

Thomas, W. I., "The Behavior Pattern and the Situation," *Publications of the American Sociological Society*, Vol. XXII, 1928, pp. 1-2.

―――, "The Problem of Personality in the Urban Environment," *Publications of the Twenty-first American Sociological Society*, Vol. XX, University of Chicago Press, 1926, p. 31.

Thurow, Mildred B., "A Study of Selected Factors in Family Life as Described in Life History Material," *Social Forces*, May 1934, pp. 562-570.

Towle, Charlotte, "Evaluation of Homes in Preparation for Child Placements," *Mental Hygiene*, July 1927, pp. 460-481.

Ward, Anne, "The Only Child," *Smith College Studies in Social Work*, September 1930, pp. 41-65.

Weidman, Jerome, "My Father Sits in the Dark," *Story Magazine*, November, 1924.

Wheeler, Olive A., "Variations in the Emotional Development of Normal Adolescents," *British Journal of Educational Psychology*, February 1931, pp. 1-12.

White, William A., "Childhood: The Golden Period for Mental Hygiene," In Bossard, James H. S., "Child Welfare," *The Annals of the American Academy of Political and Social Science*, November, 1921.

260 FAMILY SITUATIONS

Wile, Ira S., "Behavior Difficulties of Children," *Mental Hygiene*, January 1927, pp. 38-53.

Wirth, Louis, "Culture Conflicts and Delinquency," *Social Forces*, University of North Carolina Press, Vol. IX, 1931, pp. 484-492.

Witmer, Helen Leland, "The Childhood Personality and Parent-Child Relationships of Dementia-Praecox and Manic Depressive Patients," *Smith College Studies in Social Work*, June 1934, pp. 289-377.

———, "Parental Behavior as an Index to the Probable Outcome of Treatment in a Child Guidance Clinic," *American Journal of Orthopsychiatry*, October 1933, pp. 431-444.

———, and others, "The Outcome of Treatment of Children Rejected by Their Mothers," *Smith College Studies in Social Work*, 1938, 8, 187-234.

Woodhouse, Chase Going, "A Study of 250 Successful Families," *Social Forces*, June 1930, pp. 511-533.

Yeomans, Edward W., "Salvaging the Family," *Progressive Education*, October-November-December 1926, pp. 283-288.

Young, Donald, "Some Effects of a Course in American Race Relations on the Race Prejudices of 450 Undergraduates at the University of Pennsylvania," *Journal of Abnormal and Social Psychology*, October-December, 1927, pp. 235-242.

Zeligs, Rose, "Children's Worries," *Sociology and Social Research*, September-October 1939, pp. 23-32.

INDEX

Adjustment: child's to authority, 54; child's to family, 52; child's to living, 51

Adler, Alfred, 10, 51, 52

Adrian, Edgar Douglas, 6

Affection: a basic need, 49-50; discrimination in, 123-30; displacement of, 132-34; excess of, 114-20; inconsistency of, 130-32; lack of, 135-40; normal, 120-23

Allport, F. H., 46

Anderson, Christopher, 86

Anderson, John E., 18, 29, 51, 56, 92, 238

Anderson, Nels, 17

Angyal, Andras, 29

Appel, Kenneth, 8

Attitudes: role of family in determination of, 52-55; toward culture differentials, 237

Austin, Jane, 173

Beach, Allen, 166

Beach, Walter G., 166

Behavior: child's introduction to study of human, 52; cultural conditioning of, 233-34; rise of the term, 3-5; role of environment in, 9-11; sciences of, 5-9

Bernard, L. L., 14, 23

Blackey, Eileen, 186

Blanchard, Phyllis, 92

Bloodgood, Ruth S., 203

Blumer, Herbert, 16

Boll, T. E. M., vii

Bossard, Gertrude, v

Bossard, James H. S., 11, 17, 134, 151, 161, 164, 184, 186, 229

Bougle, C. Celestin, 176

Buck, Frank, 22

Buhler, Charlotte, 104, 122, 123, 124, 187

Burgess, Ernest W., 13, 44, 46, 63, 99, 121

Burke, Thomas, 182

Burlingham, Susan, 146, 164

Canfield, Dorothy, 136, 169

Carpenter, June, 93

Carter, William T. Foundation, vii

Classification: beginnings of, 69-71; evolution of, 76-77; in biology and medical science, 75-76; in botany, 73-75; in field of human relations, 77-83; of concrete family situations, 241; of dramatic situations, 79-82; of family situations, 111-12; of family situations, historical review, 85; of marriage situations in the drama, 82-83; of personal relationships and external factors, 99-101; of tone of family situation, 101-4; progress of, 71-73

Colcord, Joanna C., 92, 163

Coleman, Kathryn, v

Collip, James B., 7

Competition: protected and unprotected, 50

Conklin, Edwin G., 9

Content: cultural, of family situations, 28, 56-67, 227, 234

Cottrell, Leonard S., vii, 25, 56

Crouse, Russel, 120

Cultural Conflicts: between elements in family culture, 235; between family culture and larger society, 235-37; resulting from cultural change, 237

Cultural Pattern: class, 60-62; Ethos, or national, 58-59; regional, 59-60; status, 62-64

Culture: alien, 58-59; class, 60-62; expressed, 240-41; induction of child into, of family, 238; repressed, 240-41; transmitting function of family, 57

Dashiell, J. F., 18

Davis, Allison, 17, 236

261